WOLVES AT THE DOOR

WOLVES AT THE DOOR

Migration, Dehumanization, Rewilding the World

Peter Arnds

BLOOMSBURY ACADEMIC
NEW YORK • LONDON • OXFORD • NEW DELHI • SYDNEY

BLOOMSBURY ACADEMIC
Bloomsbury Publishing Inc
1385 Broadway, New York, NY 10018, USA
50 Bedford Square, London, WC1B 3DP, UK

BLOOMSBURY, BLOOMSBURY ACADEMIC and the Diana logo
are trademarks of Bloomsbury Publishing Plc

First published in the United States of America 2021

Copyright © Peter Arnds, 2021

For legal purposes the Acknowledgements on p. ix constitute
an extension of this copyright page.

Cover image © Rick Mousseau Photography / Getty Images

All rights reserved. No part of this publication may be reproduced or transmitted in any form or by any means, electronic or mechanical, including photocopying, recording, or any information storage or retrieval system, without prior permission in writing from the publishers.

Bloomsbury Publishing Inc does not have any control over, or responsibility for, any third-party websites referred to or in this book. All internet addresses given in this book were correct at the time of going to press. The author and publisher regret any inconvenience caused if addresses have changed or sites have ceased to exist, but can accept no responsibility for any such changes.

Names: Arnds, Peter O., 1963- author.
Title: Wolves at the door : migration, dehumanization, rewilding the world / Peter Arnds.
Description: New York : Bloomsbury Academic, 2021. | Includes bibliographical references and index. |
Summary: "A literary and cultural history of the wolf that provokes readers into finding new ways to think about migration, the environment, and the language of dehumanization"– Provided by publisher.
Identifiers: LCCN 2020015561 | ISBN 9781501366765 (hardback) | ISBN 9781501366758 (paperback) | ISBN 9781501366789 (pdf) | ISBN 9781501366772 (ebook)
Subjects: LCSH: Wolves in literature. | Immigrants in literature. | Nomads in literature. | Racism in literature. | Human-animal relationships in literature. | Wolves–Folklore. | Wolves–Behavior.
Classification: LCC PN56.W59 A76 2020 | DDC 809/.933629773–dc23
LC record available at https://lccn.loc.gov/2020015561

ISBN: HB: 978-1-5013-6676-5
PB: 978-1-5013-6675-8
ePDF: 978-1-5013-6678-9
eBook: 978-1-5013-6677-2

Typeset by Integra Software Services Pvt. Ltd.

To find out more about our authors and books visit www.bloomsbury.com
and sign up for our newsletters.

To Jerri and Jonas

CONTENTS

List of Figures   viii
Acknowledgements   ix

Chapter 1
INTRODUCTION: WOLF IN THE SANCTUARY: MYTH,
LITERATURE, BIOPOLITICS   1

Chapter 2
FEAR OF THE PACK: JEWS AND GYPSIES AS WOLVES   25

Chapter 3
WOLVES AND INDIGENOUS CULTURE: MIGRATION OF
A METAPHOR TO THE COLONIES   53

Chapter 4
WOLVES AND WAYWARD WOMEN: BETWEEN
CONDEMNATION AND EMPOWERMENT   79

Chapter 5
THE WOLVES OF WAR: FASCISM, TERRORISM, RESISTANCE   105

Chapter 6
NO TRESPASSING: WOLVES, BORDERS AND IMMIGRANTS   137

Chapter 7
WOLF TRAILS: REWILDING THE WORLD IN THE AGE OF
MIGRATION   163

Chapter 8
EPILOGUE: DREAMING OF WOLVES: THE CHILDREN OF
LYCAON IN THE AGE OF PSYCHOANALYSIS   189

References   202
Index   213

FIGURES

1.1 Rainer Opolka's Wolf Statue 'NSA Man'. Courtesy of Rainer Opolka — 4
2.1 The Werewolf or the Cannibal, Lucas Cranach the Elder *c.* 1512. Courtesy of the Metropolitan Museum of Art — 51
3.1 George Catlin, Buffalo Hunt under the Wolf-skin Mask, *c.* 1832–3. Courtesy of the Smithsonian American Art Museum — 56
3.2 Billboard Erected by the Washington Residents against Wolves. Image by Matthew Weaver, courtesy of the Capital Press, Salem, Oregon — 77
4.1 Gustave Doré, *c.* 1862. Courtesy of National Gallery of Victoria, Melbourne. Gift of Mrs S. Horne, 1962 — 87
5.1 Soviet Propaganda Poster by Kukryniksy depicting Nazi Germany as a Wolf, *c.* 1930s — 105
5.2 Propaganda poster from the Second World War: 'Der Polnische Wolf begehrt eure Heimat!' 'The Polish wolf covets your country!' © IWM — 106
5.3 Capitoline Wolf, Pisa, Italy. Photo by Peter Arnds — 113
5.4 Capitoline Wolf, Cluj-Napoca. Photo by Peter Arnds — 114
5.5 Alfred von Wierusz-Kowalskim, The Lone Wolf. Date unknown — 117
5.6 Rainer Opolka's Wolf Statue 'Anführer'. Courtesy of Rainer Opolka — 132

ACKNOWLEDGEMENTS

Putting this book together has been an exciting project that has been facilitated by a number of people and institutions. First of all, I would like to thank my wife, Jerrilynn, for her endless support in all matters revolving around the wolves, for her endurance with werewolf lore, her great patience in listening and giving me feedback. Thanks also to Trinity College Dublin for generously supporting my research with one of their Benefaction Funds; to Professor Prasad of JNU, Delhi, the former Director of the Jawaharlal Nehru Institute of Advanced Study (JNIAS); and to Professor Jennifer Rutherford, the Director of the J.M. Coetzee Centre for Creative Practice at the University of Adelaide for their generous support during my research leave in 2016. I remember with great fondness the many inspiring conversations about wolves I have had with the students and colleagues in both locations.

My gratitude is also due to the German artist Rainer Opolka, images of whose unflagging fight against racism and xenophobia can be viewed at www.diewoelfesindzurueck.de and who has kindly offered me the use of some of his photos. Moreover, I wish to thank Joseph Beach, Editor and Publisher of Capital Press, and the journalist Matthew Weaver for allowing me to use their billboard photo 'The Wolf – Who's next on their Menu?', originally published on 5 January 2015. I owe particular thanks to Professors Susan Bassnett (Warwick), Jennifer Rutherford (Adelaide), and Tabish Khair (Aarhus) for reading and commenting on my manuscript. Without their great generosity this volume would not have reached its destination. Finally, I want to thank my good friend Eva Wollschläger for visiting the wolves of Ernstbrunn with me, for her keen photographic eye and her astute journalistic comments that keep making sure I don't get lost in any overly detached academic ivory towers.

Credit needs to be given to the following publications as I have discussed some material from this book in two of my previous articles: "The Absent Mother and the Wolf in *Little Red Riding Hood*," *Neophilologus*, 101 (2), 2017, 175-85, and "Tracking Wolves: Cross-Border Inequality in Cormac McCarthy's *The Crossing*," in Critical Insights series *The Literature of Inequality*, Ipswich, Salem Press, Greyhouse Publishing, 2018, 144-58. A few ideas from this book were also taken forward and appear in a different context in my article "Rewilding the world in the postcolonial age: On the nexus between cultural production and species politics" in the *Journal for Postcolonial Writing*, vol 56.3 (summer 2020).

Chapter 1

INTRODUCTION
WOLF IN THE SANCTUARY: MYTH, LITERATURE, BIOPOLITICS

International migration is a complex phenomenon that touches on a multiplicity of economic, social and security aspects affecting our daily lives in an increasingly interconnected world. Migration is a term that encompasses a wide variety of movements and situations that involve people of all walks of life and backgrounds. More than ever before, migration touches all states and people in an era of deepening globalization. Migration is intertwined with geopolitics, trade and cultural exchange, and provides opportunities for states, businesses and communities to benefit enormously. Migration has helped improve people's lives in both origin and destination countries and has offered opportunities for millions of people worldwide to forge safe and meaningful lives abroad. Not all migration occurs in positive circumstances, however. We have in recent years seen an increase in migration and displacement occurring due to conflict, persecution, environmental degradation and change, and a profound lack of human security and opportunity. (United Nation's International Organization for Migration 2018 *World Migration Report* – https://www.iom.int/wmr/chapter-1)

In this era of deepening globalization migration impacts all nations, and research studies demonstrate the positive long-term socioeconomic benefits it provides (Maxmen 2018). Although the World Migration Report may instil a sense of hope in the success of global migration, the populist front has been increasingly eager to denigrate migrants and undocumented aliens as 'animals' breaking through borders and 'infesting' our Western nation states. The language and imagery used for migrants reinforce the perception of them as trespassers and criminals, implying fears of their appearance in large numbers or as lone crazed terrorists. This has, in particular, been the case in recent political rhetoric that casts migration as a criminal act, equating migrants with parasitic, predatory animals and warning against being 'flooded' or overrun by 'hordes' or 'swarms' of people. The current president of the United States regularly refers to migrants from the global South as 'animals,' labelling them as 'invaders infesting America', and 'slicing and dicing young beautiful girls' (Gupta 2017; Schanzer 2019), while David Cameron famously invoked images of biblical locust infestations by comparing migrants with '*swarms* of people coming across the Mediterranean' (BBC News, 30 July 2015: http://www.bbc.com/news/uk-politics-33716501). It is a rhetoric that has become an integral part of what Fintan O'Toole (2018) has described as the 'new pre- rather than old post-fascist' political climate. According to the prominent Irish journalist, we live in a new era of preparation for widespread fascism and political violence towards minorities. He defines fascism as building 'a sense of threat from a despised out-group' in the context of claims such as the one that immigrants 'infest' our well-protected nation states, a strategy he views as a 'test-marking' of whether the voters of populist politicians are ready for the next step-up in language, which is to call undocumented aliens 'vermin'. Once that has happened, O'Toole reminds us, anything is possible.

The animal that has a particularly close relationship with migration, homelessness, exile and crime is the wolf. What migrants and wolves share is the search for sanctuaries, and it is such sanctuaries which xenophobia and what I call *lycophobia* (fear and hatred of wolves) prevent and destroy. The root of both evils is territorialism, found in excess in right-wing politics and its populist rhetoric. Wolves, too, however, are fiercely territorial. Like humans they travel long distances in search of new territories, communicating their territoriality. Feared and demonized due to their long-standing cultural history they have become a global metaphor. The time-worn human fear of wolves, of their alleged hunger, greed and bloodlust, metaphorically of a predator attacking the nation's body, seems to offer itself as a suitable image to reflect fears of foreigners invading our well-guarded nation states – migrants coming in from the wild, craving our food, even our children, as is suggested by ancient superstitions about 'Gypsies' and Jews as vagrant predators and child stealers. Ironically, in recent times it has been US policy that separated children from their families at detention camps along the US–Mexico border.

The political rhetoric likening migrants to trespassing wolves has been on the rise especially in areas where wolves have produced long-standing negative associations, as in Central Europe, where they have now reappeared, coinciding with the arrival of large numbers of refugees and immigrants. As wolf debates loom large in the United States and Central Europe, with wolves entering new territories that had so far been wolf-free, the metaphor has experienced increasing media coverage. This is particularly true in the context of fears relating to immigration and terrorism, from attention-grabbing headlines such as 'Donald Trump Supporters Tell Immigrants "The Wolves Are Coming, You Are the Hunted" as Race Hate Fears Rise' (Adam Lusher, *The Independent*, 9 Nov 2016) to commentaries on rogue politicians and world leaders such as 'The Wolf of Pyongyang' (David Kang, *Foreign Affairs*, 9 Aug 2017), to articles discussing 'lone-wolf' attacks: 'We Must Track and Trap Lone Wolf Terrorists' (Micah Halpern, *The Observer*, 25 Nov 2014).

At the same time, however, wolves stand in as a metaphor for those who are adamantly opposed to welcoming refugees and other migrants. Wolves are thus appropriated as a metaphor either for humans debased as trespassers and criminals or for those in power trying to fend migrants off from our gates. The image of the wolf has been usurped for a politics of excessive nationalism and at times of war as a positive symbol standing in for strength, courage, aggressive invasion of new territories, pack organization and even berserk movements such as the desperate 'total war' scenario carried out by the Nazis at the end of the Second World War.

Hitler identified very closely with wolves, Turkish nationalists call themselves 'Grey Wolves', their greeting, the so-called *Wolfsgruß*, which was recently banned in Austria, and for the invasion of Ukraine Putin allegedly recruited members from what has been described as his 'shadow army', the *Night Wolves*, an ultranationalist paramilitary biker gang. The wolf has been appropriated for ideological purposes since the dawn of humanity, in legal and political discourse, folklore, and in artistic representations in myth, literature, the visual arts and film. In the visual arts, for example, it has recently had a comeback in the anti-fascist messages of German artist Rainer Opolka, who has warned against racism against refugees with his highly successful art installation entitled 'The Wolves Are Back', featuring a series of metal wolf statues, some giving a Nazi salute, others blindfolded to represent blind hate.

The wolf metaphor is consequently ambivalent in its tension between reverence and hatred for wolves. Populist discourse seems to link the time-worn fear and hatred of wolves especially to acts of trespassing. As wolves are once again entering Central Europe, sparking heated debates as to whether they should be protected or hunted down and driven away, some right-wing groups and political parties – the *AfD* (Alternative for Germany) or the Danish People's Party – have likened them to the new surge of migrants, labelling them as trespassers,

Figure 1.1 Rainer Opolka's Wolf Statue 'NSA Man'. Courtesy of Rainer Opolka.

parasites, and un-reformable and blaming the EU for its open borders to wolves and migrants (Bennhold 2019). While the loudest voices in the Danish wolf debate speak of outlawing 'burqas and wolves' (Nors 2018), in a profoundly xenophobic article on the website *bürgerstimme.com* Marko Wild (2015) mentioned in particular Muslim migrants whom he compared with marauding wolves, emphasizing the need for both foreigners and wolves to be hunted down and removed from German soil.

If we compare these populist uses of the metaphor, we notice that in the headline 'Donald Trump Supporters Tell Immigrants "The Wolves Are Coming, You Are the Hunted" as Race Hate Fears Rise' (Lusher 2016) the wolf features as a hunter of immigrants, a stereotypically aggressive beast of the Western frontier and American patriotism, while European populism taps into people's phobias about the new presence of wolves as a symbol of open borders, advocating that they be hunted down, that Europe be made wolf-free as a model for it becoming immigrant-free. This duality of the wolf as hunter and being hunted reflects the ways in which this particular metaphor has been used over millennia, the wolf in its biopolitical ambivalence on the one hand as sovereign aggressor, despot and invader, and on the other hand the wolf as vermin, and the lycanthrope as a human being without peace and outlawed by the community.

The recent populist rhetoric shows that metaphors do indeed matter if they become a form of hate speech that helps to inspire violence. The wolf metaphor has done extreme damage to wolves and humans alike, with both being demonized and, in the case of humans, being dehumanized to a level that aims to make violent reactions justifiable. By tracing the history of this metaphor via myth, literary texts, political rhetoric, film and visual culture this book aims to raise awareness about xenophobia, racism and the damage the wolf myth perpetuates for these animals and humans alike. The following pages offer an interspecies comparison which examines and warns against the twofold practice of anthropomorphization of the wolf going hand in hand with the dehumanization of individuals or ethnic groups and the destruction of their cultures. Straddling the boundaries between the humanities and the natural sciences this book will add to existing discourses on racism and other forms of political violence (e.g. Hannah Arendt, Étienne Balibar, Seyla Benhabib). It comes at a critical time in view of ongoing debates over migration in Europe, the racially charged political climate in the United States and the global spread of neo-fascist groups promoting racial divides. In order to destabilize the use of such volatile metaphors in the politics of exclusion, neo-fascism and the mythologization and demonization of wolves, this study takes a novel approach by comparing European with indigenous cultures, keeping in mind environmental, cultural and psychological modes of destruction under not only colonial, totalitarian, but also current forms of governance.

Thinking about wolves and migrants produces a range of questions: How are time-worn fears of the wolf linked to the migrant as alien Other over time and cultural space, and in contemporary political rhetoric? How does the metaphor of the wolf shape the way we treat it and humans associated with it? What are the psychological and actual effects of dehumanizing metaphors? How does the wolf metaphor itself migrate over time and through space and what happens interculturally, inter-ethnically during that process? How do colonial power structures and wolf fears imported from Europe compare with indigenous perceptions of the wolf in North America? Can indigenous and environmentalist wolf politics positively affect the migrant integration processes? Can biodiversity be redefined to include humans and multiculturalism? Can the idea of finding sanctuaries be applied to both animals and humans? This notion of sanctuary is key to this project. The wolf metaphor reflects a persistence over time and space in biopolitics that strips both migrants and wolves as well as migrants seen as wolves of their right to obtain sanctuaries.

Jon Mooallem has argued very persuasively in his 2014 Ted Talk that the stories we tell about animals are shaped by the times and places in which they are told, and affect extermination and preservation of various species tremendously. In examining the cultural history of the wolf this book will heed his words while proceeding both diachronically through the ages and across different cultural spaces. It will follow the history of this metaphor from its beginnings in Greek myth via its significance as a legal concept in the Middle Ages, to texts in which wolves appear in the context of race, gender and colonialism in North America, to its uses in National Socialism, to immigration, environmental politics and ecocritical literary responses today.

Keeping in mind that there is extensive literature on both cultural diversity and biodiversity but very little on the relations between the two (Heyd 2010), this book is an experiment in deconstructing the boundaries between human and non-human animal as well as between biodiversity and cultural diversity. We have seen that sanctuary cities for migrants, in which local politics may stray from federal politics, and places like Yellowstone offer some alternatives to the grim history of persecution and extermination that characterizes both wolves and humans seen as wolf-like predators. They are parallel models holding hopes for a regeneration of the planet, for what as early as 1795 the philosopher Immanuel Kant called *Weltfrieden*, the idea of world peace based on his understanding of hospitality: 'Hospitality means the right of a stranger and as long as he behaves peaceably not to be treated as an enemy upon arrival in another country. This right of a visitor is common to all people due to their shared ownership of the surface of the planet, upon which, owing to its spherical shape they cannot disperse ad infinitum, so that they are forced to tolerate each other's presence' (Kant 1923 [1795]: 21; my translation).

World peace has of course always been utopian. It is threatened in many ways and yet, as important as they are, our imagination, our story telling and metaphors may perpetuate certain myths that are responsible for destroying peace among humans, between humans and animals, and lead to the extermination of species. Our imaginary projections of nature onto culture affect nature and its creatures, as the way we see a species, the way we feel about an animal, can impact its standing on the planet more than anything covered in ecology textbooks (Mooallem 2014). The current 'wolf wars' in Europe and the United States are for the most part a product of the mythification of an animal, having produced a great deal of tension between farmers, environmentalists and, in the United States, Native Americans. Although the reintroduction of wolves has shown certain benefits such as an increase of biodiversity, the time-worn fear and hatred of wolves are very much alive in the United States as much as in Germany, France and other countries in Western Europe, where the animal has reappeared since the 1990s and been killing livestock.

Historically, the strife between humans and wolves has largely been territorial and over natural resources, a competition for food, especially in times of war when food is scarce. As the current wolf debates are also about land use and ownership it may therefore not surprise that xenophobia towards immigrants wishing to share territory with those who have held it for generations is in the mentality of a faction of people in places like the Western United States, as opposed to many countries in Northern and Central Europe where there is a 'right to roam' providing public access to natural areas even when the land is privately owned. In areas where nearly all trespassing is a crime and individualism is the rule, a greater eagerness to see the wolf removed from the endangered species list is also often seen, leading to policies that entail their widespread extermination as 'varmints'. The current aggressive immigration politics in the United States parallels the equally aggressive turn in environmental politics under the current regime (in 2019), which considers ending the endangered species status for the American grey wolf.

A place like Yellowstone National Park has demonstrated, however, that wolves can be ecologically curative when re-introduced in locations from which they had disappeared. Moreover, the extermination of wolves in an area resulting from its removal from the endangered species list causes tremendous damage to indigenous cultural identities that are traditionally closely linked to its presence. To what extent indigenous self-understanding may depend on the presence of wolves is evidenced, for example, by the rehabilitation of the grey wolf in Idaho where it has significantly reshaped the cultural identity of the Nez Perce tribe. The neo-colonial implications of a headline such as the one appearing in the UK's Independent newspaper on 9 November 2016 'Donald Trump Supporters Tell Immigrants "The Wolves Are Coming, You Are the Hunted" as Race Hate Fears Rise' cannot be fully understood unless we keep in mind the plight of the traditionally nomadic native population, their genocide and the reduction of their land rights to mere pockets of the land they used to populate.

The discussion of divergent attitudes between migratory, nomadic cultures towards their environment in general (and wolves in particular) and sedentary farming cultures forms a part of this project, as the wolf's persistently negative image as a parasitic trespasser results largely from the experiences of agrarian cultures and settlers claiming land as property. One of the main problems about wolves reappearing in places like Germany is that they are entering what Germans call a *Kulturlandschaft*, land transformed from nature into culture and no longer owned by all living creatures. Transforming wilderness into culture is a quintessentially colonial experience in which animal politics and human politics converge.

From the perspective of the early colonizers arriving in North America, who took possession of the land they found, indigenous tribes and wolves were almost-identical enemies in this land quest, so that, according to Jason Mark, the 'war against wolves and the wars against the Indians overlapped and were all but undistinguishable'. At the start of an 1865 campaign against the Northern Plains tribes, a US Army general told his troops that the Cheyenne and Lakota 'must be hunted like wolves' (Jason Mark 2015). If we compare this statement with the headline quoted above about Trump supporters featuring as hungry wolves hunting immigrants, we recognize how easily the metaphor can switch between wolf reverence and wolf hatred, in colonial and post-colonial power structures, and in different contexts of dehumanization.

The current trend in populism of employing metaphors for the purpose of dehumanizing its targeted groups is of course not a new phenomenon. We do not need to go all that far back in the history of persecution of undesirables to see how such metaphors contributed to genocide, if we think of Nazi ideology labelling Jews and other undesirables as typhoid-spreading rats. While wolves were revered in the Third Reich for their strength, organization and purported aggression, yet another animal metaphor was reserved for those the Reich deemed undesirable and *lebensunwert*, life not worth living: the metaphor of the insect, the louse in particular. In the final solution, various practices of dehumanization and killing, above all the gas chambers, point to this conceptual eradication of humans as lice. It is

1. Introduction

what in the first sentence of *Die Verwandlung* (Metamorphosis 1915) Franz Kafka calls the *Ungeziefer* – the animal that in its etymology implies that it is not clean enough to be sacrificed but which can be killed by anyone with impunity – that forms the basis of this ideology of hatred in Nazi Germany towards traditionally migratory groups such as the Jews and Sinti and Roma people. In the current political climate, as toxic discourses are being mobilized, the use of discriminating language to compare immigrants to animals – the recent misnomer of migrants 'swarming' into the UK (Elgot 2016), or as 'animals that slice and dice beautiful teen girls' (Gupta 2017) – is a sinister reminder of that connection (Shariatmadari 2015).

The *Ungeziefer* (parasite) shares with the wolf a widespread perception as vermin whose killing is believed to benefit humanity. This animal that can be killed by anyone, the parasite believed to cause harm and whose benefits humanity is blind to, has a long metaphorical tradition in myth, literature and public discourse describing migrants in search of asylum. There is no sanctuary for such animals that can be killed by anyone with impunity, although at least since the days of the early nineteenth-century American environmentalist Aldo Leopold some rights of conservation have also been granted wolves. These rights now seem to disappear again, especially in the United States where rampant wolf culling, even of wolf pups in dens, and killing hibernating bears have been on the agenda for legalization under the current government, a step that would undo an Obama regulation that prohibits these practices. There is also no sanctuary for migrants seeking it abroad, as long as their migration is considered a criminal act, criminalized to the point these days that in the eyes of the US government seems to justify separating thousands of children from their parents. From its very beginnings in myth the wolf metaphor has been closely tied to crime. Because of their mythologization as rapacious killers wolves have traditionally had difficulties in finding sanctuaries. If this concept is then applied to humans who run away from crime and war in search of better lives and are being turned into criminals because of such quests, we are facing a history of persecution that denies the basic human right to shelter and protection.

The wolf metaphor feeds itself from myth, folklore and superstition rather than actual scientific knowledge of wolves. It has little to do with the reality of wolves, their biological presence that suffers substantially from this kind of mythification. Even benevolent publications on the general benefit of wolves as social animals to be emulated by human society such as Elli Radinger's recent bestseller *The Wisdom of Wolves*

(2019) and many other texts, whether ecofeminist or literary, tend to be anthropocentric, perpetuating myths about this animal (cf. Robisch 2009: 340–2). But when did wolves turn into myth? When did, using Robisch's terminology, corporeal wolves become ghost wolves?

The metaphor's literary roots reach back in time to folktales, to medieval outlaws expelled from the community as wolves, as far back as Greek antiquity. Although an area of much speculation, it could even be argued that humans' persistent fear of wolves linked to sedentariness and territory takes its beginnings much earlier, at the dawn of humanity possibly when the bond between humans and wolves – that time-worn lycanthropy – may have taken centre stage in the evolutionary step from hunters and gatherers to sedentary farming communities. The history of migration and sedentariness reflects sentiments towards the wolf, both *lycophobia* and *lycophilia*, fear and love of wolves. It is conceivable that in the Palaeolithic period, wolves and other predators were not only feared but also revered, that hunting and gathering societies mimicked these predators, hoping to incorporate their admired faculties, particularly their stealth and strength. By donning wolf skins the hunter may have been able to imagine what it was like to be a wolf, resulting in a heightened awareness of what it meant to be human. Since the dawn of humanity the wolf has inspired mixed emotions. It is an animal of fruition and perdition, and migration and sedentariness play a substantial part in this scenario (Douglas 1993: 36).

In primordial communities the search for food during the hunt necessitated extensive wanderings, which became even more expansive and urgent if the food sources had dried up and the whole clan was forced to move on in search of new hunting grounds. This nomadic hunting lifestyle finally gave way to a more settled one, as hunters and gatherers started growing crops and became farmers. It is after this transition period that the admiration for the wolf for its hunting techniques and the necessity to emulate it began to wane, and that the idea of trespassing onto one's communal territory became more prevalent. Henceforth the fear of the wolf as an intruder may have overshadowed its former glory so that it became increasingly seen as a threat to the community and its homesteads, as humans became more and more alienated from their natural environment and all its living creatures. To this day we can see this discrepancy between sedentary cultures that subjugate nature and nomadic indigenous cultures that are still closer to nature by believing they form a part of it rather than being in possession of the land. No longer perceived as nurturers wolves became associated primarily with rapaciousness, a binary that stays with us in myth and literature over time and is at the root of the biopolitical metaphor for humans on the run outside of law as human wolves.

Wolves had to be killed, as they started threatening the clan and their livestock. It is sedentariness that links the wolf to cunning and evil and causes the emergence of heterotopias, the separation between civilization as the space of settlement and that of nurturing, and wilderness as the space outside of that settlement. David Hunt also concludes in his research on perceptions of the wolf among Eastern European and Central Asian cultures that there is a 'correlation between the mode of life of the people and their attitude to the wolf' (Hunt 2008: 331), that the more people live outdoors the more positive their attitude to wolves is, while a more sedentary lifestyle increases the fear of the wolf. The wolf became a symbol of uncontrollable nature outside of the space of dwelling, which had so far mentally incorporated its spirit as a good luck token for the great hunt. As the wolf came to be considered a parasite, so were invasive tribes, since with settlement came property and with property came strife over turf and theft. It is thus conceivable that in the transition from the hunting clans of the Palaeolithic period (until 10,000 BCE) to sedentary farmers in the Mesolithic period (10,000 to 5,000 BCE) wolves were associated with human raiders, with outlaws and crime. The larger the settlements grew, the wider the gulf between civil and wild terrain became.

Early humanity's ambivalent attitude to the wolf image as nurturer and destroyer filtered into the first form of storytelling: myth. The nurturing principle prevails in Native American creation myths or the story of Romulus and Remus, while one of the central European myths in which the wolf becomes demonized is that of Lycaon, the king of Arcadia, transformed into a wolf for breaking the taboo of cannibalism. As T. P. Wiseman has demonstrated, the Roman foundation myth has its roots in the ancient Greek myth of Lycaon, with extended links between the Lykaios rites and the Roman Lupercalia and their respective celebrations of the eternal cycle of death and life, their topographies of Mount Lykaion in the Peloponnese and the Palatine Hill of Rome, as well as between the Greek God of the Hunt Pan Lykaios, the Roman Mars as the rapist father of the wolf children and the shepherd Faunus who raises them (Wiseman 1995: 4). While the Greek myth of Lycaon features a destructive wolf, the Roman she-wolf is nurturing; in both cases, however, the wolf is responsible for a new beginning, as myths often invoke origins.

Expelled from the community of men for his crime Lycaon, however, is also an oral blueprint for the biopolitical practice associated with the Roman tradition of the *homo sacer*, the human cursed and set apart from the community, and in search of shelter. The poet Ovid, for example, who writes about Lycaon, Callisto and Io, and their loss of sanctuaries and transformation into animals, was himself such a *homo sacer*, banished by Augustus to the outer confines of the empire. Expelled from home to an area Ovid must initially have deemed savagely barbarian, if we listen to David Malouf's novel *An Imaginary Life* (1978), the poet has a special relationship with Lycaon. The first myth on display in his *Metamorphoses* is the Arcadian king's transformation into a wolf after dishing up human meat to the god Jove:

> He took a hostage sent by the Molossians, and after severing his windpipe, cut his body into pieces and then put the throbbing parts up to be boiled or broiled. As soon as he had set this on the table, I loosed my vengeful bolts until that house collapsed on its deserving household gods! Frightened he runs off to the silent fields (*silentia ruris*) and howls aloud, attempting speech in vain; foam gathers at the corners of his mouth; he turns his lust for slaughter on the flocks, and mangles them, rejoicing still in blood. His garments now become a shaggy pelt; his arms turn into legs, and he, to wolf while still retaining traces of the man: grayness the same, the same cruel visage, the same cold eyes and bestial appearance. (Ovid 2004: 13)

The Lycaon myth exists in different versions, even within the range of translations of Ovid's text. English translations include those by Sir Samuel Garth, John Dryden et al. (1717), George Sandys (1632), Brookes More (1922), A. D. Melville (Oxford UP, 2008) and Charles Martin (Norton, 2010). I am using the latter here. In his *Book of Werewolves* (1865) the renowned nineteenth-century and early twentieth-century Anglican priest and hagiographer Sabine Baring-Gould (1834–1924), one of the early critics on lycanthropy, quotes Ovid in this version:

> In vain he attempted to speak; from that very instant his jaws were bespluttered with foam, and only he thirsted for blood, as he raged amongst flocks and panted for slaughter. His vesture was changed into hair, his limbs became crooked; A wolf – he retains yet large trace of his ancient expression, hoary he is as afore, his countenance rabid, his eyes glitter savagely still, the picture of fury. (Baring-Gould 2007 [1865]: 15)

Both versions stress the trauma Lycaon experiences upon the expulsion that leaves him transformed, dehumanized and cast into utter loneliness.

Becoming wolf is associated with fits of rage, especially in the second translation, but also with melancholia, depression and, above all, the loss of language that in many philosophical traditions is seen as the principal distinction between non-human animals and humans. Lycaon shares the moment of 'running off to the silent fields, attempting speech in vain', with Callisto turned into a bear and Io turned into a heifer. It is of particular interest, as it defines the moment of exclusion from the human community as one in which a human being is deprived of speech (*logos*) while, however, retaining an animal voice (howl).

Moreover, becoming a wolf is associated with lust, greed, madness and above all fear ('frightened he runs off') in the face of change, metamorphosis and the power of the gods. These emotions expressed in the myth may reflect Ovid's own, his fear of Roman power and his loss of identity due to his expulsion from urban life, that centre of the world called Rome, and of subsequently being forced to wander in the outer reaches of the empire. It is this wandering of the proscribed human in search of a sanctuary inspired by the lone wolf in search of new territory that is at the heart of this project, which traces the descendants of the Lycaon myth over time and space in world literature by focusing on the motif of migration, loss of home, exile and its ensuing trauma.

Expulsion and wandering are the consequences of crime in this myth, the wolf an image for the undesirable. Lycaon's hostility to the gods and the human race necessitates his being set apart from both. His abandonment and subsequent migration 'in the silent fields' are inextricably linked to his crime, his wanderings being the consequence of crime but also reinforcing his status as a criminal. To this day, migrants try to escape from crime mostly in the form of war in search of a better life but in doing so are made criminals by regimes that do not provide sanctuaries for them. It is the fate of Lycaon that has stayed with us over millennia.

The moment in which the mythical transformation of man into wolf became a metaphor in the context of a concrete biopolitical reality was in the Germanic Middle Ages where criminals, murderers for the most part, were outlawed beyond the confines of the community and perceived as wolves, also known as the *vargr i veum*, the wolf in the sanctuary (Grönbech 1976: 130). This figure implies the idea of the human wolf (*vargr*) expelled from the community and in need of a sanctuary (*veum*), while at the same time threatening the community as the safest form of sanctuary. The Lycaon myth thus became a sinister reality for the *homo sacer* or *Friedlos* (human without peace) sentenced to what Giorgio Agamben calls *nuda vita* (naked or bare life), banned and rendered free (*wolfsfrei*) to be killed by anyone. Their loss of sanctuary coincided with a dissolution of the right for dwelling, the '*dissolutio civitatis* inaugurated by the state of exception' (Agamben 1995:106), which corresponds to the Hobbesian state of nature in which, based on Plautus's *homo homini lupus est* in his play *Asinaria*, 'man to man is an errant wolf'. This is a key concept that still has its validity for the contemporary global migrant or refugee situation with its scenario of abjection, loss of identity and the conceptual lupization of man. The primary trauma of migrants on the run is that loss of peace that can only be found within the community.

If we apply these concepts to today's refugees, then the space and time between their loss of home and finding a new home resembles the exile of the medieval *Friedlos*, as they tend to come from war-torn countries. Contemporary migrants remain without peace if kept in a space that prevents them from going back or forward. That space does exist currently, for example, in detention camps off the coast of Australia in which refugees are detained for undetermined periods of time. These people could indeed be described as modern-day *vargr* or *Friedlos* in a state of exception that, paradoxically, has the tendency to become the norm. They find themselves in what Marc Augé has termed 'non-places' (2009), spaces that are set apart without the protective function of a sanctuary. They are spaces of exception, a term that is highly ambivalent, as are sanctuaries. Like the state of exception the sanctuary can both provide shelter from violence and be the location where violence reigns supreme, an ambiguity that becomes observable as early as in the myth of Callisto, the nymph who gets raped by Jove inside the grove (the grove being the classical sanctuary of Greek antiquity).

Possibly some of the most extreme spaces in which the sanctuary is lost, however, are the concentration camps of the twentieth and twenty-first centuries. Place matters in this literary history, as do other phenomena that characterize the *homo sacer*'s dehumanization in the state of nature, such as their voicelessness, their loss of speech. 'Frightened [Lycaon] runs off to the silent fields and howls aloud, attempting speech in vain', as Ruth Franklin has argued a primary mechanism of dehumanization of the camp victims consisted in 'taking away the essential tool of humanity, their language' (Franklin 2011: 55). Auschwitz, says Agamben, 'is the radical refutation of every principle of obligatory communication [...] In some camps communication was taken by the rubber whip, ironically renamed der Dolmetscher (the interpreter) [and] [...] not being talked to was the normal condition in the camp, where 'your tongue dries up in a few days, and your thoughts with it (Levi)' (Agamben 2002: 65).

With the *homo sacer* of the camps we have come a long way from the wolf as itinerant expellee. According to Greek thinking, however, the *polis* is also a *polos*, the pivotal axis around which the conflict unfolds between *lethe* and *aletheia*, leaving those outside – in *lethe* – who do not have the word. Heidegger's thoughts in his *Parmenides* lectures on *lethe* and *aletheia* reflect the lupization of man. This condemnation of man to the field of *lethe* in the sense of forgetting, concealment and destruction is the plight shared by uncounted expellees. They are expelled from the polis – the place in antiquity where humanity was centred – excluded from being or *Dasein* itself. This exclusion impacts on the medieval *vargr*, the inmate of the concentration camps, and today's migrants suspended in that uncertain state between the home they left and the home they seek but may never find. Like Lycaon they tend to be deprived of speech, dehumanized, running in *silentia ruris* (the silent fields). It is an exile from language itself, traditionally seen as a key defining element of what it means to be human.

What is it in the wolf that inspires narratives of abandonment, homelessness, rootlessness, the silencing of the migrant and the clamour of the sovereign who decides over the fate of those on the run from him? The perception of wolves as migratory no doubt stems from the vast range they cover in their daily wanderings. Nonetheless, wolves are not nomadic creatures but territorial, staying mostly within the boundaries of their territories, with the sole exception of lone wolves, so-called dispersers, that split from the pack generally after losing a fight with the alpha male. It is the image of this lone wolf rather than the pack that points to the human without roots and that seems to haunt various cultures from antiquity on as a metaphor for not only human migration, exile, the permanent loss of home, crime associated with rootlessness, but also the power of resistance, for lone wolves need to be particularly shrewd and strong if they want to survive without the support of the pack. They tend to be stronger and more aggressive because they have to hunt alone. Nonetheless, there is a certain mystique about them which is not evidenced by reality. According to Barry Holstun Lopez (1978: 64–5), lone wolves may leave the pack in search of new territory; they may eventually join other packs, but in any case, territories are flexible and shifting, and in no way defined in human terms. However, wolves in search of territory run the risk of encountering hostile wolves or humans; it necessitates increased vigilance without the protection of their packs. This elusiveness, their purported stealth and cunning, is a motif to be found in literature throughout the ages.

Lopez argues that 'there is a common belief among wolf biologists working in the field that wolves like to travel' and that 'one reason for maintaining large territories is to have the space to travel freely and widely' (1978: 66). Indeed, the elusive wandering of wolves, their straying from one territory to another, became a trope for centuries in racism towards ethnic itinerant groups and individualists leaving their communities and thus no longer trusted by them. The wolf's demonization since the Middle Ages once Christianity moved into Northern Europe evolves over time from a metaphor for expelled criminals into a religious metaphor decrying women as she-wolves and witches in the early modern age, into a racist metaphor aimed at minorities with a traditionally mobile understanding of home, primarily Jews and Gypsies. While committing a crime led to expulsion in the case of medieval outlaws, inversely, in the history of humanity crime has been seen as a result of migration, of homelessness and of being perennially uprooted. For centuries so-called Gypsies, the Romany, and other vagrants and vagabonds (*Landstreicher* in German, people roaming the land) have been associated with crime due to their perceived evasive lifestyle. The negative images of such people fill political ideology and its rhetoric contributing to their persecution but also literature itself. Literary texts from the early modern period to the early twentieth century demonstrate, for example, how the Romany were stereotypically defamed as child-devouring itinerants and marauders, and how Jews – living in the diaspora – were labelled as wolves.

The uses of the wolf metaphor in European literature as a reflection of race politics show how persistent it is over time and how it develops in expressing social anxieties about minorities, a topic explored in depth in Chapter 2 – 'Fear of the Pack: Jews and Gypsies as Wolves'. The Gypsy-as-wolf paradigm pervades texts from the European picaresque tradition – e.g. Hans Jakob Christoffel von Grimmelshausen's *The Adventures of Simplicius Simplicissimus* (1668) – to Victor Hugo's *The Hunchback of Notre Dame* (1830), Bram Stoker's *Dracula* (1897), as far as Hermann Löns's scathing anti-Ziganist novel *The Werewolf* (1910). I also discuss literature in which Jews are maligned as wolves, such as William Shakespeare's classic *The Merchant of Venice* (written between 1595 and 1599) and Wilhelm Raabe's realist novel *The Hunger Pastor* (1864). This selection of literature will demonstrate the development of racism from religious superstitions in the early modern period to late nineteenth-century fears of invasion and racial pollution by migrants, how such literature then feeds into totalitarian ideologies, but also how some of these authors show a critical and at times ironic stance vis-à-vis these stereotypes.

With the colonization of the New World the metaphor was transported overseas for the purpose of dehumanizing the colonized Other. As early as in his 1596 publication 'A View of the Present State of Ireland' the poet Edmund Spenser maintained that the Irish all turned into wolves for one year, and in the American settlements wolves and indigenous people were considered 'creatures of the godless wilderness that the colonists believed they had a moral duty to subdue' (Fogleman 1989: 66). The wolf signified a frontier phenomenon and the boundary between civilization and wilderness, Europeanness and indigeneity. In a letter to James Duane from 7 September 1783 George Washington himself compared Indians with wolves, 'both being beasts of prey tho' they differ in shape' (Washington, *Letters*, Founders' Archive).

Continuing the discussion of wolves and race in Chapter 3 – 'Wolves and Indigenous Culture: Migration of a Metaphor to the Colonies' focuses on the wolf metaphor's links with the colonial Other in a selection of historical sources and literary texts, including Daniel Defoe's *Robinson Crusoe* (1719), Rudyard Kipling's *Jungle Book* (1894), Willa Cather's *My Ántonia* (1918), Jack London's portraits of dogs and wolves in the context of the civilizing mission in *Call of the Wild* (1903) and *White Fang* (1906), Michael Blake's *Dances with Wolves* (1989) and Louise Erdrich's *The Painted Drum* (2005). The chapter begins with an analysis of Crusoe's wolves as a reflection of the colonial subaltern and Kipling's good wolves as an imperialist image steeped in the Roman foundation myth. It then showcases the views of early settlers in North America to demonstrate how the metaphor itself migrates to a colonial context that equates wolves with indigenous people. The chapter proceeds to examine how literature perpetuates and deconstructs such equations and how indigenous wolf lore differs from Euro-American perceptions. It discusses how traditional indigenous views of living among other species rather than in separation from them can be read alongside similar Western philosophies of cosmopolitanism and in the context of the contemporary migrant situation.

The Euro-American authors analysed in this chapter develop an authorial stance that either supports the negative metaphor or distances itself from the deeply racist views that associate the purported savagery of the indigenous tribes with that of wolves. How, on the other hand, are wolves portrayed in Native American myth and literature? Is there an indigenous world view that can fruitfully inform the politics of migration and race, and a trajectory from exclusion to inclusion?

Wolves form a substantial part of a vision in indigenous culture of universal peace among all creatures and that Mother Earth cannot be bought, owned and must not be recklessly exploited, a view expressed, for example, in John G. Neihardt's *Black Elk Speaks* (1932). How do indigenous writers, especially women, question writing about wolves as a clichéd image of Native American or First Nations traditions, wilderness and constructions of masculinity?

That the association of humans with wolves in the context of migration is also a gender paradigm is further examined in Chapter 4 – 'Wolves and Wayward Women: Between Condemnation and Empowerment'. Migration and exile are defined here in terms of women straying from the community, living alone, being persecuted for their choices and seeking sanctuaries in the company of wolves. The romantic fairy tale in Germany offers us a sinister reminder of the treatment of such 'she-wolves' for centuries, the persecution of women perceived as a threat to the patriarchal world order and burnt as witches on the stake. From the late Middle Ages on, the wolf became synonymous with the devil. Wolves and child-devouring witches frequently blended together in this process of demonization as early as the Great Werewolf and Witch Hunt initiated by Pope Innocent VIII in the *Papal Bull Summis Desiderantes Affectibus* in December 1484 and immensely propelled by the publication of the *Malleus Maleficarum* (Hammer of Witches 1486; Zipes 1983: 69). By and large, these women's choice of leaving the community and choosing to exile themselves to a solitary life in addition to their age was the sole reason for being persecuted (Baschwitz 1963: 139–47). According to Hannah Arendt, 'isolation may be the beginning of terror', and women living outside of the community experienced this terror over centuries. As Lycaon's daughters without a place in the community, by which they were pronounced dead, and trying to survive in a heterotopia outside the social contract meant 'to have no place in the world' (Arendt 1973: 474–5).

Devouring wolves and other canine predators seem to be entirely male projections, the amalgamation of wolves and femininity in patriarchal cultures reflecting male fears and contempt for women, except for the wolf mother's role in nurturing great leaders, the material of myths such as the Roman *lupa* suckling Romulus and Remus. The negative she-wolf as witch, however, pervades European literature from Dante's *Divina Comedia* to the patriarchal folktales, to nineteenth-century texts such as Giovanni Verga's short story 'La Lupa' featuring the 'lupine whore' (Robisch 2009: 20). This chapter examines what prompted this change from a positive she-wolf in myth to her demonization in Christianized

Europe, in comparison also with her role for society in other parts of the world, and how the she-wolf survives via the folktales and their feminist rewritings into our times. Adding to the countless readings of the 'Little Red Riding Hood' tale, I suggest that the appearance of the wolf is inextricably linked to the fates of the three women the tale features, their intergenerational conflict, the girl's wandering and loss of sanctuary, and a patriarchal denigration of women as witches or she-wolves. That the trope of the absent and neglectful mother as predator still reverberates into our times can be seen by the media coverage of the case of Lindy Chamberlain, who, travelling to the Australian outback, lost her baby daughter to another canine predator, a dingo, but was, when first indicted for the murder of her child, decried as a devouring witch mother.

This chapter then proceeds to discuss how women writers have tapped into the wolf myth for its potential for liberating, sheltering and empowering women. This has been explored in ecofeminist texts by women 'running with wolves' in women's adaptations of folktales, most notably perhaps in Angela Carter's *The Bloody Chamber* (1979), in Nicolette Krebitz's recent film *Wild* (2016) and in Misha Defonseca's fictionalized Holocaust memoir *Surviving with Wolves* (2005). The latter shows a young girl's wanderings through war-torn Europe in search of her deported parents. The text debunks traditional perceptions of wolves as evil creatures, a process also explored by Krebitz's film about a solitary woman's romance with a wolf in East Germany, as well as in a range of non-fiction texts, such as by Clarissa Pinkola Estés's *Women Who Run with Wolves* (1992), Hélène Grimaud's *Wolfsonate* (2004) and Elli Radinger's recent bestseller *Wisdom of Wolves* (2018).

In parallel to the previous chapters on race, Chapter 4 follows a similar trajectory of de-demonization of wolves. Once again, this trajectory shows literature's potential to liberate wolves from their stigmatization as devourers and highlight their nurturing qualities. I will, however, also analyse to what extent the wolf is an engendered construct, romanticized and cast into anthropocentric moulds, so that these narratives end up reinforcing the wolf myth and have little to do with actual corporeal wolves.

The wolf metaphor has served many cultures and ideologues as a totem animal for power and resistance. While traditionally nomadic indigenous cultures in North America and Central Asia honour the wolf for its hunting prowess, in fascist regimes the wolf has served as a metaphor for both migration as invasion and defence against foreign invaders. In this regard the Nazis' use of this animal image is similar to other fascist and populist uses. The image of the aggressive and intrusive lone wolf has especially left its mark, as a metaphor not only for terrorists but also on a range of political leaders who have likened themselves to wolves, such as Adolf Hitler and Kemal Ataturk (the Grey Wolf). Current populist rhetoric that describes sovereign power as wolfish is embedded in a history that reaches back to ancient myths and medieval Germanic law, but is specifically rooted in Europe's history of racism, colonialism and totalitarianism. In contrast to the human wolf as an intruder and devourer of children and young women, the wolf's admired qualities of strength, ferocity and intelligence have caused the appearance of the werewolf (literally, man [Latin *vir*] wolf) in literature and the German *Wehrwolf* (defence wolf), as a figure of resistance against immigration and invasion.

Chapter 5 – 'The Wolves of War: Fascism, Terrorism, Resistance' – discusses the wolf metaphor's persistent history of nationalism, imperialism and fascism. It follows a trajectory from the wolf as a symbol of nationalist resistance and invasion to the metaphor's prominence in anti-fascist, pro-migration art. The wolf's renewed demonization in the twentieth and twenty-first centuries includes such moments as Adolf Hitler's obsession with these animals, the Nazis' wolf cult in the final years of the war, Benito Mussolini's 'children of the wolf' in Italy's Fascist Youth Organization *Opera Nazionale Balilla*, the figure of the lone wolf terrorist and the Turkish ultranationalists 'Grey Wolves'. In the context of fascism and resistance to it the lone wolf also features in Ernst Jünger's philosophical-political figure of the *Waldgänger* steeped in the medieval understanding of wolves and Jünger's reaction to the Nazi years. How can this concept be applied to anti-fascist art? This chapter showcases the work of novelist Michel Tournier and sculptor Rainer Opolka, two *Waldgänger* in Jünger's sense, who have appropriated the Nazis' lupine metaphorics for the purpose of their anti-fascist messages and in defence of nomadism (Tournier) and immigration (Opolka).

Weaving out of history back into myth and literature, one French text in particular demonstrates how the werewolf myth is paired with National Socialism. As revisionary mythopoesis Michel Tournier's novel *Le Roi des Aulnes* (1970; translated as *The Ogre*, 1972) amalgamates the history of the fifteenth-century serial killer Gilles de Rais with the Nazis' clandestine berserk movement *Operation Werwolf* which drew thousands of under-aged recruits into the war machinery of destruction. Tournier's novel shows us a lycanthrope who advances from nefarious, totalitarian sanctuaries to potential redemption and salvation, a vision that contrasts sharply with the heinous crimes addressed in this novel, especially the camps of the Holocaust.

While Tournier's novel contains a warning against the international appeal of fascism, the German artist Rainer Opolka has recently also warned against the 'return of Nazi wolves' with his *Sieg Heil* saluting bronze sculptures exhibited in Germany. In the end, Tournier and Opolka may return to time-worn superstitions and stigmata surrounding the evil wolf image, but they do so for the cause of their anti-fascist art. With the book's overall intention of debunking the wolf myth while pointing to what Benhabib called 'the rights of others' this chapter takes a close look at the concept of the 'lone wolf' in zoology, literature and political rhetoric as well as fascist wolf imagery – the body language of the Hitler salute and the wolf salute of the ultranationalist Turkish Grey Wolves – to demonstrate how literature and the visual arts use this controversial iconoclasm to fight racism and xenophobia.

Chapter 6 – 'No Trespassing: Wolves, Borders and Immigrants' – analyses the use of the metaphor in the context of current migrant scenarios, specifically in contemporary literature responding to the catastrophic situation at the US–Mexican border and immigration into Europe from the global South. Embarking from a juxtaposition of Kant's idea of hospitality and world peace with media sources in which immigrants are denigrated as wolves attacking the nation state, I proceed to analyse the uses of the metaphor in current immigration rhetoric. I then discuss several literary texts in view of the wolf metaphor's role in the context of immigration and borders: Sarah Hall's novel *The Wolf Border* (2015) about rewilding England, British identity and an impending Brexit; Roland Schimmelpfennig's novel *One Clear, Ice-Cold January Morning at the Beginning of the Twenty-First Century* (2016) about a lone wolf approaching multicultural Berlin; the Hungarian 2015 Man Booker Prize winner László Krasznahorkai's one-sentence novel *The Last Wolf* (2009) about the last wolves of Extremadura; and two texts about the US–Mexican border – Cormac McCarthy's novel *The Crossing* (1994) and Francisco Cantú's memoir *The Line Becomes a River* (2018).

These texts demonstrate that as wolves are exterminated or maintain a fragile presence in areas where immigration of people never ceases, the animal becomes a metaphor for either destruction or negotiation and reconciliation. The stark realism of McCarthy's novel, in which a pregnant wolf reflects the absence of any sanctuary also for humans, contrasts sharply with the recovery of the metaphor's nurturing qualities in Cantú's exploration of the idea of 'Brother Wolf' in the context of migration from the global South. With its focus on cross-border migration this chapter then leads over to the following chapter, which makes clear that cultural diversity and biodiversity are inseparably linked in the regeneration of the planet.

The central research question examined in Chapter 7 – 'Wolf Trails: Rewilding the World in the Age of Migration' – is the link between wolf politics, the environment and migration, be it the colonial destruction of an ecosystem along with its local nomadic cultures or the hostility with which groups on the extreme right treat both wolves and immigrants, versus the impact the reintroduction of wolves can have on biodiversity and cultural diversity. The chapter begins by showcasing Robert Winder's theory in *The Last Wolf: The Hidden Springs of Englishness* (2017) that Peter Corbett's killing of the last wolf in 1290 in England had a massive effect on English identity, the economy and (im)migration. Winder argues that the initial thrust towards changing the British landscape was done by *de*-wolfing it, which coincided with the expulsion of England's entire Jewish population and led to Britain becoming a vast sheep farm, where sheep were happy and able to multiply causing large-scale immigration of a new labour force and paving the way for Britain's rise to a global empire. 'England,' Winder says, 'was built by foreigners', and this is linked to the disappearance of its wolves, an interesting argument in light of Brexit and closed borders.

Winder's theory is rare among the spate of voices that decry the effects of the disappearance of wolves from an ecosystem. The necessity of creating biodiversity in an environmental and demographic sense is reflected in particular in literary texts that focus on the destruction of specific areas in which local traditional cultures were once in a harmonious relationship with their environment. In his novel *Wolf Totem* (2004) the Chinese author Jiang Rong has detailed the devastating consequences of wolf extermination in Northern China for the environment and its indigenous population. Debates about rewilding show that unlike the nomadic culture of Inner Mongolia, as Rong depicts it, sedentary attitudes to land ownership, be it the ranch or the nation, often view both wolves and immigration as invasive and are steeped in time-worn fears and prejudices. Such attitudes can then shape political preferences that affect the local treatment of the environment and relationships between ethnic groups, resulting in an overall loss of hospitality towards human and non-human animals. Wolf rewilding in Germany, for example, demonstrates this complex link between environmental and immigration politics. I discuss the case of Lusatia along the German–Polish border, an area that has remained fertile ground for far-right political movements such as the 'AfD', *Alternative für Deutschland* (Alternative for Germany) or the *Pegida* (Patriotic Europeans against the Islamization of the Occident), which compare 'trespassing' wolves with immigrants. On the other hand, research has shown that wolf rewilding has had positive effects on biodiversity in the double sense of the recovery of the environment and the diversity of cultures. To illustrate this I will address the controversial history of wolf reintroduction in Yellowstone National Park and the benefits of such reintroduction in redefining the identity of the Nez Perce tribe in Idaho. Chapters 6 and 7 engage with fictional and non-fictional responses to the presence versus absence of wolves in our environment to gain an understanding of the links between wolf politics and their effects on human populations in terms of identity, migration and trauma in precarious parts of the world.

The epilogue entitled 'Dreaming of Wolves: The Children of Lycaon in the Age of Psychoanalysis' examines a series of narratives that involve dreams and fantasies about wolves and how the idea of Brother Wolf in which indigenous culture and psychoanalysis merge is engaged to come to terms with exile, its enforced peregrinations and the subsequent transformation of identity. My brief readings, partly psychoanalytical, partly philosophical, of texts by Hesse, Kafka, Jung and Freud as echoes of the ancient Greek myth of Lycaon open out to a reading of David Malouf's Australian novel *An Imaginary Life* (1975) as a key text offering us an alternative vision to the traumatic scenarios described by these modernist narratives. Malouf's poetic reflections on Ovid's exile contain the story of the poet's encounter with a boy raised by wolves who takes him on his ultimate pilgrimage across the Danube, from South to North, from life to death. This final discussion of metaphor and metamorphosis in literature links my book back to its introductory discussion of Ovid's Lycaon version and will reveal that not all stories of exile are as dire as Kafka's or McCarthy's. Metaphors and myths around wolves have caused much damage to actual, corporeal wolves, as well as to humans. But there is a dimension of hope in this book for the species *canis lupus* and for the migrant coping with trauma, depression and separation. Despite the persistent loss of sanctuaries for animals and humans who are being characterized as invasive predators, the following chapters will highlight those artistic and actual attempts that resist and act against the wolf's demonization and the language of dehumanization.

Chapter 2

FEAR OF THE PACK: JEWS AND GYPSIES AS WOLVES

The boundaries between religion, politics and race are blurred in the wolf metaphor. While in the Middle Ages the metaphor was used in the context of religion, evil, deceit, sovereignty and outlawry, some literary texts from the early modern period to the early twentieth century associate the wolf with matters of race and ethnic and religious alterity. The metaphor dehumanizes not only Jews but also Gypsies and Eastern Europeans with what was thought of as a Gypsy lifestyle. This happens as early as in the seventeenth-century German picaresque novel *The Adventures of Simplicius Simplicissimus* (1668) by Hans Jakob Christoffel von Grimmelshausen, and persists well into the nineteenth century, in novels by Victor Hugo and Bram Stoker. Even in Hermann Löns's extremely anti-Ziganist novel *Der Wehrwolf* (1910, The Werewolf) Gypsies are still defamed as being void of humanity, hunted by the hero, who features as a werewolf or defence wolf. The novel has now sunk into oblivion but was hugely popular in the Third Reich.

Finally, the metaphor was also transported to the American colonies, where the indigenous population was equated with wolves coming in from the wilderness and threatening the European civilizing mission and conquest of the New World. As Coleman argues, 'Wolves symbolized the frustrations and anxieties of colonization, and the canines paid in blood for their utility as metaphors' (Coleman 2004: 11). While the literary lycanthrope appears in the context of race throughout the second half of the nineteenth century, at the beginning of the twentieth century it changes into a psychological paradigm. This happens in Jung's discussion of the Wotan myth and the shadow, Freud's wolf man case and in literature primarily in Hesse's *Steppenwolf* (1927). In all these texts, the wolves and the humans they metaphorically signify show traces of the medieval *vargr i veum*, the human wolf exiled and isolated from the sanctuary of the community, but now in the context of their impact on the nation.

How does literature employ the motif of the human wolf breaking into the sanctuary of home and the *polis*, the latter as city, the nation at large or even European civilization versus the wilderness of the colonies? This and the ensuing chapter argue that the use of dehumanizing metaphors in this literature contributes to culturally preparing the ground for the xenophobia and racism of the twentieth and twenty-first centuries, from genocide to the anti-immigration rhetoric and politics of today. What are the seeds in the medieval wolf metaphor from which its racial connotations develop in the early modern period? What types of migration are associated with this metaphor? What human fears does it convey and what are the links between the ethnic alterity it expresses in the nineteenth century with earlier, more time-worn fears and with twentieth-century fascism, nationalism and even today's anti-immigration rhetoric?

The literary wolves this chapter foregrounds are despised and persecuted as aliens with a migratory background, threatening the peace of the community, whether the family or home, the city, the civilizing mission or the nation. In nineteenth-century literature in particular, where nation building becomes a key motif, the wolf metaphor undergoes a shift from its former religious and moral contextualization to a paradigm by which the presence of minorities who were perceived as threatening to communities and the nation at large is fictionally represented. Some of the literature of the second half of the nineteenth century associated wolves not only with foreign invaders (Heinrich von Kleist, for example) but specifically with Jews, the Romanies and Slavs. The wolf's demonic aura becomes a reflection of an increasing preoccupation with matters of race in the context of the topography of home versus world and an increasingly rootless, migratory population. Literary texts in the nineteenth century that feature this dehumanizing metaphor include Victor Hugo's *The Hunchback of Notre Dame* (1831), Charles Dickens's *Oliver Twist* (1839), Wilhelm Raabe's historical novella *The Children of Hamelin* (Die Hämelschen Kinder, 1868; discussed at length in Arnds, 2015) and his Bildungsroman *The Hunger Pastor* (Der Hungerpastor, 1864), and Bram Stoker's *Dracula* (1897).

The racial aspects of these literary texts do not appear out of the blue, but have their origin in the early modern age's demonization of minorities such as Jews and Romanies, who were condemned for their rootlessness, their subsequent purported inclination to crime, especially their thievishness and abduction of children. The Great Werewolf and Witch Hunt initiated by Pope Innocent VIII and by the *Malleus Maleficarum* (Hammer of Witches, 1486) gave rise to a racism that links the wolf not just with any religious non-conformity but specifically with Jews, unassimilated and seen as rootless wanderers.

2. Jews and Gypsies as Wolves   27

As Jack Zipes has pointed out, in 'all the religious diatribe of the 16th and 17th centuries there were constant parallels drawn between the devil and his associates, the Jews, witches, and werewolves, and this had a profound effect on the popular imagination' (Zipes 1983: 68). It is specifically the links between rootlessness, foreignness and crime with wolves threatening communities that become thematic in equations of wolves with migrants from nineteenth-century literature to internet sites and populist rhetoric today.

This fixation with the wolf as a metaphor in matters of race, nationalism and imperialism in the nineteenth century and also under National Socialism, as we shall see, not only is psychologically motivated but also has its roots in philosophical thinking. In philosophy, the tension between wilderness and its wolves and civilization with its human communities has a long tradition. Philosophers ranging from Aristotle to Agamben have linked the *polis* to a number of paradigms: the notion of being, *Dasein*, to inclusion versus exclusion, and to the idea of peace. Exclusion from the *polis* has traditionally resulted in a loss of peace and subsequent survival in the state of nature. One of the perceptual consequences of such individuals excluded from political life has traditionally been their reduction to the level of animals through dehumanizing metaphors. Agamben has detailed this in his chapter 'The Ban and the Wolf' in *Homo Sacer: Sovereign Power and Bare Life*, where he argues that this reduction of human political life to bare life, from *bios* to *zoe* in the state of nature can be a principle not just outside of the city but also within city walls, where the state of nature can correspond to the state of exception and the state of war (Agamben 1995: 106). We will see examples of both scenarios in the canonical texts I am looking at.

Exclusion from the *polis* as well as within the *polis*, which nowadays functions as the larger polity, the nation state, has been a biopolitical process from antiquity on. Aristotle distinguished those humans living in Athens from the 'idiotes' outside, who did not hold any political office and were speechless. Aristotle also considered a person who says nothing as a vegetable (Aristotle 1993: 8), a thought that may evoke the speechlessness of the migrant and recalls myths and literature of transformation from Lycaon to Kafka.

As outlined briefly in Chapter 1, the Lycaon myth may give us one of the blueprints for the biopolitical reality of expulsion, the trauma of exile and persecution. Here, the *homo sacer*'s exclusion from the city as the community of men happens at the moment when Jove turns the Arcadian king into a wolf, and when 'frightened he runs off to the silent fields and howls aloud, attempting speech in vain' (Ovid 2004: 13). Lycaon's abjection to the level of animality is closely tied to his crime of cannibalism, which excludes him from the *polis*, from human being (Ancient Greek: *pelein*) itself. Thus abandoned by humanity implies a solitary life beyond the pale of the social contract with its reach of laws and rights. As early as in ancient Greek thinking the state of abandonment implied that human existence *per se* was cast into doubt, since human 'being' was closely linked to dwelling within the community, inside the *polis*. The ancient Greeks considered the wolf as the symbolic antithesis of the city and its ideology of dwelling in peace (Mainoldi 1984: 127). The loss of *autochthony*, of being rooted in one's home soil, would imply a loss of peace.

As mentioned, the permanent exile in wolf shape in most versions of the Lycaon myth became a historical biopolitical reality in the Germanic Middle Ages. The myth of the wolf, however, does not disappear from it. The human perceived as a wolf to the community on account of a crime, usually murder, expelled from the community and on the run seeking some kind of sanctuary, appears to us in its perhaps most prominent manifestation at the seam of myth and biopolitics in this Old Germanic figure of the werewolf, in Scandinavian cultures referred to as the *vargr i veum*, the wolf in the sanctuary (Grönbech 1976: 130). This figure implies the idea of the human wolf (*vargr*) expelled from the community and in need of a sanctuary (*veum*), while at the same time threatening the community as the safest form of sanctuary.

The primary trauma of migrants on the run is that loss of peace that can only be found in a community. If, however, the community is at war within itself, migrants become refugees seeking sanctuary in another community that can offer them peace. The idea of sanctuary derived from the concept of the *vargr i veum* can take on different shapes. Traditionally, it is a holy place like the church, but in our modern context migrants and refugees seek refuge and sanctuary within the *polis*, either as the city or as the nation state. Its contrast is the migrant's or refugee's loss of sanctuary in the state of nature, where man is a wolf to man: forests, deserts, the sea. In a contemporary context, the Sonoma Desert and the Mediterranean Sea quickly come to mind as migrants are struggling for survival in these natural spaces.

What is it that turns the wolf in particular into a metaphor for race? If we look at the medieval outlaw or *vargr*, the notion of moral impurity stands out, as well as his ensuing homelessness and migration in wilderness, his crossing the boundary between civilization and the Hobbesian state of nature. To the community he is henceforth not only a

2. Jews and Gypsies as Wolves   29

stranger, but, what is more, it considers him dead, as he has been banned to the night side of life. To what extent wilderness in the Middle Ages was a conceptual threshold associated with wolves has been explored in great detail by Alexander Pluskowski, who points, for example, to the Anglo Saxon *Beowulf*, where the royal hall as civilized realm contrasts with the wolf-infested slopes outside, with lupine Grendel at its centre (Pluskowski 2006: 58).

The *vargr* was outlawed for a crime, usually a murder he committed, a deed combining bloodlust with cunning and preying on the community. This biopolitical act of dehumanization is reflected in various written and oral tales employing the idea of 'an archetypal wolf characterized by unbridled cruelty, bestial ferocity as well as literal-mindedness and gullibility, driven by his ravenous hunger – overall an avatar of vice' (Pluskowski 2006: 132). Such lycanthropes preying on the community, drawing the life blood of their fellow citizens, is a topic in the medieval bestiary, where the wolf stands metaphorically for human greed, but beyond that also specifically for clerical hypocrisy (Cf. Morton 2010: 976–97), for the monk who has renounced carnal desire but yields to it. In the late twelfth-century story of *Reinhart Fuchs* by the Alsatian writer Heinrich der Glîchezâre, showing Reinhart the fox dupe Isengrin the wolf, the latter is described as 'beschnitten' (circumcised) after a fishing accident in which his tail has frozen off. Heinrich adopts this motif from Pierre de Saint-Cloud's earlier *Roman de Renard*. The word refers primarily to the tonsure of monks, with whom Isengrim is closely associated, although as 'circumcision' it could very well carry anti-Semitic undertones: 'According to the Old Testament the wolf Isengrim is circumcised' (Glîchezâre 2011: 73).

While the wolf metaphor carried positive associations such as those of the stalwart warrior and of fallen nobility, specifically in Marie de France's fables from the mid-twelfth century (Pluskowski 2006: 88), it did stand for vice but not necessarily for the devil who had a different iconography. I would argue that bloodlust and greed are the primary motifs that transcend the religious aura and contribute to the metaphor's later use in matters of race. In the literature of the early modern period the memory of the biopolitical practice of abandoning criminals in addition to the metaphor's various negative qualities in medieval literature then transitions smoothly into racial dehumanization, specifically for the vagrancy of the Roma and Sinti as well as the mercantile cosmopolitanism and homelessness of Jews perceived as threats to the community. So-called Gypsies and Jews are stigmatized as wolves trespassing upon sedentary communities, appearing as marauding thieves, cannibals, child devourers and seducers of young women.

Wolves and anti-Semitism: From Shakespeare to Dickens

The idea of the rapacious, bloodlust-driven wolf as an anti-Semitic image for a Jew's fragile sanctuary within the city features perhaps most prominently in Shakespeare's moneylender Shylock in *The Merchant of Venice* (written between 1596 and 1599). He is repeatedly denigrated to a dog and, in Gratiano's speech during the trial scene, to a wolf:

> Thou almost mak'st me waver in my faith
> To hold opinion with Pythagoras,
> That souls of animals infuse themselves
> Into the trunks of men. Thy currish spirit
> Govern'd a wolf, who, hang'd for human slaughter,
> Even from the gallows did his fell soul fleet,
> And, whilst thou lay'st in thy unhallowed dam,
> Infus'd itself in thee; for thy desires
> Are wolvish, bloody, starv'd, and ravenous. (IV. I)

It is a strange image indeed, the wolf hanged for human slaughter, which has puzzled critics over time. Animals did have trials and were sentenced, punished and even hanged, as is well documented from the fifteenth to seventeenth centuries by E. P. Evans's *The Criminal Prosecution and Capital Punishment of Animals* (1906). As these were mostly domestic animals so that wolves were generally not hanged, there may be a different story behind Shakespeare's image.

One argument has been that Shylock may have been inspired by Roderigo (Ruy) Lopez, physician-in-chief to Queen Elizabeth I. A convert to the Anglican Church upon his immigration to England from his native Portugal, where he had been accused of secretly practising Judaism, he was found guilty of plotting to poison the Queen and executed in 1594. There is a possibility that Shakespeare had Lopez on his mind when he has Gratiano mention the hanged wolf (due to the homophonic Lopez or lupus), although Ralph Nash has convincingly shown that for his wolf passages Shakespeare may have been indebted to Vergil (Nash 1959: 125–8). In particular, Antonio's comment about Shylock that 'you may as well use question with the wolf; why he hath made the ewe bleat for the lamb' (IV.I 73–4) evokes two passages in the

Aeneid, Book 9, line 52ff.: 'And as a wolf prowling about some crowded sheepfold, when, beaten sore of winds and rains, he howls at the pens by midnight; safe beneath their mothers the lambs keep bleating on; he, savage and insatiate, rages in anger against the flock he cannot reach, tired by the long-gathering madness for food, and the throat unslaked with blood'; and line 570: 'The wolf of Mars snatches from the folds some lamb sought of his mother with incessant bleating.' By the same token, Shylock's greed as sin also evokes Dante's she-wolf, whose diet consisting of 'terra e peltro' (lands and lucre) is a reference to her desire for earthly rather than spiritual goods, money (peltro) in particular.

Shylock's proverbial wolfishness reveals itself at the moment when he wants to cut a pound of flesh from Antonio's body as payback for the outstanding debt. It is the custom of usury that is associated with the wolf, Shylock's bloodlust an allegory for this association. Usury was a dubious concept in Shakespeare's days. While the Church classified it as sinful and it was generally considered a despicable act, it was not entirely forbidden during the Elizabethan age, as the government also depended on borrowing money from the rich (Draper 1935: 41). Ethically speaking, however, it implies lending money out of greed and for personal gain rather than out of generosity or empathy for the need of others. Paradoxically, however, usury in the Middle Ages was only tolerated from Jews who were otherwise not allowed to own or till land. While they were allowed to charge interest on their loans, there were fiercely anti-Semitic attacks made against this practice, above all by religious leaders such as Martin Luther in Germany, to whom the usurer was essentially a werewolf:

> A usurer is no real person, his sins not human! He must be a werewolf, worse than all tyrants, murderers, and thieves, as evil as the devil himself. For he enjoys the protection and peace of the community not as an enemy but as a friend and fellow citizen, robbing and murdering worse than any enemy. If therefore one tortures and beheads robbers and murderers how much more should one torture and murder all usurers! (Fabiunke 1963: 229)

This myth of the werewolf must have also guided Shakespeare, Shylock's desire to have his debt repaid with interest in the form of a pound of flesh rendering him inhuman, a cannibal. It is primarily mental cannibalism, Shylock's greed, his *gaudium alterius doloris*, *Schadenfreude*, pure malice, all conveyed by his unrelenting insistence on being recompensed, which is then translated into an act of physical cannibalism, bringing him on to the side of an animal predator. We encounter this mentality also in Ben Jonson's *Every Man out of His Humour* (1599), in the character Sordido, whose *dolor alienae felicitatis* makes him a consummate villain and 'wolf in the Commonwealth' (Gifford 1816: 46). Jonson implies the wolf in the polis or sanctuary, although without the anti-Semitic context, for he who enjoys the pain of others is a *lupus hominem*, a wolf to man, in the Hobbesian sense. Needless to say, this is a grossly exaggerated projection of human qualities into the wolf, any animal for that matter. It is known that animals can feel empathy, but I leave the answer to the question whether they can also enjoy cruelty to the experts in zoology.

As an act of quasi-cannibalism Shylock's 'crime' evokes Lycaon and his expulsion from the human community for the crime of dishing up human flesh to the God. The idea of expulsion of undesirables certainly seems to be a backdrop to this play. While Jews were banished from England in 1290 following the Edict of Expulsion and not openly readmitted until the 1650s, they were allowed to live in Venice, although without obtaining citizenship. Other than the case of Ruy Lopez, a converted Jew, the plight of Jews was practically not a firsthand experience for Shakespeare. Nonetheless, the problem of human expulsion from their communities and subsequent immigration to England may have been on his mind in the 1590s, as has been suggested by interpretations linking Shylock's status in Venice to the problem of refugees and immigrants of Shakespeare's time. As Andrew Tretiak pointed out, Shakespeare may have cryptically tried to address the situation of Huguenot immigration in the wake of the Edict de Nantes in an attempt to appeal to Elizabeth I to show mercy to non-citizens. Shylock the Jew would then stand in for these refugees as Venice stands in for London. Much like Othello, Shylock is allowed to live in Venice but both are denied citizens' rights, and in the end he is punished under 'alien law'. Tretiak once argued that by portraying the anti-Semitism vis-à-vis a Jew in Venice Shakespeare tackles the foreign immigrant question, of Huguenots who while not being citizens enjoyed the same rights and were subject to the same principles of justice as the natives of England (Tretiak 1929: 405). If we consider, however, that in the wake of anti-Huguenot riots five rioters were hanged on Tower Hill in 1595 after Elders of the Huguenot Church had requested their condemnation from Queen Elizabeth I, then Shakespeare's wolf metaphor can also be understood as a comment on Old Testament politics of unforgiveness and revenge. In that case, his play can be read as a warning for the Huguenot refugees to relinquish their rioting and as an appeal made to the foreign immigrants to assimilate to their host culture, much as Shylock's transformation from a 'lone Jewish wolf' into a Christian lamb signals his assimilation from someone standing apart from the social contract to a more social human being.

In the nineteenth century then this figure of the werewolf is revived in the context of anti-Semitism and as part of a fascination that writers especially of the gothic genre had with lycanthropy. Chantal Bourgault du Coudray has shown convincingly in her book on werewolves in the nineteenth century that 'a composite Otherness gave expression to anxieties about working class degeneracy, colonial insurrection and racial atavism, women's corporeality and sexuality, and the bestial heritage of humanity' (Bourgault du Coudray 2006: 50). Novels redolent with anti-Semitism and orientalizing fears of invasion such as George W. M. Reynolds's *Wagner the Werewolf* (1846) and Bram Stoker's *Dracula* (1897) reflect this especially for the Victorian Age. In Germany it was in particular the bourgeois realist author Wilhelm Raabe who used the wolf metaphor in the context of Jews and migrants from Eastern Europe threatening small communities. They are narratives that ought to be read in the context of nation building and how the nation views its Others. Although firmly rooted in his region of Lower Saxony from where he rarely moved, Raabe was a rather cosmopolitan author by interacting intertextually with a large international body of literature in his novels and stories. In his Bildungsroman *The Hunger Pastor* (1865), which he based to some extent on Charles Dickens's *David Copperfield* (1849) with which it shares the concept of a nefarious anti-hero, as I have shown elsewhere (Arnds 1997), Raabe portrays one of the least likeable Jews in German literature. While Dickens's novel, however, is not openly anti-Semitic, Raabe's alongside with Gustav Freytag's *Debit and Credit* (1855) is, although the author himself was not.

His Jewish character Moses Freudenstein, modelled in part on Heinrich Heine and his exile in Paris, represents the kind of rootless cosmopolitanism that poses a persistent threat to those who have stayed at home in their rural German community. Here is a new version of the wolf in the sanctuary, the Jew who in order to assimilate needs to accumulate considerable wealth and embrace the existence of a *Weltbürgertum*. Moses explains this to the naïve protagonist Hans Unwirrsch: 'We Jews are the only true cosmopolitans, citizens of the world by the grace or rather disgrace of God' (Raabe 1953a: 128). His cosmopolitanism goes hand in hand with an insatiable greed for money and status, products of a need he feels to assimilate to the German and French bourgeoisie. Moses's drive for assimilation, however, is a perversion of his father's admonition to his young son that if he has the choice between a piece of cake or a book he should choose the latter, encapsulating the popular belief that *Wissen ist Macht*, knowledge is power (Raabe 1953a: 60).

Little does Father Freudenstein know at this point that his message gets translated in his son's mind into pure greed for wealth. At the moment of his father's death, Moses displays excessive greed in one of the most anti-Semitic passages that puts him in line with Shylock. The fact that Shakespeare's play voices public opinion and the author's own critical stance vis-à-vis the immigration crisis of his time brings it close to Raabe's concerns about anti-Semitism in *The Hunger Pastor* and his fictional analysis of Eastern European refugees in his novella *The Children of Hamelin*. In the nineteenth century, anti-Semitism shifted from the early modern age's superstition and religious demonization of Jews to bourgeois anxieties about Jewish assimilation, their social climbing and their purported 'voraciousness' concerning the accumulation of vast material wealth, which guaranteed political power. This voraciousness, a central attribute of the wolf as early as in medieval beast narratives, appears in the mid- to second half of the nineteenth century as the trademark of other characters and outside Germany, for example, in Dickens's Fagin in *Oliver Twist* (1838) and Uriah Heep in *David Copperfield* (1849).

Moses's greed and ruthlessness ultimately lead him to abduct Kleophea, a young bourgeois daughter. After he has seduced and eloped with her, he is directly being compared with a wolf: 'Oh Unwirrsch […] You let the wolf into the house' (Raabe 1953a: 375). This motif of abduction of the young, especially of children and young women, has for millennia been associated with wolves, and is a prominent motif in literary texts featuring lycanthropes. What is new in Raabe is that Moses is described as an urban wolf disrupting the provincial bliss of the non-Jewish community. He resembles closely the old notion of the *vargr i veum*, the wolf breaking into a sanctuary. The nineteenth century thus no longer associates the human wolf expelled by the community with the forest, but the lycanthrope increasingly becomes an urban phenomenon. His loss of roots, originally linked to the ban from the *polis*, has become a part of the urban landscape, where the individual experiences loneliness within the crowd. Poe's 'Man of the Crowd' (1840), a werewolfish night prowler, is another literary example of this exile among the rootless urban proletariat. Moses Freudenstein's survival in the cosmopolitan jungle of Paris, far away from the stultifying German provinces that Raabe's novel celebrates as the ideal place to live, is, however, also a reference to Heinrich Heine's exile in that city, his banishment from German soil.

We encounter the human wolf as an urban prowler also in the work of Charles Dickens from whom Raabe, an avid reader of world literature, borrowed extensively for his novels. Moses Freudenstein is partly modelled on Dickens's Uriah Heep from *David Copperfield* (1849) whom Dickens describes in dehumanizing, vaguely anti-Semitic tones. Although there is no clear consensus in criticism as to whether Heep is Jewish, two factors can be named in support of the argument that he is a Jew and consequently the product of a disguised anti-Semitism: his name and his red hair. That Dickens gave the good Jew in *Our Mutual Friend* (1864/5) the name of *Riah* can be interpreted as the author's intention to counterbalance not only his bad Jew Fagin but also the bad portrait of *Uriah*. Moreover, Uriah's last name *Heep* may imply *Hebrew*. It has been shown that Jewish figures in visual and literary works of art have traditionally been depicted with red hair. While Mellinkoff has argued that Uriah may not be Jewish, but that 'the Jew as an evil, red-haired figure was given its most striking delineation by Charles Dickens' (Mellinkoff 1982: 45), L. Jane has claimed that Heep is most likely a Jew (Jane 1958: 97).

In *Oliver Twist*, Dickens's anti-Semitism is unconcealed and applies the same metaphor of the wolf for demonized Jewishness that we see in Raabe's novel: Sikes calls Fagin 'a black-hearted wolf' (Dickens 2000: 295) and Fagin's address to Oliver 'delighted to see you looking so well my dear' has been interpreted as evoking the Grimm Brothers' wolf in 'Little Red Riding Hood' (Dellamora 1996: 70). The old motif of the wolf seducing and abducting children persists in Dickens's novel, but it occurs as part of the pan-European anti-Semitic view in the late nineteenth century of Jews as ruthless money grabbers, as thieves in the middle of national communities.

The character of the urban wolf-like prowler is, however, well-disguised under a varnish of German-style *Bildung* in Raabe. Moses's cosmopolitan *Bildung* contrasts sharply with the provincialism of the other characters. In the end, Hans Unwirrsch's self-confinement within a village vicarage not only reflects Raabe's own choice of provincialism over world travel but also reveals Freudenstein's negatively perceived cosmopolitanism as a persistent anti-Semitic perception of Jews as lacking clear home boundaries and being itinerant. In the 1920s, Werner Sombart, for example, saw the Jews as 'an "Oriental" or desert people who wandered to and then throughout the European, Nordic north, thereby producing the economic-cultural synthesis called modern capitalism' and that 'it was the fate of the Jews to have remained a wandering and desert people' inclined to repress 'character traits associated with rootedness to the soil [...] in favour of those linked to the nomad or urban merchant' (Herf 1984: 140). And Hannah Arendt points out that the Jewish community is based on the concept of people rather than territory, Jews being an

> example of a people who without any home at all had been able to keep their identity for centuries and could therefore be cited as proof that no territory was needed to constitute a nationality. If the pan-movements insisted on the secondary importance of the state and the paramount importance of the people, organized throughout countries and not necessarily represented in visible institutions, the Jews were a perfect model of a nation without a state and without visible institutions. (Arendt 1973: 239–40)

This statelessness allows for the kind of cosmopolitanism that Kant propagated in his 1795 essay on 'Perpetual Peace', where he states that world peace rests on the concept of the *Weltbürgerrecht*, the right of the world citizen to enjoy hospitality beyond national boundaries (Kant 1923 [1795]: 443). In Kant's view hospitality is a right that every world citizen can enjoy wherever they decide to go, as the planet is the property of all human beings regardless of boundaries ('das Recht des gemeinschaftlichen Besitzes', Kant 1923 [1795]: 320). This exterritorialization is at the heart of Jewish world citizenship, but has also contributed to the anti-Semitism that has existed for centuries.

'Gypsy' wolves between child abduction and racial infection

Nineteenth-century anti-Semitism differs substantially from contemporaneous views and the treatment of so-called Gypsies, the Romany and Sinti, whose presence was considered a *Landplage*, a scourge plaguing the land, and became increasingly subjected to police control (Saul 2007: 61). In Germany, thoughts of deporting them arose as early as 1900. From the mid-nineteenth century on, ethnologists and linguists had become increasingly concerned with the question of their original home and were eager to return them there. Their non-sedentary lifestyle is the primary category of alterity that caused their seclusion from civil rights in the eighteenth and nineteenth centuries. Vagrancy, homelessness, crime, seduction and abduction combine also in literary representations of discrimination against 'Gypsies'. In the folk superstition of the early modern age they were often grouped together with Jews, witches and wolves as child stealers and child devourers, and their biopolitical exclusion can be documented in literature from the seventeenth century to the early twentieth century.

Other than greed and a voracious appetite the wolf metaphor also implies cunning mixed with the power of taking a human life. It is easier for wolves, however, to kill children than adults. Wolves have been known to kill children for millennia, especially at times when the rural population was less protected in their dwelling places than they are now. It is not surprising then that child murder, the abandonment of children and the wolf come together in folk superstition and many literary texts drawing from these. We encounter this motif as early as in some versions of the Lycaon myth, where child murder and cannibalism are the main triggers of Lycaon's transformation into a wolf:

> Lycaon, son of Pelasgos, first king of Arcadia, founded on the mountain Lycosyra the oldest of all cities (the first that sun saw), gave Zeus the name of Lykaios and instituted games in his honor, entitled 'Lykaia'. All went well until he sacrificed a child and sprinkled the altar with his blood. Upon this act, he was instantly turned into a wolf. (Smith 1894: 14 and Poulakou-Rebelakou et al. 2009: 469)

According to a different version:

> Lycaon, son of Pelasgos, was the father of fifty sons. To test them Zeus once appeared among them in the form of a weary traveller. They slew a child, mingled his entrails with the usual offering and served it up to the guest; whereupon Zeus overturned the table and struck Lycaon and his sons with the thunderbolt. Nyktimos (the youngest son) was the only one who was spared, for Gaia (the goddess Earth) stayed the hand of Zeus. (Kakridis 1986: 240)

This motif of child deprivation that turns man into a wolf continues to fill the European imagination from the Middle Ages on, wolves becoming derogatory metaphors not only for women suspected of witchcraft and child murder but primarily for Gypsies and, as we have seen, also Jews as purported child stealers and seducers of the young. In folk superstition vagrant thieves, Gypsies and wolves as child abductors, seducers and devourers of the young are often placed within one category, and the motif of abduction is closely linked to these outsiders' migratory way of life perceived as a threat by sedentary communities. In his *Expulsion de los Gitanos* (1619) Sancho de Moncada, professor of theology at the University of Toledo quoted Cain's words from Scripture: 'I shall be a vagrant and a wanderer on Earth, and anyone who meets me can kill me' as a justification for condemning Gypsies to death, not even sparing women and children. Moncada argued that there 'is no law which obliges us to bring up wolf-whelps, to the assured future detriment of the flock' (Fraser 1992: 162). As Miriam Eliav-Feldon has shown in her work, the perception of vagrants as vermin was widespread in seventeenth-century Europe as it became plague ridden. Especially Gypsies were considered vermin, disease spreaders and poisoners of drinking water. The wolves with which they were sometimes associated were in the seventeenth century still not free from their religious connotations and pointed in particular to their alleged thievishness with which even someone like Miguel de Cervantes credited them in the first sentence of his story *La Gitanilla* (The Little Gypsy Girl, 1613):

> It would almost seem that the Gitanos and Gitanas, or male and female gipsies, had been sent into the world for the sole purpose of thieving. Born of parents who are thieves, reared among thieves, and educated as thieves, they finally go forth perfected in their vocation, accomplished at all points, and ready for every species of roguery. In them the love of thieving, and the ability to exercise it, are qualities inseparable from their existence, and never lost until the hour of their death.

Prior to the nineteenth century, epidemics were not linked to vermin or parasites. Gypsies were, however, frequently associated with syphilis and the sweating disease (Eliav-Feldon 2009: 289). One of the major fears linked to parasites is that they are a kind of animal that cannot be domesticated. The notion is partly linked to today's view among ranchers that wolves are 'varmint', although of course the history of dogs tells us otherwise, namely that dogs had at some point evolved from wolves that became domesticated. As Eliav-Feldon points out:

> Plague might not have been caused by vermin in early modern medical theories, but both epidemics and invasions of harmful creatures spread at the same frightening rate, and the expression 'a plague of godless vagabonds infesting the land' seemed to appear only when Gypsies were involved. Although Gypsy companies in the sixteenth and seventeenth

2. Jews and Gypsies as Wolves 39

centuries seldom numbered more than a few dozen people, they were 'swarming', and 'infesting' and 'plaguing' and 'flooding' in all published warnings, whether in legislation, in literary texts, or in local chronicles. And like these pests, Gypsies, it was believed, were thieves by nature. They poached on human territory and stole man's food (at the time when famine was always at the doorstep), and could no more be civilized than locusts or lice. (Eliav-Feldon 2009: 289–90)

It is alarming that a word like 'swarming' demonstrates that the contemporary rhetoric – David Cameron identifying immigrants as people swarming across the Channel – still echoes seventeenth-century racist jargon.

In literary texts depictions of vagrant Gypsies as marauding corruptors of innocent youth and as wolf-like creatures appear as early as in the picaresque tradition of the seventeenth century. In Hans Jacob Christoph von Grimmelshausen's *The Adventures of Simplicius Simplicissimus* (1668), for example, the wolf retains his medieval reputation as a cunning rogue, uniting in himself traces of the historical expulsion of criminals with the wolf's nature as portrayed in the medieval bestiary, where Isengrim appears as voracious and stupid.

The wolf metaphor in this novel reflects early anxieties about idleness, robbery, mental illness and crime. In the course of his life, Simplicius follows a career that progresses from youthful folly to vagrancy and crime, to an unsteady life in the forest, until he finally matures and, disillusioned with life and the world, withdraws from it. Raised by peasants, for whom he tends sheep, he is repeatedly warned by his putative father against the cunning wolf at a time when the young boy witnesses the skirmishes of the Thirty Years' War. Never having encountered a real wolf, Simplicius surmises when a band of marauding soldiers burns down the family farm that these raiders must surely be that wolf. In its childish naivety the thought reflects the time-honoured practice of expelling criminals as human wolves. After being forced to run away and growing up as a feral child in the forest, of aspect half human-half animal and deprived of all *logos*, speech and reason, he advances to the position of a court fool; subsequently, he becomes a huntsman, and finally the Thirty Years' War turns him into a berserk-like marauder, a wolf in the eyes of man. The wolf metaphor is an integral component of this picaresque novel with its religious denigration of human idleness and crime.

The link becomes strongest when Simplicius joins a *pack* (Grimmelshausen 1999: 320) of Merode's Brethren, a pivotal moment in the text where Simplicius becomes a wolf to other men. The Merode's Brethren are marauding deserters of the army, soldiers without honour 'best compared to Gypsies' (G 319) and *Gesinds* (G 364, vermin), prone to rest on their 'bear skins' (G 364, an expression that has survived in German to this day for someone who is lazy). These pernicious marauders are described in no uncertain terms as *homines sacri*, cursed individuals who can be killed with impunity, like vermin:

> The harm a large number of such vermin can do their general, their comrades, and the army itself is beyond description. The most bungling raw recruit who can do nothing but forage is more use to his commander than a thousand Merode's Brethren who make a profession of malingering and spend all their time sitting on their backsides doing nothing [...]. They ought to be leashed together like greyhounds. (G 320-1)

Grimmelshausen's vocabulary is an early literary example equating the idle (the useless eaters) with criminals and both these groups with vermin, thus preconfiguring the kinds of nineteenth- and early twentieth-century literary texts as well as National Socialist ideology that label Gypsies and Jews as *Ungeziefer* (vermin), but also current populist rhetoric of immigrants as being a drain on the national budget, of robbing those with an innate right to be on national territory of precious resources. The fear of idleness, however, expressed in this text concerns a wide range of groups: the lower classes, the insane, Gypsies, thieves and other vagrants as much as the aristocracy, which is ultimately also associated with banditry and wolfish voraciousness.

The links between wolves, child abduction and Gypsies survive as a cultural memory of earlier ages perhaps most prominently in Victor Hugo's novel *Notre Dame de Paris* (Notre Dame de Paris, 1832). Hugo's version of the Beauty and the Beast story shows us the close symbolic union between Quasimodo, the Gypsy child (Hugo 2004: 182-4), taken in and raised by Frollo the priest, and Esmeralda, abducted as a young girl and raised by Gypsies. Set in the Middle Ages, the text reflects that period's superstitions that have survived over centuries and resulted in a racism towards the Sinti and Roma believed to abduct and devour children. Quasimodo and the allegedly Gypsy girl Esmeralda are targets of this folk superstition which marginalizes them within the city.

The name Quasimodo is a reference to Low Sunday, the Sunday after Easter on which the malformed (Quasimodo literally means 'almost in shape') boy was found by Frollo, the priest. Hugo repeatedly refers to his liminality between the animal and the human. His dehumanization and demonization conjoin in the derision and physical violence he experiences at the hands of the people of Paris, who see in his animal ugliness an incarnation of the devil. He is, however, given shelter and thus recognized as human. Unlike the human wolf of medieval proscription, the *vargr* (wolf or outlaw) banned from and feared within the *veum* (sanctuary), Quasimodo is the *homo sacer* who finds a sanctuary inside the Cathedral of Notre Dame, where persecution and even the communal law do not reach him. His sanctuary includes him within the city while also excluding him from it, in line with Agamben's repeated argument that the outlaw is never entirely outside of law but always tied to it so that exclusion never works as being excluded from the law (Agamben 1995: 39).

Traditionally the grotesque or monstrous is excluded within the city by being relegated to the market place, where it can be displayed outside the sacred realm, the Church. Quasimodo, the Lord of Misrule with 'the ugliest face' (H 36), seen as the Devil incarnate (H 40), is paradoxically, given shelter by the Church. He is a monster and a saint, subhuman and superhuman at the same time, with 'awe-inspiring vigour, agility and courage' (H 40). His dual position of being crowned and uncrowned, Prince of Fools one day (in the opening scene) and tortured the next (H 191), ironically evokes the duality of the beast as sovereign ruler and demon underdog. The carnival scenes of the novel, however, are ritual replications of the original ban (Agamben 2005: 71–2). It is through these anomic acts that the city with its law and order as part of the social contract becomes temporarily dissolved, because as a state of exception carnival acts never last long. It could be argued persuasively here that the carnival rite is in itself a sanctuary, however one that is diametrically opposed to the kind needed by Quasimodo. Carnival rites are sanctuaries from the oppressiveness of Church and State, a security valve for the people at large, their sinister side drawing on rituals of expulsion of those singled out as scapegoats.

Quasimodo's position inside the cathedral, which he comes to resemble in all its grotesque hybridity of architectural styles ranging from the Roman to the Gothic – Hugo elaborates on this extensively – is necessary as the Church wants to control evil. His sanctuary thus has the twofold purpose of protecting him from outside and of protecting the Church from the evil that may assail it from the secular realm. In that sense, he functions very much like one of the church's stone gargoyles he also resembles in his hybrid physique. As a foundling who becomes the living gargoyle of the Church of Rome he shares much in common with those twin foundlings of Rome raised by the *lupa romana*. The Church of Rome is ultimately built on this foundation myth. Like the foundling children of Rome who were reared by a wolf in her duality of devourer and a nurturer, Quasimodo too, as a Gypsy child, is the offspring of wolves in the metaphorical sense, who according to folk superstition were believed to be devourers of children. As it turns out in the end, they prove that superstition wrong by raising, and not eating, Esmeralda, the purported Gypsy girl Quasimodo is in love with.

Although Quasimodo is described as a raging predator who 'roars, foams, and bites' (H 61), he is extremely sensitive and loving. He is filled with great devotion for Frollo, the priest and true monster of the story, and he is the only one capable of truly loving Esmeralda, whom he rescues into his sanctuary. Like Saint Christopher, who is depicted as a cynocephalus (dog-head) in Eastern Orthodox icons, Quasimodo is associated both with the Devil and with saintliness, truly the *homo sacer* as the one set apart from society and sacred in the sense of being cursed. Both the monster and the saint fall under this principle of exclusion. Monster and saint, Quasimodo becomes the protector of Esmeralda in life and beyond, when at the end of the story his skeletal remains are found in an embrace with her in their tomb (H 429). As such a protector on the threshold of the temple he also resembles Anubis, the jackal-headed god who protects the dead on their journey to the afterlife: 'Egypt would have taken him for the god of this temple' (H 130). This too is a reference to his Gypsy or Egyptian background, as is his love of Esmeralda, who was inspired by Cervantes's *Gitanilla* (Moore 1942: 259).

She, too, is in the position of *homo sacer*, but rather than being expelled from the city she is tied to it, as the city needs her as permanent scapegoat. Persecuted as a witch because of her alleged Gypsy background Esmeralda becomes the victim of sacrificial violence, but when Quasimodo rescues her into his ecclesiastical sanctuary she is also temporarily immune to that violence. 'When once he had set foot within the asylum the criminal was sacred; but he must beware of leaving it; one step outside the sanctuary and he fell back into the flood' (H 308). Their sanctuary in church, where they are immune to community law, emphasizes their animal nature: 'occasionally', the narrator points out, the tradition of sanctuary even 'extended to animals. Anymoin relates that a stag, chased by Dagobert, having taken refuge at the tomb of Saint Denis, the hounds stopped short barking' (H 309).

The novel is set around the time when the *Malleus Maleficarum* appeared (1486), the cause of condemnation of thousands of women as witches in Germany and France. Esmeralda's goat Djali is part of this scenario of purported devil worship and it points to her position as sacrifice as does as her sympathy with Quasimodo pilloried in the market square 'like a calf whose head hangs dangling' (H 192). Esmeralda becomes the sacrificial victim for the Parisian mob, the community's sacrifice to restore order. She is literally the scapegoat, that outcast of the community first mentioned in *Leviticus* and then ritualized in ancient Judaism (Yom Kippur). Her sidekick while performing magical tricks, the goat Djali, reinforces this impression. In line with this sacrificial aura Esmeralda ends up in the vault of Montfaucon, 'an edifice of strange form, much resembling a Druidical cromlech, and having, like the Cromlech, its human sacrifices' (H 428).

Claude Frollo embodies Derrida's wolf as sovereign. The priest who takes Quasimodo in after he is abandoned by Gypsies is truly demonic. He stabs Phoebus Apollo, Esmeralda's great love, and manages to direct the blame for his deed onto her. Moreover, his secret alchemical studies evoke the pact with the devil, in his resemblance with Dr Faustus (H 223). Hugo's account of the fifteenth century makes abundantly clear that while the art of magic was condoned in men it brought women to the stake. As Baschwitz explains, magicians and other devil worshippers were generally not feared and hated, while witches were shown no mercy (Baschwitz 1963: 51).

Like Quasimodo, who 'stole with the stealthy tread of a wolf' (H 422), Frollo is also repeatedly likened to animal predators, birds of prey and tigers (H 252), resembling them in his habit of being a 'nocturnal prowler about the streets of Paris' (H 244). Frollo is the true monster of the story, and the roles of monstrous-looking but gentle-hearted Quasimodo and the priest become completely reversed the moment Esmeralda appears in the church and Frollo loses his mind and tries to rape her (H 326). He is the *vargr i veum* reminiscent of the mythical Jove in the grove, the sovereign god, in this case a representative of God breaking into the sanctuary and spreading violence inside it. In contrast, Quasimodo, upon seeing her beauty, is overcome with modesty and as is typical of the lycanthrope stays on the threshold. In this carnivalesque inversion the priest is the monster, the monster is the saint. Frollo is the wolf in sheep's clothing, indicating that Hugo may have been aware of the medieval monk or priest as wolf theme in the Ysengrim bestiaries, while Quasimodo is the sheep in wolf's clothing, as given in Matthew 7.15: 'Beware false prophets, who come to you in sheep's clothing, but who are inwardly ravening wolves.' The two characters thus reflect the sanctuary's ambiguous nature of providing shelter and precarity.

The wolf metaphors in this novel extend even further, to Pâquette La Chantefleurie, Esmeralda's mother, but completely unaware that she is. She is described as having 'the wild air of a caged she-wolf' (H 284). In her hatred of the Gypsy girl she is not only the devourer but also nurturer of her own daughter. After her daughter disappeared as a little girl, Pâquette went insane and now hates all Gypsies whom she blames for her loss. They are child-stealers in her eyes, and from her underground cell she keeps watching Esmeralda in the market square, not knowing that she is her daughter.

'Father,' asked she, 'whom are they about to hang yonder? [...] There were some children that said it was a gypsy woman.' [...] Then Pâquette La Chantefleurie burst into a hyena-like laughter. 'Sister,' said the archdeacon, 'you greatly hate the gypsy women then?' 'Hate them,' cried the recluse. 'They are witches, child stealers. They devoured my little girl, my child, my only child! I have no heart left, they have devoured it.' (H 284)

The two traditional roles of the wolf perceived in most cultures as both nurturer and devourer clash at the moment when she finally recognizes her daughter. Her emotions swivel from hatred to love, but it is too late for the mother and daughter to be reunited, as King Louis XI has ordained that Esmeralda be killed, seeing in her the cause of the mob's insurrection which needs to be crushed. Upon entering Pâquette's cell to seize Esmeralda the henchman Tristan, the executive of the King, is also described as a wolf, his face resembling that of a wolf when he grins (H 413). Pâquette calling him a 'he-wolf' (H 416) evokes the traditional union between the henchman and the criminal whom he kills as being set aside by the community as no longer among the living. In medieval Germanic law they were united by the location of hanging, the so-called *vargtre* (wolf tree), but while the henchman was only temporarily pronounced dead by the community, the criminal was permanently pronounced dead, regardless of whether he was expelled as *Friedlos* or hanged.

One may wonder why Hugo addresses the late medieval persecution of minorities like Gypsies and the physically deformed in the 1830s. The text with its realistic tapestry of social classes, even featuring beggars, which no other novel had done before in France, is first and foremost a reaction to the July 1830 revolution, which deposed the Bourbon family and tried to reassert the values of the 1789 revolution, the liberty, equality and brotherhood of all citizens. These were ideals the restorative monarchist period after Napoleon's defeat at Waterloo in 1815 had been trying to sweep under the carpet. Hugo thought that the 1830 revolution did not go far enough in establishing a constitutional monarchy and would have preferred to see a republic, hence his depiction of social classes and the inequality that reigns between them in his novel. What he describes for the late fifteenth century still to an extent held true in the early nineteenth century, thus his message, but the racism towards Gypsies and physically deformed outsiders is only one aspect of this widespread absence of the great ideals of the 1789 revolution.

By the late nineteenth century the image France and Germany had of the Romanies was almost entirely negative, and the rationalists saw in them 'depraved vagabonds, deprived outcasts or a 'useless race'' (Clark 2004: 239). While the fairy tales show the wolf as a seducer outside of the context of race, in the second half of the nineteenth century the motif of the seduction of innocent youth, especially the dutiful bourgeois daughter, is performed by Romanies, Jews and Slavs. Hugo contextualizes this racism and xenophobia in his portrait of Paris and specifically the Cathedral of Notre Dame as chief protagonist of the novel and sanctuary to the undesirable monstered by the community. As a portrait of the *vargr i veum* as the wolf who has found a fragile sanctuary in the city, a portrait of individuals deemed alien to the community and its *polis*, Hugo's novel on xenophobia and anti-Ziganism still has much to offer us today as migrants are seeking sanctuaries in the Western world.

Late nineteenth-century fears of migrants perceived as invading and infecting the nation are, in literature, perhaps nowhere as prominent as in Bram Stoker's *Dracula* (1897). Stoker's bloodsucking vampire who enters Britain in Whitby, traditional territory for Viking raids, is feared 'perhaps for centuries to come [...] amongst its teeming millions, [to] satiate his lust for blood, and create a new and ever-widening circle of semi-demons to batten on the helpless' (Stoker 2000: 45). The novel is clearly the product of the discourse on racial hygiene and eugenics that emerges at the end of the nineteenth century in Germany, France and England, and the Count a projection of late nineteenth-century British phobias of invasion, contagion and racial pollution, of the nation being drained by Eastern European immigrants, primarily Jews and Romanies (Zanger 1991: 36). Between 1881 and 1900, the number of foreign Jews in England increased by 600 per cent (Zanger 1991: 34: quoting Paul Johnson's *History of Jews*). Although the Count embodies English fears of mass immigration, an island trait that has persisted to this day, the wolf-man Dracula bleeding late Victorian England is partly also the product of the anti-Semitic climate in the wake of the series of unresolved murders in 1888 accredited to Jack the Ripper, who at one point was suspected to be a Jewish kosher butcher. Old prejudices were coming alive when this man was openly accused in an article in the *Times* so that the chief rabbi of England, Dr Hermann Adler, wrote an official response targeted at allaying popular apprehensions (Sharkey 1987: 114–15).

Count Dracula is hence yet another wolf who breaks into the sanctuary of the nation state. Wolves are at his constant beck and call in his 'wolf country' of Transylvania or Romania, as are even their more domestic relatives, Bersicker, the London Zoo wolf and all dogs, it seems. The Count controls wolves just by holding up his hand in silence, and he can turn into a wolf or bat in the twilight hours. In the final showdown between Van Helsing and Dracula, the close connection between Gypsies, wolves and the vampire culminates. The Gypsies and wolves are connected through forming circles around the hunters of Dracula, but as soon as Dracula is finished they also disappear. This trinity of wolf, Gypsy and vampire is closely associated with the Count's family and race. From the beginning, British fears of racial pollution by Eastern invaders of Oriental provenance form a stark contrast with the Count's own perception of his noble and ancient lineage steeped in Northern Europe. The Count's understanding of his race is quite different from the way he and his kind are seen in civil Western Europe. His identification with the allegedly superior Nordic race, however, contains the ambivalence of the beast as sovereign and outcast specifically in his insistence on his family's origins in the berserks, aligning him with marauding Vikings, with predators, and thus a much older threat of invasion than that experienced by the British from the nineteenth-century migration waves of Jews and Gypsies.

Descended from berserk warriors, as he explains to the lawyer Jonathan Harker who visits him, Dracula is the classical *vargr* as wolf and outlaw (once outlawed in the early Middle Ages the *berserkr* became synonymous with the *vargr*). As such, he is contrasted with Harker, who embodies English law but suddenly also finds himself outside of its reach in that state of exception where man is a wolf to man and where the idea of human sacrifice is closely linked to ritualistic violence: 'I am shut up here, a veritable prisoner, but without that protection of the law which is even a criminal's right and consolation '(S 38) [...] a man's death is not a calf's' (S 40). 'I was to be given to the wolves" (S 43). Harker's position as the Count's prisoner, suddenly

2. Jews and Gypsies as Wolves 47

reduced to *homo sacer*, has all the qualities of a rite that will initiate and facilitate the great hunt for blood and souls upon which Dracula embarks as he sets out for England. As the ruler of his lawless terrain and the one who vindicates the right to sacrifice humans, be it Harker or the children he feeds to his female fellow vampires, Dracula is the primordial hunter. Since he is the one who in turn eventually becomes hunted, he finds himself in the typical dual position of sovereign and *homo sacer*, both hunter and hunted, while for Harker, who advances from initial sacrificial victim to becoming one of the hunters, this process is inverted.

In line with the fear of the West that sees itself as civilized and considers the East as uncivilized – that 'mysterious East! The poisonous East – birthplace and home of an ill wind that blows nobody good', as George Du Maurier calls it in his novel *Trilby* – the two locations of the novel, Transylvania and Britain, reflect the tension between the wild and lawless versus the civil, domestic space in which law and order prevail. Dracula, a sort of evil *homme naturel* not least because he knows how to shape-shift into animals, is obviously aware of England's domesticating and civilizing mission. While associated with wolves back home, as soon as he lands in Whitby – classical terrain of Viking invasions – he sees the need to camouflage his uncivil nature. He does so by shape-shifting into the domesticated version of the wolf, a dog. However, like those Viking marauders a long time before him from whom he claims to be descended, he is a dog gone berserk, immediately engaging in a fight with a home dog, a scene in which the hierarchy between the alleged superior race of the West and the alleged inferior races of the East is inverted in that Dracula, the noble and 'evidently fierce brute', kills the 'half-bred' English mastiff (S 69).

England is the country that killed all wolves a long time ago, in 1290 according to Robert Winder's theory in *The Last Wolf* (2017). The only wolves still present are the domesticated ones, the one's whose natural spirit has been thoroughly whipped out of them. This can be seen primarily in the irony surrounding Bersicker, the Norwegian wolf living in a London zoo. He belies his own name, implying ferocity, in that 'the animal was as peaceful and well-behaved as that father of all picture wolves, Red Riding Hood's quondam friend' (S 117). Old and no longer used to the wild, he is a pathetic creature instilling pity rather than fear. When Dracula arrives in London, however, Bersicker seems to develop a memory of the distant past of his erstwhile nature and tearing himself from years of domestication breaks from the zoo and follows that call of the wild that the Count's presence has sent him telepathically.

As a descendant of the berserks Dracula exerts special control over Bersicker as he does over all wolves and those given to lunacy, like Dr Seward's patient Renfield and Jonathan Harker's fiancée Lucy Westenra. Victorian fears of racial contagion are especially inscribed into Lucy who, in getting bitten by the Count, becomes racially polluted.

Dracula's presence in the city of London is thus a case of the wolf breaking into the sanctuary, the *vargr i veum*. It is a sanctuary that has a civilizing and domesticating mission, where lunatics and real wolves are tamed, their muted instincts suddenly reawakening upon the arrival of the creature from the wilds of Transylvania. His castle there, although a trap to Harker, is a sanctuary to the Count, whose ultimate sanctuary is the coffin. By leaving his castle for the metropolis of London, where he quickly reinstalls a sanctuary for himself in the House of Carfax with its coffins filled with consecrated earth, he simultaneously destabilizes the sanctuaries of others, the city itself at the heart of Victorian England but also the mental asylum from which Renfield escapes, as well as the London zoo, both sanctuaries and places of enforced domestication.

Authors like Victor Hugo, Bram Stoker but also the German Wilhelm Raabe in *The Hunger Pastor* (1864) and his novella *The Children of Hamelin* (1868, cf. Arnds, 74–83) thematically interact with historical phobias and folk myths about the alleged abduction and cannibalism of children or youth by vagrant Gypsies and Jews, thus retaining some of the Gothic horrors steeped in myths that were also typical of the Romantic period. All three authors compare Gypsies and/or Jews with wolves threatening the community. A comparison of their texts, however, reveals that there is an evolution of the vagrant-as-wolf theme from text to text, that is, from the 1830s to the very end of the nineteenth century: while Hugo's Gothic novel is still steeped in the demonization of Gypsies in the Middle Ages, Raabe explores racism towards Jews and, in *The Children of Hamelin*, of Slavs and Gypsies in the context of modernity's loss of roots and the displacement of these groups. Stoker's *Dracula* at the very end of the nineteenth century is already part of the discourse surrounding racial pollution that becomes prominent in the first half of the twentieth century. These texts demonstrate specifically what treatment the *homo sacer* experiences when he enters the civic space from which he is traditionally expelled. The Gothic elements in these narratives arise from the fact that the *homo sacer* now resides within the community, his presence threatening the city as a reflection of the nation state from within. Moreover, he becomes a catalyst for authorial frustration and fear, from Hugo's frustration with the restoration of monarchist conditions, his discussion of absolutist power and abandonment, and his social engagement in the wake of the revolutions of 1789 and 1830, via Raabe's concern about racism towards Slavs and Jews, to the phobia of racial contagion and invasion in Stoker's late Victorian Britain.

Modern homelessness is a key motif tied to the wolf metaphor, perhaps best embodied by Wilhelm Raabe's cosmopolitan Jew in *The Hunger Pastor*, the kind of rootless character the German *Bildungsroman* as a literary instrument in the construction of the nation state does not tolerate. Although the Nazis became particularly fond of this novel, Raabe, much like Shakespeare, seems to indict anti-Semitism by satirically juxtaposing German provincialism with Jewish worldliness. Moses Freudenstein, the nefarious *vargr i veum*, embodies the rootlessness of Jews that Hannah Arendt has identified in her *Origins of Totalitarianism* as one of the chief reasons for the anti-Semitism spreading among the bourgeois class. He represents the homelessness of modernity as does Hermann Hesse's *lupus urbanus* Harry Haller. Hesse's *Steppenwolf* (1927) demonstrates lycanthropy as a densely psychological phenomenon, making the wolf one of modernism's metaphors for homelessness. While in Hugo, Raabe and Stoker the wolf metaphor is closely tied to the threat for the city and community as sanctuary, Hesse's *Steppenwolf* uses the metaphor for the impossibility to find roots within a community, but also as a mild form of anarchy vis-à-vis the nation-building class, the bourgeoisie. It is typically modernist in that regard, a text in which homelessness is closely connected to the idea of lycanthropy. Lycaon's transformation into a wolf running in the silent fields where his speech turns into howls emitted in vain has metamorphosed into urban loneliness in modernism.

At the beginning of the twentieth century the wolf's time-worn association with drawing the blood of the community undergoes a transformation in itself. While the wolf survives as a metaphor for rootless individualism in Hermann Hesse's *Steppenwolf*, as a figure for expulsion and human abandonment, it shifts to a creature far less glamorous than the *canis lupus*. This shift has its roots in the early twentieth-century's technological advancements in microbiology and bacteriology alongside with a ubiquitous fear of contagion that had haunted Europe since the various episodes of the plague and other disease from the Middle Ages. The so-called *Ungeziefer* (vermin), literally the animal that is not clean enough to be sacrificed but can be killed by anyone with impunity, was used in the context of marauding Gypsies as early as in Grimmelshausen's novel without, however, the presence of a scientific understanding of the role played by parasites and micro-organisms in spreading epidemics like the plague. *Ungeziefer* is the word by which Hermann Löns in his fiercely anti-Ziganist novel *Der Wehrwolf* (1910) then, as did Grimmelshausen in the seventeenth century, still labels the so-called Tatern (Romani; Löns 2007: 48) and Marodebrüder, dispersed lone-wolf soldiers during the Thirty Years' War, who go around plundering the villages. And it is the word that Kafka uses for Gregor Samsa, the young man who one morning wakes up and finds himself transformed into a monstrous *Ungeziefer*, generally poorly translated as 'insect', 'cockroach' or 'bug'.

While Kafka's *Metamorphosis* (1915) may be expressive of the anti-Semitism of his age, Löns's novel is one of the worst literary testaments regarding the treatment of so-called Gypsies on European soil. And while Kafka's text heralds the racist discourse of the Third Reich, its labelling of Jews and other minorities as *Ungeziefer*, Löns's aggressive description of the 'tartars' as criminal vagabonds foreign to German soil made this novel particularly popular among Nazi ideologues and for the werewolf movement towards the end of the Second World War, as we shall see in Chapter 5.

I would argue that in reflecting the anxieties of their time these texts from the nineteenth and early twentieth centuries form part of a seedbed for the use of dehumanizing metaphors in the contemporary migrant crisis with its loss of community and the *polis* as sanctuary: sanctuary cities and sanctuary nations. The kind of rhetoric we hear today – with words like 'marauders' or 'swarming' for migrants entering our well-guarded national fortresses (Shariatmadari 2015) – is a distant echo of a use of language and imagery that has over the centuries taken hold of how Europe and North America (with its European cultural heritage) have viewed and indeed 'wolfed' their Others. Raabe's orientalizing anti-Semitism and Dracula as the lycanthrope from Transylvania, the place beyond the forest, reflect deeply ingrained prejudices that come alive again when the right-wing *AfD* (Alternative für Deutschland), also in orientalizing fashion, compares Muslim and other Eastern immigrants with wolves that have crossed the German–Polish border (more about this in Chapter 7). Stoker's novel in particular evokes that fear of infestation that was recently mentioned by Donald Trump saying that 'Democrats want immigrants to "infest" the U.S.' (Grahan 2018). Comparing current scenarios of biopolitics with these canonical texts demonstrates how contemporary politics in its dehumanizing rhetoric and practices has reached a level at which the lines between fiction and reality become strangely blurred.

The trauma of the *homo sacer* is a key element in these texts and in its metaphorical construction – their animalization, demonization and expulsion from sanctuaries resulting in homelessness. The plight of this figure in literature is persistently relevant to the current construction of narratives in which the *polis* as city and above all as the nation state has become fractured to the point of no longer offering a sanctuary. The horror of such narratives is neo-mythical but has its roots in ancient myths of transformation, Callisto, Io and especially the story of Lycaon, the king of Arcadia, whom Jupiter expels as a wolf to the 'silent fields' where 'attempting speech' is 'in vain'. These myths about the transformation of a human being cast into liminality between the human and non-human accompany us through literature over time. Lycaon's profound depression and speechlessness resurface in fiction – in Mary Shelley's *Frankenstein*, in Hugo's *The Hunchback of Notre Dame* and in Kafka's *Metamorphosis*. They will appear again in the concentration camps and gulags of the mid-twentieth century,

Figure 2.1 The Werewolf or the Cannibal, Lucas Cranach the Elder *c.* 1512. Courtesy of the Metropolitan Museum of Art.

in literary representations of their conditions such as Primo Levi's memoirs, where he describes the trauma of humans caught between life and death, physically still alive but mentally in a state of abandonment to fate. And as we shall see in the chapter on the wolf and immigration today, these paradigms of dehumanization and the extreme trauma of being caught in liminal states of being are still the material of literature today as a representation of contemporary migrant conditions.

Chapter 3

WOLVES AND INDIGENOUS CULTURE: MIGRATION OF A METAPHOR TO THE COLONIES

In his 1596 publication *A View of the Present State of Ireland*, the poet Edmund Spenser maintained that the Irish all turned into wolves for one year (Helfer 2012: 254). It is this metaphor for the colonial Other that gets transported also to the New World, especially the American colonies where the Christian mindset of the first agrarian settlers clashed with indigenous cultures. Wolves became 'symbolic participants in the humans' escalating conflict over land and political ascendancy' (Coleman 2004: 36), and in their extermination policies and practices the colonizers and pioneers relied substantially on negative images gleaned from the Bible (Coleman 2004: 41), causing the wolves' criminalization in places like New England but also further afield. Guided by religious demonization some of the worst phases of extermination of wolves took place on the North American continent, such as the Mormon wolf hunts that intended to rid the new Zion of wolves. With all its biblical connotations this was a key event in the colonization of the Far West, the new settlers taking the Bible all too literally (Coleman 2004: 148). The desire to rid the American West of its alleged vermin did not abate until the appearance of an environmental conscience, with people like Aldo Leopold whose appeal in 'Thinking Like a Mountain' (1944) was the kind of writing that became known as the last wolves' nostalgia. Not until the sort of realization Leopold expresses in his famous passage on how he saw the fierce green fire dying in the eyes of a wolf mother he had shot do we see the birth of an environmentalist land ethic that had been triggered by the gradual extermination of the wolf.

> In those days we had never heard of passing up a chance to kill a wolf. In a second we were pumping lead into the pack, but with more excitement than accuracy [...]. When our rifles were empty, the old wolf was down, and a pup was dragging a leg into impassable slide-rocks. We reached the old wolf in time to watch a fierce green fire dying in her eyes. I realized then, and have known ever since, that

there was something new to me in those eyes, something known only to her and to the mountain. I was young then, and full of trigger-itch; I thought that because fewer wolves meant more deer, that no wolves would mean hunters' paradise. But after seeing the green fire die, I sensed that neither the wolf nor the mountain agreed with such a view. (Leopold)

In the early phase of settlement of the North American colonies wolves and natives soon became seen and treated in similar terms. Wolves and Native Americans were considered 'creatures of a godless wilderness that the colonists believed they had a moral duty to subdue' (Fogleman 1989: 66), the wolf thus standing in for a frontier phenomenon and the boundary between civilization and wilderness, Europeanness and indigeneity. As Shipman has argued:

> Before the designation of Yellowstone as a national park in 1872, many of the indigenous tribal peoples who once inhabited the area – Shoshone, Bannock, Nez Perce, Flathead, Crow, and Cheyenne – were killed or run off in a series of brutal military campaigns known collectively as the Indian wars […]. The presence of 'wild renegade Indians,' as they were characterized, was seen as incompatible with white settlement, and many, largely successful, attempts were made to exterminate the tribes or confine them to reservations. (Shipman 2015: 89–90)

It is not all that difficult to agree with Shipman's argument that the white human settlers arriving on the American frontier were the actual invasive predators. Not only were they competing with the indigenous population for food resources but also with the wolves. 'In 1915, Congress established the Federal Bureau of Biological Survey and its Division of Predator and Rodent Control, with the express mission of eliminating wolves and other large predators from all federal lands […]. Grey wolves had been part of this ecosystem for millennia but were effectively extinct by the 1930s' (Shipman 2015: 90). The North American history of the extermination of the indigenous population thus displays parallels in its homo sacer or wolf analogy to European history.

From the early colonists' perspective the way Indians sang, talked, as well as their migrations was seen in terms of wolves. Even their surprise attacks were interpreted as wolfish behaviour. Moreover, Indians and wolves were known to inhabit wild places such as swamps as safe havens, a spatial association that fed the Europeans' habit of seeing them as metaphorically equivalent (Coleman 2004: 59). The association of Indians with wolves was further strengthened by the custom introduced by the colonizers demanding that, as an expression of their submission to colonial rule, natives were to present annual tributes of wolves' heads to the authorities. These tributes functioned as tokens of power and domination, helping colonizers to mark their territories (Coleman 2004: 45–63). However, they were also misunderstood by the natives. The Algonquin, for example, understood this symbol as one of alliance and equality, a fundamental misunderstanding between the colonizers and the colonized in the use of metaphors. At a symbolic level these tributes echo the ancient Anglo Saxon tradition of identifying criminals with wolf heads, especially the ritual of placing the *wulfesheud* (wolf head) on to the bandit who was to be expelled from the community. Agamben has argued that 'what had to remain in the collective unconscious as a monstrous hybrid of human and animal, divided between the forest and the city – the werewolf – is, therefore, in its origin the figure of the man who has been banned from the city' (Agamben 1995: 105). One of the shortcomings of Agamben's book on the *homo sacer* is its Eurocentrism, as the Italian philosopher is quick to build bridges between medieval practices and the camps of the twentieth century, thereby completely ignoring the genocidal atrocities in places outside of Europe. For the ancient Aristotelian notion of not being human outside of the *polis* and the Anglo Saxon ban from the Middle Ages also became European biopolitical practices in early colonial America, with its immediate distinction between European civilization establishing itself in the East of that continent and the vast frontier filled with 'savage natives', more like animals than humans in the perception of the colonists. That concepts like the *vargr* and *friedlos* discussed by Agamben also apply to colonial America is evidenced by the fact that the tribute of wolves' heads even coincided with the decapitation of Indians treated as *homo sacer* whom anyone could kill with impunity. Coleman convincingly argues that these quasi-sacrificial rituals created the illusion of regeneration through violence, which was to become the guiding myth of the conquest of North America and in overpowering its purported savagery (Coleman 2004: 106).

In the clash of civilizations between Europe and the indigenous world the wolf is consequently a densely political animal in discourses of nationalism, colonialism, territory, migration, genocide and environmentalism. The wolf is located at the intersection of migration on the one hand and the protection of home, territory and the nation-state on the other, a scenario that makes evident that indigenous cultures tend to view the wolf very differently from European ones.

Although the Navajo, for example, share gruesome werewolf stories and the fear of wolves as witches with medieval and early modern Europe, they have healing ceremonies in which the wolf features prominently. Unlike in Europe and among European Americans, the wolf is generally not demonized and despised as vermin in indigenous views. It is described as cunning and deceptive at times, in proximity to the trickster archetype, typically Coyote in tribal cultures, a perception that reflects these canines' astute survival skills, but overall, indigenous cultures largely revere the wolf for its hunting skills, intelligence and pack organization. The respect for the wolf goes so far for some tribes, like the Ojibwe or the Pawnee, that he is considered a Brother Wolf and plays a significant role in these cultures' creation myths. The Pawnee of Kansas, for example, the so-called wolf people, show conscious identification with wolves to the point of feeling the spirit of wolves inside themselves, especially when hunting buffalo, as can be seen by George Catlin's famous painting about two Plains Indians donning wolf skins while stalking a herd of unsuspecting buffalo (1846).

Figure 3.1 George Catlin, Buffalo Hunt under the Wolf-skin Mask, *c.* 1832–3. Courtesy of the Smithsonian American Art Museum.

Is it possible to go so far as to maintain that the widespread absence of demonizing images of the wolf as well as the perception of interspecies similarities among native tribes results from their traditional lifestyle as hunters and nomads and consequently from a closer proximity to the natural world? Lopez has claimed that 'it was naturally among the hunting tribes that the wolf played the greater mythic-religious role, because the wolf himself was a great hunter, not a great farmer' (Lopez 1978: 102). This argument would tally with Daniel Quinn's philosophical novel *Ishmael* (1992), where he maintains that the story of Cain and Abel is a metaphor for the destruction of people with a biocentric world view by agriculturalists. The latter assume the role of God by placing themselves above other species and exploiting nature, seeing their relationship with her as one of ownership. This clash of civilizations between the indigenous world and logo-centric European culture which in following the Cartesian dictum of *cogito ergo sum* assumes god-like domination and ownership of the planet, a crime of comparable status to the one committed by Lycaon, results in an alienation from nature – the biblical fall from Eden – and ultimately the demise of the planet.

Once the biocentric world view that recognizes a deeper bond with other species ceases, negative mythologization can be one of the consequences that endanger some of our species, such as the wolf. Fogleman has argued that as soon as interactions with wolves ceased, attitudes towards them 'became based on folklore and myth rather than on reality' and, as generations passed, those 'who had never encountered real wolves transferred the horrifying characteristics of the imaginary wolves to their real-life counterparts' (Fogleman 1989: 64). It is this cultural-symbolic legacy that conservationists are still up against today, and although the image of the wolf in the Euro-American mind has undergone some radical shifts, old ways of thinking do not easily disappear (see also Chadwick 2010: 34–55).

Colonial wolves from Crusoe to Kipling

Although the wolf has been persistently demonized, cultures around the world have recognized its role as nurturer and preserver, from the Roman foundation myth to Rudyard Kipling's *Jungle Books* (1894), its potential for the liberation of women from the yoke of patriarchy, to Mongolian wolf totem cults, its role as environmental healer and Native American identifications with wolves. Scholars like Fuhr

(2016) and Zimen (1993), too, have pointed out that nomadic and hunting communities tend to see the wolf with greater positivity than agrarian ones. How does literature reflect the association of wolves with indigenous culture in a colonial context?

In European literature, the proximity of wolves and the indigenous people is imagined as early as in Daniel Defoe's *Robinson Crusoe* (1719). The wolves in this novel could be read as a symbolic representation for the sovereignty of the colonizer vis-à-vis the colonized, for Robinson's relationship with 'his man' Friday, one of the *Savages*, as he calls the locals of the island. The very end of the book presents its readers with a vicious wolf attack. It happens on European soil when Robinson and Friday travel from Spain to France and their guide is being set upon by three monstrous wolves. Robinson instantly asks Friday to help the guide and deal with the creatures. The triadic union between Robinson, Friday and the wolves reflects the colonial relationship of power, the master–slave link, the wolves symbolically signifying the colonist as both sovereign lord and the colonial subaltern. As their guide gets attacked by the wolves and Robinson asks Friday to act, the latter 'rode directly up to the poor man and with his pistol shot the wolf that attacked him in the head' (Defoe 1994: 210). Despite the triadic union a detail such as this one moves the wolves, nature's allegedly uncivil beasts, into closer proximity both physically and metaphorically with the colonial subaltern. Robinson's comment that Friday is 'used to that kind of creature in his country' (D 210) can be read as a reference to their symbiosis as 'man eaters', Friday coming from a tradition of cannibalism. The scene shows the native caught between the civilizing mission he is subjected to and the savage conditions Europeans see in his origins, personified by the wolves he needs to defeat (the wolf inside him) in order to become more civilized. His function in his interaction with beasts of prey is twofold, however, for the wolf attack is followed immediately by an attack from a truculent bear, with whom Friday engages in a kind of game that blurs the boundaries between animal, man and who eats whom. By insisting that he will eat the bear rather than the other way round Friday's role is that not only of conqueror of the beast (within himself) but also of the slave entertaining the master: 'Me make you good laugh' (D 212). It is a scene that may recall the traditional master–slave scenario of the court fool entertaining the King, but is now transferred to a colonial situation, with Friday also engaging in a mimicry of the colonizer's incorporation of him.

This colonial contextualization of wolves is very different in Rudyard Kipling's *Jungle Book* (1894). Wolves are not immediately associated with India, although there are of course many wolves in the subcontinent and, what is more, many wolf children. The tiger, panther, monkeys, elephants – these are first and foremost the animals in *The Jungle Book* that Europeans associate with India. It is possible that when Kipling describes his nurturing wolf pack that raises Mowgli, the wolves of Vermont where he lived at the time of writing the Mowgli stories may have been on his mind. But there is a deeper personal story to these wolves than the mere memory of the Vermont wolves.

As we have seen, the idea of abandonment is a pivotal component for the European iconography of wolves, occurring both in the concept of the wolf as abandoned outlaw in medieval Germanic law and in the context of racial dehumanization for Gypsies and Jews. For Kipling abandonment was an acutely personal experience, a traumatic memory the author tried all his life to work through by way of his writing. Kipling's own childhood trauma has filtered through to his wolves and Mowgli's twofold abandonment, once by his human parents as Shere Khan invades the village and the second time by his new family, the wolf pack.

As Jad Adams has shown in *Kipling: A Life*, the Kiplings left India in 1871 for a visit to England, where they abandoned their children Rudyard, aged six, and his younger sister Trix, aged only two, to the care of a complete stranger, a Mrs Sarah Holloway, who 'made a living by taking in children whose parents were in India' (Adams 2005: 8). Although it remains a complete mystery why the parents would not leave the children with relatives, the primary reason for this abandonment was to avoid bringing up their children in India, fearing they would 'go native' and become culturally more Indian than English. Kipling's *Kim* is the story of precisely such an Anglo-Indian child who grows up owing more to the bazaars and temples than the tea parties (Adams 2005: 8).

The experience left lifelong scars with Rudyard and especially Trix, whose nervous condition never fully healed. They called the place in Southsea they had been dropped in the House of Desolation, and never understood why they had been abandoned, what had led their parents to leave them to the horrors of emotional and physical maltreatment at the hands of Mrs Holloway and her son Harry (Adams 2005: 9). Rudyard himself only got along with Captain Holloway, a gentle but weak man who did not resist the terror dealt out to the children by his wife and son. When he died in 1874, Kipling felt abandoned for the second time, a memory adapted fictionally in the scenes when Mowgli, after first having lost his human mother, then also goes astray from his wolf mother and her pack.

All his life Kipling was deeply troubled by the loss of shelter and parental protection. He became a writer who was at home on four continents but felt forever nostalgic about the India he lost as a child. His wolves, one could argue, offer him a kind of liberation from this sense of loss. They follow law and order thanks to which Mowgli can embark on shaping his identity in the jungle. When kidnapped by the monkeys he is being drawn away from the nurturing pack and the maturity and responsibility the wolves have cultivated in him. The monkeys represent the inchoate side of the jungle, in Kipling's rather racist symbolic language a battleground between the British colonizers (the wolves) and the colonized Indians (the monkeys), with Mowgli caught between both sides.

There are at least two types of wolves in this text: Mother wolf Raksha and the lone wolf Akela. While in Hindi Raksha means the *Defender*, Akela signifies *alone*. Raksha is modelled on the Roman she-wolf that raises Romulus and Remus, a key myth of nurturing and the foundation of an empire that Kipling translates to imperial India. Mowgli, after all, as has been pointed out many times, grows into a man with imperial authority, especially in the story *In the Rukh*. Akela, on the other hand, is the lone wolf, excluded from the pack. In nature the lone wolf is often an older one expelled by younger wolves and subsequently in search of new territory. Because of his confinement in solitude the lone wolf is typically stronger and more aggressive than others, but he is also more challenged when it comes to hunting, as he cannot rely on the pack and is therefore reduced to hunting smaller prey. Mowgli in a sense becomes that lone wolf at the moment he is expelled from the pack and being caught between humanity and animality, the village and the jungle. As colonial sovereign who masters the 'jungle' Mowgli also resembles Akela, under whom he enjoys the protection of the pack, who is sovereign over his pack but gets ousted by the younger wolves with the help of Shere Khan and Tabaquis the jackal.

While Kipling's good wolves represent empire, the wolf in American literature generally stands for the opposite, a threat to empire and nation building. Narratives, however, are often filled with a mix of fear and awe of wolves which in turn are also a symbol of the challenging frontier. Perhaps one of the most famous North American wolves in this regard was the so-called king of Currumpaw, whose story is told by Ernest Thompson Seton in his 1898 book *Wild Animals I Have Known*. It is the story of Lobo, who eludes all the traps but finally dies from a broken heart for his love Blanca, a rather anthropocentric romanticization of two wolves. It is an early document, however, that challenges the traditional view of wolves as mere vermin, while also being a quintessential story of the American West, the conquest of its native creatures, both animal and human, and the disappearance of its wilderness.

Dances with wolves in North American literature: Willa Cather, Jack London, Michael Blake

There are numerous fictional accounts in which wolves are described as bloodlust-driven creatures threatening the well-being of people on the open road. In terms of posing a threat to immigrants, one prominent text in North America is Willa Cather's *My Ántonia* (1918). It features an episode in which a dying man tells Cather's narrator Jim the story of a Russian bridal party chased by hundreds of wolves, and which ends with the two surviving members Pavel and Peter, the two Russian immigrants Jim meets near his prairie town of Black Hawk, who throw the bride and the groom to the wolves so they can escape. In this gruesome tale of human sacrifice the positions of sovereign and *homo sacer* are reversable. While Pavel and Peter are sovereign in their decision to sacrifice the bride and groom, they in turn subsequently become the *homines sacri* of the entire Russian community, which abandons them from their middle, forcing them to emigrate to the New World. Their interaction with the wolves renders them doomed forever, as even here, in Nebraska, they fail to prosper. The wolves as godheads to whom the humans of six sleighs are sacrificed are central to Cather's classic and her rich animal world consisting also of rattlesnakes, prairie-dogs and even insects, all of them described in great detail in their relationship with the humans who have made the stark prairie their new home. The wolves may be in Russia but they are significant for Nebraska as well, as Antonia becomes abandoned by her first boyfriend, thrown to the metaphorical wolves as it were. For the narrator protagonist Jim, the wolves also become meaningful, as he too abandons women for the sake of his career (cf. Cohen 2009: 52).

There is a close symbolic relationship here between wolves and immigration. This is one of the few stories in which the wolves become the cause for exodus and a search for exile. The wolves are the ones that are ultimately sovereign in Russia, and humans like Pavel, Peter, or the bridegroom and his bride their victims. But the American West too, its frontier, is described as wolf country, metaphorically, a place that stirs eerie feelings in young Jim as he migrates west to the frontier, that he had suddenly left 'the world [...] behind, that we had got over the edge of it, and were outside man's jurisdiction' (Cather 1993: 10). When first setting eyes upon the stark landscape of the prairie, he cannot feel homesick, thinking that 'if we never arrived anywhere it did not matter. Between that earth and that sky I felt erased, blotted out' (C 11), a place to which, he ponders, even the spirits of the dead cannot follow. It is a place, in other words, not only in which wolves do have a substantial biological presence but where the concept wolf implies the constant interplay between sovereign and *homo sacer*, and where sacrifices have to be made for the sake of survival.

Three other texts stand out in highlighting how wolves have become a catalyst for issues of ethnicity, territory and the frontier in the North American colonial project: Jack London's *Call of the Wild* (1903), *White Fang* (1906) and Michael Blake's *Dances with Wolves* (1988, film version 1990). While Cather's wolves, however, are a clear import from Europe with its perception of the wolf as miscreant, London and Blake demonstrate a more nuanced picture of the animal, although both still reflect upon wolves within a colonial context. Blake's critical stance vis-à-vis the colonial enterprise is unsurprising given the fact that he wrote in the second half of the twentieth century, whereas London's perception of wolves, which is closer to the indigenous world than was generally displayed by his contemporaries, is no doubt based on his own long-term exposure to the Yukon during the Klondike gold rush. It was here that he became intimately acquainted with human survival, the local environment, as well as the indigenous population (Kershaw 1997: 57–73).

Possibly no other American author of his time has written about wolves with as much detail. *Call of the Wild* describes a process of retrogression (London 1998: 16) from civilization to the primordial, the latter receiving greater appreciation by the author than the former. The protagonist Buck is the chief catalyst for this process from white to native America, from the soft Southland to the rigours and freedom of the Arctic wilderness, where all men and animals blend together in a conglomerate of savages ruled by the 'law of club and fang'. It is a place that knows 'neither peace nor rest, nor a moment's safety' (L11), where the domesticated generations fall from all creatures, most of all Buck's owner Thornton, who though white and thus part of white man's vision of the civilizing world feels more at home in the Yukon wilderness than elsewhere. There is of course a good deal of romanticizing of primordiality and the frontier as a last place of freedom for men, London celebrating his fantasies of exaggerated masculinity (Cf. Gurion 1966:

112–20). The wolf is central to these male fantasies, as are the natives, Rousseau's *hommes naturels*. As Thornton dives deeper and deeper into the natural environment he displays tendencies of 'going native', as both he and Buck become negotiators between white and native America:

> John Thornton asked little of man or nature. He was unafraid of the wild. With a handful of salt and a rifle he could plunge into the wilderness and fare wherever he pleased and as long as he pleased. Being in no haste, Indian fashion, he hunted his dinner in the course of the day's travel; and if he failed to find it, like the Indian, he kept on travelling. (L55-6)

As Thornton increasingly embraces the state of nature, Buck the dog becomes more and more wolf-like. As enamoured as London may have been of the great North, however, Thornton's vision of primordial masculinity embodied in wolves alongside with indigeneity never quite abandons white man's civilizing mission, thus betraying a degree of authorial distance to all things wild. This is revealed primarily in the final showdown where Buck awakens to memories of his roots in white man's civilization and defends his master's camp against the Yeehat Indians, killing 'man, the noblest game of all [...] in the face of the law of club and fang' (L65).

London's racist attitude is well established. Immigrants from Asia he famously described as the 'yellow peril' during his coverage of the Russo-Japanese war in 1904 and, as has been argued by Richard Vanderbeets who called London a 'Nietzsche of the North' (Vanderbeets 1967: 229-33), in some of his early short stories, the cycle called 'The Son of the Wolf' (1900), wolves form part of his vision of Nordic supremacy over half-breeds and Alaskan Indians.

Buck's transformation from a dog to wolf offers a variety of interpretations in view of race and biopolitics. He displays a liminal status between dog and wolf, between the domestic and the wild, between his dog allegiance to his master John Thornton and his wolf freedom from the yoke of domestication. Buck is thus a border phenomenon between the city and the forest, but by 'going native', as it were, as well as berserk in the act of killing natives, he is the creature, much like the *homo sacer* of ancient proscription, who is set apart from the community of men residing inside the *polis*. In this case the idea of the *polis* represents the civilizing mission on the North American continent, from which London's characters want to escape. As dog turned wolf, Buck ends up being closely tied conceptually to the natives as they are perceived through the racist lens of white man, whom, however, he still defends against the natives. He is thus strangely caught between two worlds and a creature in which nature and race are in close proximity.

In his feral wolf status, Buck has become beast and sovereign at the same time, to borrow an equation from Derrida's famous seminar series. The freedom he acquires in wilderness implies his sovereign status, a vulnerable sort of freedom albeit due to having shed his domestic ties, thus being removed from civilization and its social contract. This freedom of the wolf reflects the inherent symmetry that exists between the *homo sacer* and the sovereign, a symmetry that pertains to the relationship between the colonizer and his dog, and the dog-become-wolf (literally *canis lupus*, dog wolf) and the natives. The narrative's trajectory from dog to wolf parallels the approximation between Buck, the *canis* or *lupus sacer*, and the colonized natives as *homo sacer*, between the predator Buck as a defender of the human predators or colonizers and as their prey, the Yeehats. The natives and Buck are tied precisely through their relationship of predator and prey, Buck killing them off with ease. In the Yeehats' eyes he is a demonic figure, reminiscent of the Christian demonization of the wolf but also in his uncanny ferocity of the berserk warrior of the early Middle Ages, who became demonized and outlawed after Christianity moves into Northern Europe: 'This ecstasy […] comes to the soldier, war mad on a stricken field and refusing quarter; and it came to Buck leading the pack, sounding the old wolf cry' (L25). In final analysis, Buck assists the colonizing world in the natives' self-destruction as they are shooting arrows at each other in a frantic fit of panic. He is assisting the colonial enterprise, although he has become the wolf who will himself in the end fall victim to that enterprise. Both the Yeehats and Buck are symbiotic in their shared victim status in which genocide and the extermination of the species *canis lupus* coincide.

In London's novel *White Fang* (1906) this process is reversed. Here the wolf emerges from the depth of wilderness and is slowly being domesticated and integrated into so-called Western civilization. Somewhat loosely and perhaps a bit provocatively, London's novel can be described as a wolf's Bildungsroman in which, traditionally in the nineteenth century at least, the hero has to learn to relinquish the poetry of his heart for the prose of circumstances. In other words, the protagonist, in this case the wolf with some roots in domestication (his mother is a dog gone wild), learns to give up his wildness and subject himself to the civilizing mission. It seems that he becomes a metaphor here for the twofold process of either destruction of alterity seen as a threat to the *polis* or its absorption through domestication, ultimately also a destructive process. This process of White Fang's domestication happens in two phases: the first one is his encounter with an indigenous tribe, the second one his exposure to the white colonizers who subject all nature to their culture. Although the process of domestication begins to some extent while White Fang lives in the natives' camp, they do not deprive him entirely of his identity but allow for the core of his wolfishness to remain. The affectionate bond between him and the native tribe is a reflection of their proximity to nature in distinction to the whites who only see nature's potential for exploitation and profit.

Overall, London establishes strong parallels between the indigenous people and wolves, especially in their shared experience of hunting and survival. Although the Natives initiate his transformation into a dog, the brotherhood of wolf and Indian shows itself at the moment when White Fang and his gang of Indian dogs attack the southern dogs the white intruders bring to the Yukon, who are no match for their wilder cousins. Their attacks of these dogs and in turn the soft southland dogs' hatred of White Fang can be read as an allegorical description of the wars between Native Americans and the colonizers. The white men's dogs' hatred of White Fang and his gang of Indian dogs, which stand for everything wild that the southern dogs had left behind generations earlier, reflects their masters' hatred of the native population. Despite White Fang's initial victories over many a southland dog, however, his ultimate domestication by the white 'superior gods' is indicative of the wider context of colonial subjugation of the indigenous people, of everything wild:

> It was their instinct. He was the Wild, the unknown, the terrible, the ever-menacing, the thing that prowled in the darkness around the fires of the primeval world when they, cowering close to the fires, were reshaping their instincts, learning to fear the Wild out of which they had come, and which they had deserted and betrayed. Generation by generation, down all the generations, had this fear of the Wild been stamped into their natures. For centuries the Wild had stood for terror and destruction. And during all this time free licence had been theirs, from their masters, to kill the things of the Wild. (L164)

Some of the race matters are inscribed not only into London's use of a gradient between wolf and dog but also into his use of colours. White Fang's mother Kiche, who like Buck went feral, is a red dog, while the name of White Fang denotes his journey between ethnic groups and his gradual 'whitening' from native wolf in the arctic North to Euro-American dog in balmy California. Although London is far from ever shedding the racial views typical of his time, he seems to be aware of the fact that not all is well with the civilizing mission. This becomes discernible also in the disturbing scene of the prize fight in which the pit bull named Cherokee nearly kills White Fang. A dog from England described as more of a monster than any wolf, his relentless grip on White Fang that would surely kill him if the young gold hunter Weedon Scott did not intervene a reflection of the choking grip the colonizers have over the colonized.

Taken together the two stories, however, show London reiterate colonial fears of going native, which to the early colonizers entailed leaving the realm of God for a wilderness seen as full of savagery rather than in its prelapsarian condition. While London was full of admiration for untouched wilderness and the spirit of freedom, survival and untamed creatures of the forests, his second story *White Fang* about domestication corrects the vision about going native he had expressed three years earlier in *Call of the Wild*. Whether he did this to please his white readership or in defence of colonization and his faith in the righteous subjugation of the continent is not clear.

The symbolic symbiosis between the wolf and the indigenous people is also a key component in Michael Blake's *Dances with Wolves* (1988), a novel popularized by its movie version (1990) starring Kevin Costner. Here colonial attitudes towards nature in general and indigenous populations in particular are reflected through the prism of the growing triadic bond between Lieutenant John Dunbar, the Comanche tribe he meets and the wolf Two Socks. Exiled to Fort Sedgwick, a remote civil war outpost on the frontier, Dunbar finds himself temporarily in the position of the *homo sacer*, set apart from his own community in terms of ethnicity and military, and left at the mercy of the state of nature. He arrives from a world full of entrepreneurial spirit eager to exploit the natural resources of the new continent combined with intense racism towards the indigenous population as a reflection of the perception of his kind. In that world wolves are seen as an embodiment of native hostility, as vermin to be killed. His first impression of the natives as a 'mass of humanity that had raised a fearful howling, [...] a whole separate race of humans watching him' (Blake 122), echoing the voices of early settlers, however soon subsides. From the beginning, Dunbar is open and responsive to the nature that surrounds him, and willing to learn about and be absorbed in the new world he encounters.

3. Wolves and the Colonies   67

His encounter with an aging wolf, whom he names Two Socks due to the two white patches around the ankles of his front legs, foreshadows his ensuing contact with the Comanches living near his outpost Fort Sedgwick. His first impulse to distrust the wolf also quickly subsides as he is beginning to fathom their shared creaturely existence. That day, he writes in his diary that the wolf 'does not seem inclined to be no nuisance' (B50), recognizing that his horse Cisco and the wolf are his only company. Unlike his predecessors at the outpost, who kill animals for sport, Dunbar quickly comes to realize that he needs to live *with* the other creatures on the prairie, not against them. His love of animals grows over time to a point that he comes to understand that 'their unwavering loyalty was satisfying in ways that human relationships had never been' (B188) – a view that in his gradual immersion in Native American culture he will come to adjust, for his relationship with the Comanches will also be based on the kind of trust and loyalty he has never experienced among his own people. Although he seems to resist 'going native' by pointing out that 'he did not think of becoming an Indian' while however conceding that 'so long as he was with them he would serve the same spirit' (B217), in the end he embraces full cultural assimilation with the Comanche to the point of not wanting to return to white American culture. As the *homo sacer* temporarily abandoned by his army he has found his 'wolf brothers'. The army tries to claim him back, but he resists this return to his compatriots and ends up fully switching sides to the Comanche tribe. By naming him 'Dances with Wolves' the Comanche welcome Dunbar into their community, his name progressing from 'Jun' to 'Loo Ten Nant' to his Indian name. This naming process and his union with Christine or Stands with a Fist, whom the Comanche adopted as a child after her parents had been killed and who like Dunbar straddles the ethnic divide, are significant steps in the consolidation of his union with the Comanche and their surrounding natural world.

There is hence a triadic understanding between Dunbar, the wolf and the natives – their symbolic symbiosis and cohabitation rather than destruction and enmity. The wolf soon follows him around like a dog, its apparent domestication paralleling Dunbar's gradual cultural assimilation to the Comanche way of life. As Two Socks shows more and more trust and becomes increasingly more tame, Dunbar goes native and becomes more and more 'wild' in the eyes of white America.

Much like in London's two stories Dunbar's rapport with the wolf is heavily romanticized in its equation with his understanding of the ethnic Other, his crossing the human–animal divide in synchrony with crossing the ethnic divide. One may argue that Blake's vision of a *locus amœnus*, where cultures and species meet, is highly utopian. This cultural approximation is, however, admirably analysed and envisioned as the native world gradually opens itself to Dunbar. Dunbar soon departs from his own world in which prejudices against the native population reign supreme. He is particularly keen to observe that they are diverse, complex in character and full of wisdom, unlike his own people whom he increasingly comes to despise as intruders. He realizes that while the native population lives in harmony with nature, it is his own people who destroy that human harmony with nature. The devastation of the land and its creatures by white Americans shows itself, for example, when one day he and his fellow Comanche come across a herd of buffalo butchered only for their furs, their meat left rotting in the sunshine. In another scene they chance upon a forest grove, that traditional sanctuary in myth and literature from Greek antiquity to fantasies about *Waldeinsamkeit*, a wholesome solitude in the forest, in nineteenth-century literature from the German Romantics to the American transcendentalists. Here, however, as part of the destructive trail Euro-Americans have blazed along the American frontier, Blake shows us the complete desecration of indigenous sanctuaries and the genocidal extermination of all its living creatures. It is a scene in which his utopian vision of species interaction violently clashes with species genocide, foreshadowing the end of life on the Great Plains as it once was:

> Everywhere he looked the ground held bodies, or pieces of bodies. There were small animals, badgers and skunks and squirrels. Most of these were intact. Some were missing their tails. They lay rotting where they had been shot, for no apparent reason other than target practice. The primary objects of the genocide were deer that sprawled all around him. A few of the bodies were whole, minus only the prime cuts. Most were mutilated. In one spot the severed heads had been arranged nose to nose, as if they were having a conversation. It was supposed to be humorous. (B 348)

Such violation of the land heralding the imminent genocide of its people, the colonizers' stripping nature of its resources and blatant disrespect for all native creatures, is in salient contrast to the communicative efforts between Dunbar and the tribe. It is by eating from the buffalo liver after the Great Buffalo Hunt that Dunbar indicates he has switched sides, having become a hunter, a significant step in his cultural assimilation.

Once again, like in London's novels, this reads like dense romanticizing of the phenomenon of going native and of cultural encounters, but what is interesting for our discussion of the wolf metaphor's transfer to the North American colonial context in which wolves and the indigenous people are equated are precisely such moments in which the species divide is blurred: by becoming Comanche, Dunbar also opens himself to the nature of the wolf, a metamorphosis recognized by Two Socks as the wolf makes Dunbar the gift of a prairie chicken he has killed. The symbiosis reveals itself in moments when Dunbar is sharing food with the natives as well as the wolf, as well as in the ways they watch each other, in the reciprocal gaze between human and animal. When he dances around the fire like an Indian the wolf is watching him, and as he plays with the wolf on the prairie the Indians are watching him. This interaction with the wolf is what earns him the trust of the native tribe. They respect him for how he treats the wolf, demonstrating to them that he is one of the few exceptions among the invaders who treats nature with the same kind of respect as they do. By contrast, the European invaders are described as 'rich in goods but poor in everything else' (B61), as inferior opportunists. Kicking Bird, for example, thinks of white men as coyotes, traditionally the Native American trickster, and unsurprisingly as white America will trick the indigenous people out of their land.

The wolf in Blake's novel not only is a symbol and catalyst for crossing intercultural and interspecies boundaries but also stands for a greater nobility in the sense of a deeper rapport with nature found in Native American culture than is found in the colonizing power represented by the coyote. Two Socks' eventual killing (B365) by the advancing soldiers marks the end of Dunbar's harmony with the natural and Indian world, as civilization wants to claim him back. In its migratory invasiveness this so-called civilization that destroys sanctuaries is described with a range of metaphors, including the coyote but primarily relating to water and the flood (the 'human tide [...] rising in the East' [B384]). Such metaphors of migration also echo through recent populist rhetoric, the difference being one of colonialist invasion versus refugees' search for sanctuaries.

Dunbar's symbiosis with wolves and the natives is most prominently expressed perhaps in the image of dancing inscribed into his Indian name. His dancing with wolves parallels his dance with the Comanche, both in the real sense of the dance asking for the buffalo to return and in the metaphorical sense of a dance with their culture. It is a temporary dance, however, as Two Socks is killed by the intruding soldiers – a temporary dance with wolves as well as with indigenous culture.

Although at the end of the film a lone wolf howls, symbolically heralding the indomitable spirit of the frontier, the final caption tells us that the culture of the local tribes is all gone thirteen years later, their homes destroyed, their food source, the buffalo, on the brink of extinction and the horse culture of the plains gone forever, as is the frontier itself.

Blake's novel is a key text about the role of wolves and indigenous culture in the politics of land appropriation and agrarian land use. The wolf's persistently negative image as a parasitic trespasser results largely from the experiences of agrarian cultures and settlers claiming land as property. One of the main problems about wolves reappearing in the lower forty-eight states is that they are entering land transformed from nature into culture and no longer owned by all living creatures. Transforming wilderness into culture is a quintessentially colonial experience in which animal politics and human politics converge. From the perspective of the colonizers indigenous tribes and wolves were almost identical enemies, so that the war against wolves and the wars against the Indians overlapped and were all but indistinguishable. The convergence of genocide with specicide has its documented moments in the history of the United States, such as the one when at the start of an 1865 campaign against the Northern Plains tribes, a U.S. Army general told his troops that the Cheyenne and Lakota 'must be hunted like wolves.' (Jason Mark 2015). It is one of the great achievements of Michael Blake's *Dances with Wolves* (1988) as well as the film version to capture and remind us of this madness.

Wolves, gender and the world in indigenous perceptions

If we look beyond Euro-American literature, we may wonder to what extent these authors and their texts may differ from indigenous perceptions of nature, land use, and the wolf in myth and literature. By and large, indigenous cultures in North America have more positive attitudes towards wolves owing to their traditional proximity to nature and the wolf's role in the creation myths of some tribes, but not all perceptions of the wolf are reverential. In Cheyenne legends, for example, the wolf features as a trickster figure and is compared to white man cheating the tribe (Preece 2002: 11). The wolf as trickster, however, is an oddity in Native American myth, as that role tends to be occupied by the wolf's relative coyote (cf. Radin 1972: 3–53).

The idea of Brother Wolf is largely but not exclusively indigenous. The work of ethnobiologist Raymond Pierotti is of particular relevance in trying to explain why Native Americans may see the wolf as a brother figure. Pierotti has argued that creation stories are inherently responses to changing environmental conditions that happened millennia ago. 'Indigenous cultures,' Pierotti argues, 'were attuned to thinking about variability rather than stability in the environment. Thus, any other species that helped them navigate these changes effectively was credited with great spiritual power, and in some circumstances, identified as the protagonist of a creation story' (Pierotti 2016: 9). This role of the North American wolf helping humans to orient themselves in their survival, through sheer mimicry in the end, is radically different from the wolf in the early European bestiaries which contrast the animal's profound stupidity with the fox's cleverness and in which the impact of early Christianity is present. These bestiaries mark the beginning of a cultural demonization of the wolf that ultimately not only helps to destroy wolves in Europe but then travels to the New World where it clashes with more benevolent indigenous perceptions of the environmental role of wolves in the world.

Wolf experts like Barry Holstun Lopez have described in some detail that indigenous knowledge of wolves seems to be more extensive even than what science can offer us. This holds true especially for seminomadic hunting communities among the Inuit of Alaska and northern Canada who are facing some of the same problems in securing game and surviving in the Arctic as wolves do, so that their knowledge of wolves is based on a tradition of careful observation that would help them survive (Lopez 1978: 78). As long as their traditional hunting culture is able to survive, which for the Inuit is increasingly threatened by climate changes, humanity will be able to benefit from the vast library based on oral tradition and the cultivation of a rich memory that safeguards the survival of biodiversity in the dual sense of cultural and ecological diversity. Alongside with the wolves these cultures have a long history of vulnerability whether in North America or, as we shall see, in other places such as Inner Mongolia in northern China.

These colonial patterns also contain gender-related aspects, as the destruction of wolves and indigenous cultures, in North America at least, revolves around issues of masculinity in the conquest of the frontier. That this kind of thinking has not disappeared to this day has been explored by Sine Annahita and Tamara Mix who have shown to what extent notions of masculinity and femininity play out in Alaska's renewed wolf politics that draws on the myth of frontier masculinity. From at least the mid-nineteenth century on, they claim,

U.S. men imagined frontiers as places to which they could escape stifling civilization and feminine domestication and where they could return to an authentic masculinity tested and honed by strenuous and virtuous labor. [...] Wilderness areas are imagined as places where men can go wild and where they can experience masculine freedoms unavailable in stifling, feminized, domesticated cities. (Anahita/Mix 2006: 334)

It is a mentality that we also see enshrined in Jack London's writing with his myth of the great northern frontier. Hunting in this frontier myth is a highly gendered activity, thus Anahita's and Mix's argument, and killing 'fierce' animals like bears and wolves has long been an attribute of male virility in patriarchal societies in which 'violence is part of what it means to be a man' (Anahita/Mix 2006: 335). Since masculinity came to be increasingly challenged in the last century, state policy makers in Alaska have developed strategies to retrofit frontier masculinity, especially by vilifying the opponents of killing wolves for sport as effeminate sissies and by recasting wolf hunters as patriarchal family providers (Anahita/Mix 2006: 344). The myth making continues in places like Alaska and much to the detriment of wolves. In this light of patriarchal control indigenous attitudes to wolves as nurturers are likely also cast as part and parcel of the feminization of wolf defence. To recognize the nurturing side of wolves as indigenous cultures and some women writers tend to do deeply challenges the white male frontier mentality filled with an excess of testosterone that keeps damaging the ecosystem.

The wolf as a gender paradigm is largely a colonial European import, but while in Europe it featured in the form of medieval and early modern phobias about women perceived as werewolves or witches riding wolves, in the colonies this gendering shifts to a patriarchal frontier myth, of white men having to clear the wilderness of its ferocious beasts in order to make a safe home for their wives and children. The sports hunting mentality in places like Alaska is grounded in this myth, and men not partaking of it are viewed as being on the side of women staying at home.

Indigenous culture has also responded to the wolf in gendered terms in the sense that some myths focus on the interaction between wolves and women, and some indigenous writers, especially women, have questioned the clichéd images of wolves, be they Native American or not, in their constructions of masculinity and femininity. In indigenous folklore women are often depicted as the wives of wolves, their helpers or women may receive their wisdom from wolves. On the other hand, in similarity to the early modern European tradition Navajo tales identify women siding with wolves as witches. The wolf also plays a significant role in traditional constructions of masculinity, for example, in the rituals surrounding the Cheyenne wolf warriors. It is the wolf's intelligence and elusiveness that feed into such constructions, while the bear is accredited more with valour and strength. That such constructions of masculinity have not disappeared and that bears seem to have more of a link with masculinity than wolves have been shown by Peter Hennen and Sine Anahita and Tamara Mix for the state of Alaska, where gay men and masculinized men celebrating hairy and large men have created a subculture of 'bears' (Anahita/Mix 2006: 349; Hennen 2005).

In postmodern literature such constructions and stereotypical images are either being modified, or elaborated upon or challenged, especially in indigenous women's writing. While it has been argued, for example, that the Ojibwe author Louise Erdrich has enriched her novels 'with the mystery, power, and potential of bears as breakers of spiritual and cultural barriers, as guardians, as transformers, and as representatives of a tribal spiritual tradition alive in contemporary literature' (Barry 2000: 28), especially for her character Fleur Pillager, in her novel *The Painted Drum* (2005), she has deconstructed the idea of Brother Wolf by featuring an Ojibwe woman who throws her elder daughter to the wolves in order to save herself and the baby she has from her lover. This image of sacrificing a human life to the wolves for survival is revisionary of the patriarchal act in Willa Cather's *My Ántonia* of the two Russian men sacrificing the bride and bridegroom to the wolves to save themselves. The wolves in Cather's story reflect male aggression as they do in Erdrich; yet Erdrich's scene not only challenges the traditional nurturing quality of the wolf as a participant in creation myths of her own Ojibwe culture but also empowers her female protagonist with the sovereignty of her own decision to sacrifice her daughter. In terms of gender this is an ambivalent act showing the mother as sovereign beast (Derrida 2009) and her daughter as *homo sacer*.

As Wyatt argues, there is a certain way of reading Erdrich's book which reflects Native American philosophy of life as fluid, cyclical rather than linear and crossing boundaries. This would also apply to other texts by writers with an indigenous background. The travel writer William Least Heat-Moon, for example, describes in his classic *Blue Highways* (1989) how his journey along the small, forgotten highways of America from the centre out and then around the periphery closely follows the Hopi cycle of life. Erdrich's texts and other such narratives offer what I would call a 'migratory way of reading' that is closely connected to the oral tradition of storytelling among the Ojibwe and other tribes. In the Deleuzian sense these stories are highly rhizomatic and nomadic rather than arborescent and sedentary:

> Readers have to make associational leaps across different story lines, as listeners to oral storytellers have to listen for analogies between disparate tales in a story cycle. As we read, we begin to notice similar details occurring in the widely different contexts of the stories, and we learn to connect them. These parallels gradually build up a lived philosophy on death, loss, mourning, survival, and the continuing relation of the bereaved to the dead. (Wyatt 2011: 14)

Erdrich's books are also densely inclusive of non-human animal species in the symbolic significance they hold for Ojibwe culture: she features Coyote as trickster facilitating change and the development of her heroines and the bear as an embodiment of the healing qualities of nature. The symbolism of some of these animals, the bear in particular with his 'seasonal cycle of hibernation and renewal' (Wyatt 2011: 27), is closely tied to the notion of cyclicality of time and processes of stability that are only guaranteed through eternal change. However, by adopting the image of wolves tearing humans to pieces Erdrich not only seems to engage intertextually with Willa Cather's scene but at the same time deliberately reverts to the colonizer's perception rather than her indigenous ones. It is a strategy one could interpret as a self-reflexive and ironic way of engaging with a metaphor that has over centuries divided Euro-Americans and the indigenous people. Through the deliberate appropriation of such a metaphor by a female indigenous writer she may be signalling that in spite of all adherence to indigenous cultural icons she is still free to change such images, even if it means reverting to the stereotypical destructive side of wolves.

Thinking of Erdrich's inclusive treatment of various species one may ask if the indigenous world view can fruitfully inform the politics of migration and race in terms of a trajectory from exclusion to inclusion and the universal belief among indigenous cultures that the land cannot be owned but owns all living creatures, as expressed also in John G. Neihardt's classic *Black Elk Speaks* (1932). In his memories of the gradual destruction of his tribe, the Sioux and ultimately all Native American culture Black Elk renders a detailed account of the senseless exploitation of natural resources, such as the killing of most buffalo for their hides, tongues or mere sport, the folly of selling Mother Earth resulting in the dispossession of her people, their years of wandering on the 'black road' of misery and selfishness, and culminating in genocidal massacres such as the Battle at Wounded Knee (1890). This decline of the Indian nation contrasts sharply with the utopian vision he had as a child, his journey to the centre of the earth where he meets the Six Grandfathers of all Native American people, and where he is initiated into their secrets of making the nation flourish. His vision is 'the story of all life that is holy and good to tell, and of us two-leggeds sharing in it with the four-leggeds and the wings of the air and all green things; for these are children of one mother and their father is one spirit' (Neihardt 1979: 13).

Black Elk's great vision of circularity and inclusion is reminiscent of Erdrich but also of Immanuel Kant's concept of world peace (1795), which propagates that our planet be shared by all and that consequently refugees have an innate right of being given shelter in nations other than the ones they were born into. As Seyla Benhabib argues in *The Rights of Others*, Kant envisaged 'a world condition in which all members of the human race become participants in a civil order and enter into a condition of lawful association with one another' (Benhabib 2004: 39). His ideas of hospitality for those who want to first enter another country in conjunction with his advocacy of *Weltbürgertum* (citizenship of the world) are anti-nationalist, if one defines nationalism in its restriction of space within boundaries of a 'people who believe they share a common ancestry and a common destiny to live under their own government on land sacred to their history' (Wiebe 2002: 5). They are ideas voiced at the height of the age of rampant colonialism and exploitation of the New World. His utopian vision was directed against John Locke's theory of the *res nullius*, which implied that the planet belonged to nobody in particular, a thought at the root of ruthless imperialist appropriation of overseas territories, while Kant held that the surface of the planet belonged to everyone as it was limited and thus had to accommodate everyone, disregarding 'property relations historically existing among communities that have already settled on the land' (Benhabib 2004: 30).

This vision of absolute inclusion of all humans, and of hospitality to every citizen of the world regardless of where they decide to migrate, shares much in common with the indigenous *Weltbild* (world view) of paradisiacal conditions as expressed in Black Elk's memoirs, although this view is one of pluralism in the sense of a harmonious biodiversity that includes all living beings. A good example of an approximation of

Kant's ideals with those of Native Americans, of hospitality bestowed on those who enter new territory for the first time, would be the benevolent interaction between the natives and early European colonists remembered to this day by the Thanksgiving tradition. Needless to reiterate that this act of hospitality was soon abused by the colonizers' greed for property and territory, hence collapsing under a typically European understanding of land ownership. The claim of hospitality made by Kant and indigenous peoples is, however, still heeded in the right to seek and obtain asylum as laid down by the Geneva Convention for refugees, although it clashes vehemently with the principle of national sovereignty that guards nations and their borders.

The Universal Declaration of Human Rights (United Nations, 1948) recognizes the right to emigrate but not necessarily to immigrate (Benhabib 2004: 11). While upholding the sovereignty of states, of territories tied to kinship, the declaration propagates the freedom to cross territorial boundaries. The wolf metaphor in current populist discourse is a product of a mentality that views the encroachment of migrants and refugees upon territories tied to kinship as a criminal act, much in the same way as wolves treat the crossing of boundaries by other wolves who are not part of their own pack as an act of trespassing which then typically triggers extremely aggressive defence mechanisms. Wolves are creatures that ignore boundaries but also defend them violently, and it is perhaps due to this strange ambivalence that the metaphor lends itself so well to being employed in the context of migration of people, that is, as a metaphor describing undocumented aliens as criminals while also standing in for those defending the nation against migrants.

It is important therefore to read the literary texts presented in this chapter by bearing in mind the current populist rhetoric on migration in the United States (and Europe) as well as its 'wolf wars', which have produced a tension between ranchers, environmentalists and Native Americans in view of the benefits versus damage caused by wolf rehabilitation (cf. McIntyre 1993 and 1995). Particular attention needs to be focused on areas where after having been reintroduced wolves have had an impact on cultural heritage and identity. In Idaho, for example, the reintroduction of the grey wolf has significantly reshaped the cultural identity of the Nez Perce tribe (Wilson 1999). I will address this particular example in more detail in Chapter 7. There is mounting tension in these areas between those claiming private land use and trying to eradicate the wolf, and environmentalists defending the interests of wolves and the indigenous people. This controversy is reflected, for example, in the use of billboards along highways.

Figure 3.2 Billboard Erected by the Washington Residents against Wolves. Image by Matthew Weaver, courtesy of the Capital Press, Salem, Oregon.

Historically, the strife between humans and wolves has largely been over natural resources, a competition for food, especially in times of war when food shortages are common. As the current wolf debates are about public land use and ownership it may therefore not surprise anyone that xenophobia towards immigrants is in the mentality of a large faction of people in places like the Western United States not far removed from their eagerness to see the wolf removed from the endangered species list. A place like Yellowstone National Park has demonstrated, however, that wolves can be successfully re-introduced in locations from which they had disappeared and how they can then benefit the environment. Moreover, the extermination of wolves in an area by removing it from the endangered species list causes tremendous damage to indigenous cultural identities that are traditionally closely linked to the triangular symbiosis of human-buffalo-wolf.

The wolf is unrecognizable, says a character in Cormac McCarthy's novel *The Crossing* (1994) about the persecution of a pregnant wolf. In this novel, discussed in more detail in Chapter 6, it is the oppressed, the colonized, those guided by superstition and long memories (in this case the Yaqui Indians) who show wisdom and respect for the wolf. To these groups she is an archetype, a mythical being representing a world order:

> El lobo es una cosa incognoscible, he said. Lo que se tiene en la trampa no es mas que dientes y forro. El lobo propio no se puede conocer. Lobo o lo que sabe el lobo. Tan como preguntar lo que saben las piedras. Los arboles, El mundo [...]. He said that the wolf is a being of great order and that it knows what men do not. [...] The wolf is like the copo de nieve. Snowflake' (45) [...] 'Escuchame, joven. [...] The wolf is made the way the world is made. You cannot touch the world. (McCarthy 1999: 46)

The miserable end of McCarthy's she-wolf reflects the failure of both international and environmental politics. The respect she receives from the downtrodden and indigenous people reveals an awareness of her beneficiary role within the ecosystem, the balance between all species sharing and migrating across the various national borders of this planet, and ultimately also ties in with Black Elk's and Kant's utopian visions: 'Deer and hare and dove and groundvole all richly empanelled on the air for her delight, all nations of the possible world ordained by God of which she [the wolf] was one and not separate from' (McCarthy 1999: 127). In that sense, the wolf who has once been so persistently maligned in the context of race may indeed be recognizable for a wider politics of hospitality, cosmopolitanism and biodiversity.

Chapter 4

WOLVES AND WAYWARD WOMEN: BETWEEN CONDEMNATION AND EMPOWERMENT

Lycaon is turned into a wolf for the crime of cannibalism, for offering human meat to Jove. Despite the parallels between the Arcadian myth and its Lycaios rites and the Roman myth of the she-wolf with its fertility rites celebrated in the Lupercalia (Wiseman 1995: 4), the two wolves obviously differ in gender and intent. While one is a devouring male, turning 'his lust for slaughter on the flocks' (Ovid 2004: 13), the Roman *lupa* is the archetype of the nurturing wolf mother so significant for the prosperity and progress of Rome. The Roman myth glorifies the she-wolf as a foundation figure. It venerates the wolf as a creature of fertility and war, of nourishment and destruction, with Mars, the father of Romulus and Remus, as God of farmers before he became God of war, a shift that reflects that the possession of land in agrarian societies results in territorialism, neighbourly clashes and warfare. Destruction and regeneration are thus inseparable in the Roman she-wolf who returns to us in literature most prominently perhaps in Kipling's wolf mother Raksha, who represents British law and order in its indebtedness to Roman imperialism, the colonial mission as an act of kindness when she adopts the abandoned boy Mowgli (the 'frog') and defends (*Raksha* is Hindi for the 'defender') him against the aggressive males of the pack. No doubt, Kipling adopted this idea of the she-wolf as a defender of empire from the Roman wolf, whose nurturing and defensive qualities have been ideologically exploited time and again, more recently by Mussolini, for example, whose wolf statues gifted to places such as Romania indicated the two countries' shared *romanità*, Rome's allegiance and protection of its allies (Mazzoni 2010: 71).

What happens, however, when not the nurturing but the devouring wolf is amalgamated with femininity? Straying widely from the Roman myth Dante's *Inferno*, in line with medieval perceptions of wolves, gives us a she-wolf 'both greedy and whorish' (Davis 2000: 247), 'la bestia senza pace' (Dante, I, 58), the beast without peace, recalling the Germanic *Friedlos*. She is defeated by Veltro, the hound, their battle an allegorical one reflecting the clash between the forces of darkness (the wolf) and the light of day (the dog) in correspondence with the Latin phrase for 'dawn', *inter lupum et canem* (between the wolf and the dog), the dawn of Christian Enlightenment and the banishment of all vices embodied by the she-wolf back to Hell. In particular, the lines 'Questi non ciberà terra né peltro, ma sapienza, amore e virtute; e sua nazione sarà tra feltro e feltro' (*Inferno* 1.103–5; 'He shall not feed on lands or lucre, but on wisdom, love and power. Between felt and felt shall be his birth') refer to the defeat of the *lupa* and the expulsion of all greed from humanity, as greed (and pride) is the worst vice in Dante's view. It is not clear who the Veltro refers to as saviour, but the most likely interpretation could be that it was the German Emperor Henry VII, as Dante, in exile at the time of writing the *Inferno*, had become a supporter of the Ghibelline party and hoped to return to Florence if Henry were to take control of the city. This being one of the most obscure prophecies of the *Divine Comedy* (1427) the only thing clear is that the *veltro*, who 'shall not feed on lands and lucre', will by defeating the *lupa* and bring order to Italy and Europe, to all of humanity in the end.

Influenced by Dante's negative image of the she-wolf Giovanni Verga's short story 'La Lupa' (1880) then plays with the dual role of the *lupa romana* as either mother wolf or prostitute, as the word *lupa* also has the latter meaning. In Verga's short story about the *femme fatale* Pina who seduces her son-in-law the she-wolf becomes an allegory for male fears of being devoured by sexually insatiable women. While the devouring she-wolf is rare in myth and literature, and women in the company of devouring wolves even more so (the *vargamors*, wild women in Scandinavian myth being an exception), the bad mother archetype with predatory instincts and practices appears to us primarily as the folktale witch. In the Grimm Brothers' *Hansel and Gretel*, for example, the witch is described as a predator with animal eyes: 'Witches have red eyes and cannot see far, but they can pick up a scent like animals knowing when humans approach' (Grimm Brothers 2007: 105). Like the wolf, the witch in myth and folklore embodies the trauma of exile and reflects the reality of centuries of persecution and annihilation which have left their traces in continental European literature to date, in stories that realistically revive the archetype such as the one by Verga or in Wilhelm Raabe's novella *Else von der Tanne* (1905) about the torture and death of a young woman decried as a witch due to her isolated life, hiding in the woods from the troubles of the Thirty Years' War, or in twentieth-century parodies such as Edgar Hilsenrath's *The Nazi and the Barber* (1971), which plays with the Hansel and Gretel witch in the context of the Holocaust and the trauma of exile and post-war migration.

4. Wolves and Wayward Women

As early as in the infamous *Malleus Maleficarum* ('The Witches' Hammer', 1486-7) women decried as witches were equated with wolves eating babies: 'Contrary to the inclination of human nature and in fact in violation of the condition of all beasts (with the exception of the species of wolves), some sorceresses devour and consume babies' (Mackay 2009: 211). This highly influential and deeply misogynist book reiterates on several occasions the innate nature of so-called witches as wolfish, comparing them with werewolves, an equation offered to its readers as scientific knowledge rather than superstition. Werewolves and witches were treated alike in the widespread panic and mass hysteria in the early modern period, and in France, for example, Henri Boguet, a sixteenth-century judge, was responsible for the burning of about 600 witches and werewolves (Poulakou-Rebelakou 2009: 475).

This chapter will demonstrate how this demonization to be found primarily in the folktale where witches and wolves devour children and young women undergoes a process of deconstruction in some contemporary literature and film about women running with wolves. The contemporary authors I focus on, Angela Carter, Misha Defonseca and Nicolette Krebitz, have all produced works that debunk the myth of the demonized wolf in the context of gender, and show their female protagonists wandering away from traditional gender patterns in search of sanctuaries in the company of wolves. Women as she-wolves in the context of wandering away from the domestic space are a recurrent feature in European cultural representations in which such women form some kind of symbolic bond with wolves or other predatory canines. The Grimm tale of Little Red Riding Hood is possibly the most famous example. The wandering of Red Riding Hood and her twentieth- and twenty-first-century feminist recreations happen time and again in the absence of parental figures, in the context of abandonment or self-abandonment, and an escape from patriarchal bullies. The feminist *récriture* of the Red Riding Hood tale shows the wolf in its nurturing role, which artists like Carter and Krebitz have taken to the extreme of turning the wolf into a lover. It is perhaps not surprising that overall, women's thinking about wolves and their rewriting of the patriarchal tales can be compared with indigenous attitudes about the wolf as nurturer rather than devourer, but one has to be careful in drawing such parallels as they may be somewhat reductionist. One also needs to be careful with such revisionary writing in general, as they all too easily fall into the same trap of mythologizing the wolf as do the texts of men. To say that the engendered myth survives into our times is perhaps not an exaggeration, as there exist countless books in which women describe their life-changing encounters with wolves. By the same token, the patriarchal view of equating women who leave the domestic terrain with witches and predatorial canines may be rare today, but it has survived in one case that I will discuss in this chapter.

Although some indigenous cultures like the Navajo have at times considered women living with or being helped by wolves as witches, such associations are perhaps the strongest in Germanic culture with its myth of the Wild Hunt, which is full of wolves as creatures of valour and doom. The motifs of the devouring wolf and the end of humanity already alluded to in the Lycaon myth where Jupiter wants to exterminate the entire human race appears again in the myth of Wotan or Odin, the god of rage, the storm and, indeed, war and its ultimate destruction of the world by the gigantic wolf Fenrir at Ragnarök. However, Odin is also a god of wisdom, associated with the runes as 'ciphers of a mysterious primordial archaic time' (Gille 1993: 615). In a single poem within the Poetic Edda called Hávámál, specifically in a section called Rúnatal, Odin is described as learning the magic of runes while hanging for nine long nights from the tree Yggdrasil, upon which the nine worlds existed. The exile of *nine* nights seems to point to an Indo-European link tying Germanic to ancient Greek wolf lore, as the Arcadian initiation rites in worship of Zeus Lykaios also emphasize nine years of exile for youths symbolically turned into wolves.

Odin learns to interpret the runes, which in a modern, psychoanalytical sense implies that he gains further insight into his own self. The runes, however, are also associated with another figure from this mythological complex, with *Holle* as Earth Mother. In some versions of the myth she is Odin's wife, known by a variety of names in Germany: Holle or Hulda in central Germany; Perchta in South Germany; Herke, Gode, Freke or Frigga in North Germany (Timm 2010: 9). Like Odin himself Holle is linked to the destruction of the world, but also to replenishment, nurturing and wisdom. Holle has an ambivalent role between the Mother Earth goddess who holds the secrets of Earth and her devilish, passionate nature that connects her to war, destruction, loss of control, uncontrolled sexuality and the seduction of men.

Holle is closely associated with wolves as they share the ambivalence of nurturing and destruction. Their proximity is supported by motifs such as the cut-open belly. In folk belief, Holle typically appears during Twelve Nights between Christmas and Epiphany, when she is said to check on the weavers to make sure that they are working diligently in the weaving rooms. She punishes the lazy by cutting open their bellies and placing rocks inside them, a motif which then reappears in 'Little

Red Riding Hood' and 'The Wolf and Seven Young Kids', where the wolf is cut open to allow for the devoured children to escape and where his belly is then filled with rocks that sentence him to death.

Holle is a nurturer of humanity before becoming its devourer, an evolution replicated in the destiny of women labelled as witches or so-called *Unholde* in the early modern age. Perceived as a threat to men they became persecuted after they were thought to have transformed from the *Holde*, the fair and beautiful woman of the pagan world, to the *Unholde* (witch) demonized under Christianity, transformed, that is, from a nurturer or healer to a devourer of children and, in a sexual sense, of young men. Hansel having to stick his finger out from the cage for the myopic witch's inspection could be read as a reminder of this pairing of cannibalism with sexual deprivation and seduction, if we keep in mind such sinister folk superstitions as expressed in *The Hammer of Witches*, where sorceresses and other demons are reported to be able to 'really and truly take away the limbs of a man' (Mackay 2009: 194) and hide 'the male member through the art of conjuring' (Mackay 2009: 199).

The patriarchal view of women becoming *unhold*, morally unclean, continues well into nineteenth-century fiction, such as Ludwig Tieck's and E. T. A. Hoffmann's Venus figures who seduce young men into the mountain world. It is in particular her ability to seduce men that is seen as a perpetual threat to the bourgeois class, her uncontrolled sexual desire that transforms her from *Holde* to *Unholde*. In Ludwig Tieck's novella *Der Runenberg* (1802), for example, the *Waldweib* (woman of the forest) demonstrates this binary. Appearing at times ugly and old, at other times youthful, beautiful and highly seductive, she is a figure of perdition and fruition reflecting the eternal cycle of life, death and rebirth. While the romantic literary fairy tale, however, has a soft spot for the excesses of youth including the seduction of men by Venus figures, the cautionary folktale featuring child-devouring witches and wolves does not.

Of wolves and she-wolves: Re-reading Little Red Riding Hood

Adding to the countless readings of *Little Red Riding Hood* (Grimm Brothers [tale 026] and Perrault) I suggest here that the appearance of the wolf is inextricably linked to the fates of the three women in the tale, their intergenerational conflict, the girl's wandering and loss of a sanctuary, and a patriarchal denigration of women as witches or she-wolves. The wolf affects all characters in this tale and he is primarily destructive, but there is a nurturing side to his destructiveness.

First, we need to remember that it is the mother who sends her daughter to the wolf, and she is not a stepmother. A common pattern in folktales is that when the real, loving mother dies she is replaced by an evil stepmother, whose double is the witch in some tales. Nonetheless, the absent mother often casts a benevolent shadow over the progress of her children. For the Cinderella tale (Grimm 021), for example, Elisabeth Panttaja has argued that despite the death of the mother at the beginning of the tale it 'tells a story about a strong mother/daughter relationship' (Panttaja 1993: 90). The absent mother in the Red Riding Hood tale also makes her presence felt throughout, although often ignored by psychoanalytical theories by scholars, such as Bruno Bettelheim who shifts his attention to the figure of the father. Basing his analysis on Freudian models Bettelheim has famously argued that Little Red Riding Hood has an unconscious desire to 'be seduced by her father (the wolf)' (Bettelheim 1977: 175), and that while the mother is absent the father is present, albeit in hidden form: both as the wolf, 'an externalization of the dangers of overwhelming oedipal feelings', and as the hunter 'in his protective and rescuing function' (Bettelheim 1977: 178).

While Bettelheim has insisted that there is an acute need for the child to have a real mother, Jerilyn Fisher and Ellen S. Silber disagree, pointing out that the stepmother's destructive nature in fairy tales helps the heroine to progress. They also tell us that the mother figure's destructive drive could be the result of hidden sources of frustration and anger, arguing that the fairy-tale stepmother's 'terrifying acts of aggression toward the girl under her care' could be the result of an 'untold story of this disruptive female character, whose rebellion against the "feminine plot" of passivity and submission is repeatedly cast as the source of conflict in the tales' (Fisher/Silber 2000: 123).

Her obvious restraint in displaying her love for Little Red Riding Hood may lead to a reading that suggests yet another untold story of a discontented mother. We are assured the girl is loved by everyone, but, both in the Grimm Brothers' version and in Perrault's, slightly more so perhaps by her grandmother (Grimm 2007: 156) than her mother. It may make us wonder whether the mother, if she is the biological one, wanted the girl in the first place, what happened to her and where the actual father is, not just his symbolic doubles, the wolf and the hunter. The mother, however, initially sends out a warning to her daughter; she cautions her not to leave the path as she would otherwise break the wine bottle if she tripped. There is not a word about the wolf or the mother's fear that her daughter may come to harm in any way. Instead, she scolds the girl telling her that when she enters Grandma's house she should not 'start snooping around in all the nooks and crannies' (G 157). Submissively, the girl assures her that she will do her best, shaking her mother's hand (not hugging or kissing her) just before her departure.

The mother's ensuing absence is the first step to the girl's exile from the domestic sphere. It is meant to be cautionary and remind her of the peace to be found in staying connected to the two houses, and not to stray from the path that links them. As a liminal figure between civilization and wilderness the wolf stands at the intersection – the *crisis* – between the girl's continuation on the trail and her distraction from it, between dwelling and loss thereof. Despite the wolf's destructive nature in the tale, his enticement for the girl's decision not to heed her mother's warning and stray from the forest trail has a strangely nurturing function for the child's maturation. While the wolf may thus nurture her maturation in an educational sense, he is, however, also closely linked to her physical maturation, and it is the latter that, as scholarship has shown, may pose a problem to the mother.

Yvonne Verdier, for example, points out that the intergenerational conflict in the tale demonstrates that the mother is struggling with the fact that her daughter is of an age in which she will soon replace her as child bearer: 'What the tale tells us is the necessity of the female biological transformation by which the young eliminate the old in their own lifetime. Mothers will be replaced by their daughters and the circle will be closed with the arrival of their children's children. Moral: grandmothers will be eaten' (Verdier 1997: 110). According to this reading, the wolf would then also embody the mother's fear of being displaced by the daughter. We need to keep in mind, however, that this displacement of the mother by the daughter is not solely linked to the act of procreation but, if we follow Freudian readings of the father or daughter plot, also to oedipal desire.

No doubt, the wolf symbolizes more than this intergenerational conflict. It has been argued that the tale could in the end just be a warning against animal attacks (Sugiyama 2004: 111), while he also points to male aggressors in general, even rapists (Orenstein 2003: 145). Through his close bond with the mother he may signify a male aggressor in her own life. After all, where is the father, and why does the grandmother live so far removed from the mother's house? The tale does not explain this. What it does reveal is the wolf's function for the loss of peace within a family that seems to consist only of women.

This image of the folktale wolf as an animal with human qualities and destroyer of peace echoes the biopolitical paradigm of the medieval *Friedlos*, those humans without peace abandoned in the forest for their crimes. Metaphorically, the 'unclean' wolf embodies human sin devouring its victims and threatening to relegate them into permanent exile. Following this rationale, the encounter with wolves in folktales signals a warning against succumbing to sin as well as the impurity associated with sinfulness. While the early barbaric practice of expulsion and persecution may be but a distant collective memory in nineteenth-century folktales, it survives as an initiation rite and cautionary gesture for children, echoing the time-worn equation of actual wolves with men preying on the community.

By sending her to the state of nature, the traditional space of the *homo sacer*, the mother renders her daughter *wolfsfrei*, literally free to be taken by the wolf, whose blood-spilling instinct reflects the girl's own potential loss of innocence signalled by the red cap as a possible image for her beginning menstrual cycle. Her temporary exile in the forest and encounter with a creature traditionally associated with the Devil add the dimension of the witch to this tale. All three women, I would argue, through their symbolic bond with the wolf evoke the witch, women that pre-Enlightenment patriarchy condemned for the mere fact that they absented themselves from the domestic terrain.

Derived from Old High German *hagazussa* the German word *Hexe* (witch or hag) in the early modern age was the woman associated with the hedge or forest. By migrating across the hedge, that boundary between domesticity and wilderness, between communal law and outlawry, women eager to live outside of the community entered the space of *homo sacer* and were associated with these human wolves and their crimes. The wolf and the witch are particularly close in the context of this liminal space. For women in the sixteenth and seventeenth centuries having crossed such thresholds and left the communal space for the forest was highly suspicious. It would have easily marked them as witches, thought of as being in conspiracy with the devil and riding wolves (Jacob Grimm 1835: 593).

Although the *Little Red Riding Hood* tale does not mention witches, all three women are somehow associated with them. 'Grandmothers,' Cixous writes, 'are always wicked' (Cixous 1981: 43). Being devoured by the wolf means that Granny becomes a part of him, their physical union revealing the symmetry between woman living outside the community condemned as a witch and the *homo sacer* expelled as wolf from the community. The hagazussa or *Hexe* as woman associated with the hedge is alluded to above all in Grandmother's life in the forest, by the *Nusshecken* (Hazelnut Hedges, G157). Grandmother is absent in the sense of having withdrawn from the domestic environment and the community, 'weiter im Wald' (G157), further into the forest, into wolf space.

The wolf also forms a link between the mother and the grandmother. Although the mother is absent in a physical sense, she is nonetheless inextricably linked to the other two women; and the wolf is the knot that ties them together. While reflecting the mother's emotional and physical absence, this lone wolf shares the grandmother's isolation from the communal bond in the forest. His voraciousness also signals the devouring mother archetype, on the one hand the mother's willingness to endanger her child, on the other the grandmother's physical incorporation by the wolf; she is literally temporarily possessed by the wolf, an image that indicates her symbolic proximity to the witch. By

Figure 4.1 Gustave Doré, *c.* 1862. Courtesy of National Gallery of Victoria, Melbourne. Gift of Mrs S. Horne, 1962.

posing as the grandmother when the wolf is about to devour Red Riding Hood he manifests the devouring mother archetype through which the absent mother is still present in the grandmother, a fact supported by earlier, especially French, versions of the tale from the oral tradition in which the mother and grandmother are interchangeable (Cf. Verdier 1997: 109: 'Fricon, fricassee, le sang de ta grantasse/mérasse'). By devouring Granny and posing in her clothes (in drag) the androgynous wolf perverts her love for Red Riding Hood, any nurturing instinct it may contain, into cannibalistic love. He or she loves her so much that he or she could devour her the way the Hansel and Gretel witch as the double of the evil stepmother wants to devour the children.

In earlier versions of the tale, however, the wolf is not the only wolf to grandmother, Red Riding Hood too is a *homo homini lupus*. In most Asian and French versions from the oral tradition the wolf kills the grandmother before putting her blood in a container and placing some of her flesh on a plate to be consumed by the girl (Dundes 1991: 77). This implied cannibalism affects all three generations, and the wolf as devourer is a metaphor for it: the mother cannibalizes her daughter through her destructive instincts, the 'wolf as grandmother/ grandmother as wolf' cannibalizes her by loving her so much that he or she eats her, and the girl cannibalizes her mother and grandmother in the sense that both are past child-bearing age and thus being displaced by her fertility.

In most of these earlier versions the girl is never devoured by the wolf, but Grandmother is (Verdier 1997: 104). In the Grimm Brothers, however, the girl's incorporation by the beast seems to indicate that the girl herself is in danger of becoming a witch or wolf. In many of these folktales it is especially a young woman's awakening sexuality that marks her liminal status between innocence and her loss of innocence, with heterotopias such as the forest being typical testing grounds for her individuation. *Little Red Riding Hood, Hänsel and Gretel* and *Frau Holle* (Mother Hulda) all demonstrate that the descent into the underworld (indicated as either a walk into the forest, a plunge down the well or the descent into the belly of the beast) is closely linked to the passage from childhood to maturity, but by the same token these tales are also sinister reflections of the persecution of women as witches.

In the patriarchal Christian world represented in the Grimm tales, *Little Red Riding Hood* stands on the threshold between the innocence of a child and her awakening sexuality as a potentially sinful side of her. Her encounter with the wolf is her lycanthropic moment, in which the animal brings out her 'indulgence in sensuality and her disobedience'

(Zipes 1983: 34) to bourgeois expectations of young women. This encounter, however, also corresponds to that phase in the formation of an individual, that is, character building.

What the anthropologist Hans Peter Duerr has (1985) famously called *Traumzeit* (dreamtime) is that period spent in wilderness serving many cultures as a rite of passage and having left its imprint especially on folktales. In view of a young woman growing up, most scholars concur that *Little Red Riding Hood* embodies the need for young people to distance themselves from home and their parents and spend time in the metaphorical woods of the world. As an adolescent girl in the wild she is bound to encounter one of the most prevalent threats faced by women: rape. As is typical, however, of the patriarchal folktales in the early nineteenth century, her walk through the woods and encounter with the wolf contain the warning against a potentially immoral side of herself. Her eventual physical union with the beast that devours her contrasts sharply with her nurturing goodwill signalled by her task of carrying a basket of food to her grandmother, and, from the vantage point of a patriarchal Christian value system, accentuates the peril of her becoming morally corrupted.

Depending on what we make of her age, her walk through the forest vacillates between child neglect and an initiation ritual. If we take her as an adolescent, then the girl's awakening sexuality is the cause of her being tested to see whether she will stay on the right track in life or succumb to the sensual temptations of the forest – the sexual urges of her own body which in line with the bourgeois moral code of the nineteenth century were subject to being disciplined. Bettelheim famously interpreted this moment of temptation in the context of the Freudian pleasure principle for which Little Red Riding Hood relinquishes the reality principle. His argument is that 'deviating from the straight path in defiance of mother and superego was temporarily necessary for the young girl to gain a higher state of personality organization' (Bettelheim 1977: 181), with her absent father representing both oedipal desire and the resolution of the conflict through his double, the hunter (Bettelheim 1977: 175–8).

The father/hunter and the wolf, too, can be seen as symbiotic, reminding us of Jacques Derrida's equation of the sovereign with the beast. After killing the wolf, the hunter then skins the animal – 'der Jäger zog dem Wolf den Pelz ab und ging damit heim' (the hunter skinned the hide off the wolf and went home, G159). It is an act that marks him as a lycanthrope uniting in himself the sovereign and the *homo sacer*, the powerful patriarch torn between maintaining law and order (that is, killing desire) and breaking it (giving in to desire). As the one who breaks it he becomes the very wolf or *Friedlos* he kills, a process reflected in his holding on to the wolf skin as a trophy.

Red Riding Hood being devoured in the Grimm version is an image that according to the Christian value system inscribed into the tale shows her, however briefly, physically possessed by the tempter. Little Red Riding Hood can only be cleansed from her impending transformation into a young woman possessed by the wolf – from becoming a witch in other words – by being cut out of his belly. The tale echoes centuries of anxieties about the dangers of women young and old – Granny has to be excised as well – of becoming witches. After being liberated, the belly of the wolf is then filled with stones. In *The Wolf and the Seven Kids* it is the loving, nurturing mother who performs this act, while in *Little Red Riding Hood* the victim herself gets the big stones before being assisted by the hunter/father in filling the wolf's stomach, the cause of his death.

This image of cutting open the wolf's belly and replacing life inside it by rocks that the two wolf tales share may signify a few things. The swollen belly indicates Little Red Riding Hood's rebirth as a more mature young woman stabilizing her place in the natural generational order of reproduction. Although the rebirth of the goats in *The Wolf and the Seven Kids* and Little Red Riding Hood may be on the side of nurturing, as it implies a lesson learned, replacing the children with rocks also demonizes the wolf marking him as a 'gottlos/godless' (G54) destroyer of life, thus negating the animal's side as a nurturer of nature. Cutting open the belly, however, may also imply the desire for self-harm. It may express the refusal to become pregnant by a rapist, which makes me wonder if this is not the case in *Little Red Riding Hood*, where, unlike in *The Wolf and the Seven Kids*, it is not the mother but the patriarch, the hunter, who instead of just shooting the wolf grabs a pair of scissors and starts cutting open the sleeping wolf's belly ('nahm eine Schere und fing an, dem schlafenden Wolf den Bauch aufzuschneiden,' G159). This act of violation then prepares the way for that ultimate image of infertility, the rocks inside the belly that he and Little Red Riding Hood put inside, and that may point to the fact that the absent mother would have preferred infertility to her pregnancy.

If the hunter is another version of the absent and aggressive father, as Bettelheim claims, then his cutting open the belly could be read as a reference to his violation of the mother, the girl being the unwanted result of that rape. According to the logic of the double identity of the father as wolf and hunter, the killing of the wolf would then mean that all sexual desire, whether oedipal (between father and daughter) or otherwise (the father's possible rape of the mother), is being stifled. If

Little Red Riding Hood is indeed the result of rape, then this would explain the mother's emotional absence, her inability to show feelings of love at the beginning of the tale. Being aware of this, the girl's help in getting the heavy rocks could then be indicative of her wanting to undo her mother's pregnancy with her. Whichever interpretation we may give this final image of the tale, the absent mother never quite leaves the scene but remains present to the end. According to this reading, there is ultimately no sanctuary for women in a world in which men go about raping them. The folktale thus also recalls ancient myths such as the one about Callisto and Io who are both raped in the sanctuary by the God Jove and subsequently experience animal transformations.

Beyond Red Riding Hood: Feminist rewriting and women in search of sanctuaries

The devouring wolf seems to be an entirely male projection, the amalgamation of wolves and femininity in patriarchal cultures reflecting male fears and contempt for women. This is, however, only one side of the story of women and wolves. While folktales and other literature featuring purported witches and the proximity of these with the wolf evoke this sinister chapter in the history of genocide as gendercide, the wolf also has a potential in liberating women from repressive patriarchal structures. This has recently been explored in various adaptations of the folktales by women, most notably perhaps in Angela Carter's *The Bloody Chamber* (1979), in Nicolette Krebitz's film *Wild* (Germany, 2016) and in Misha Defonseca's fictionalized Holocaust memoir *Surviving with Wolves* (2005).

The notion of the *homo sacer*'s impurity survives in some revisionary retellings of the Red Riding Hood tale. In *The Company of Wolves*, one of her brilliant renderings of the tale, Angela Carter describes the wolf as an 'infernal vermin' (Carter 2006: 135), a creature set aside into exile and attempting to set others aside who become unclean through him. This intimate union between women and wolves is already contained in the imagery of devouring in the versions by Perrault and the Grimm Brothers, but Carter intensifies it in her story about the love her Red Riding Hood develops for the wolf so full of lice.

In her revisionary fairy tales, which emerge primarily from her reading of Perrault, whom she was translating around the time of writing the first stories for *The Bloody Chamber* (1979), Carter takes this patriarchal notion of woman's purported uncleanness to an extreme, as her Red Riding Hood commits the kind of disgrace the Inquisition saw in the union between women and the devil (Baschwitz 1963: 93). As Kurt Baschwitz has argued in his seminal book on the witches and witch trials, the war against the devil was primarily a war against old women (Baschwitz 1963: 139–47). This amalgamation of witches and wolves becomes particularly prominent in Carter's story *The Werewolf*. Here she empowers the girl in a northern superstitious and hostile country where the woodsmen's world is inclement to women all too easily perceived as witches: 'When they discover a witch – some old woman whose cheeses ripen when her neighbors' do not, another old woman whose black cat, oh, sinister! follows her about all the time, they strip the crone, search for her marks, for the supernumerary nipple her familiar sucks. They soon find it. Then they stone her to death' (Carter 2006: 126). Not only is Carter's Red Riding Hood able to defend herself against a wolf that immediately attacks her and makes her chop off one of his paws, but she then also discovers that her grandmother is a werewolf, the chopped-off paw her hand. As discussed above, the Grimm tale already contains allusions to the amalgamation of wolves and old women as witches in the wolf's physical symbiosis with grandmother, but Carter takes this further. Not only does she indict these superstitions through authorial distance and irony, but she also deconstructs the typically male projection and fear of nature as hostile.

Nonetheless, we see the wandering girl in search of a sanctuary. Kimberly Lau has argued how this opening tale to Carter's wolf stories presents us with a phallic mother symbol – the traditionally male werewolf (vir = man) as woman – and an oedipal relationship in which the phallic grandmother becomes the girl's object of both desire and displacement (Lau 2008: 81–4). This tension between desire and displacement affects the young girl herself in a masculine world in which woodsmen all too readily decry women as witches and stone them to death, so that the presence of a sanctuary is of pivotal relevance and seems to result in a fierce battle of Darwinian proportions in which granddaughters get rid of their grandmothers to find shelter in their houses, where if they are lucky, they may prosper.

While Perrault's version of Little Red Riding Hood does not contain the hunter rescuing the girl from the belly of the wolf, traditional gender divisions apply in the Grimm's version, where the liberation she and her grandmother experience happens at the hands of the hunter, the male principle. In both versions of the folktale, however, the girl is entirely a victim of male predation, her blood marking her as prey. The wolf is a werewolf, not just in the androgynous sense of being a cross-over between animal and grandmother, but between an animal that devours and a young man stalking young women.

The wolf as rapist: Carter is playing with this widespread interpretation. She takes it as a starting point for her adaptation *The Company of Wolves*, one of her rewritings which coincides with her writing of *The Sadeian Woman* (1979), where she is rather outspoken about rape: 'In the mythic schema of all relations between men and women, man proposes and woman is disposed of, just as she is disposed of in a rape, which is a kind of physical graffiti, the most extreme reduction of love in which all humanity departs from the sexed beings' (Carter 1978: 6). In another critical piece ('Notes from the Frontline') she emphasizes the importance of rewriting patriarchal language and decolonizing phallocentric visions:

> Yet this, of course, is why it is so enormously important for women to write fiction as women – it is part of the slow process of decolonising our language and our basic habits of thought. I really do believe this [...] it has to do with the creation of a means of expression for an infinitely greater variety of experience than has been possible heretofore, to say things for which no language previously existed.
> (Carter 1983: 75)

Her Red Riding Hoods form a substantial part of such decolonization and the debunking of masculine mythical visions. In *The Company of Wolves* in particular she turns Red Riding Hood into a woman who is 'nobody's meat' (Carter 2006: 138), who runs with the wolves and, unlike the girl in the folktale who needs to be saved by a man, becomes part of the hunt. That the archaic union between the two, the bloodthirsty wolf and the bleeding girl, is disrupted in the patriarchal tale is indicated in the girl's initiation, her passage through the wolf's belly from which she has to be liberated by the hunter. Hunting and slaying the animal are thus reserved solely for the man, who engages in sacrificial violence, while the girl is excluded from that hunt not only by being the prey, but also by having to learn her lesson that she should never have strayed from the forest path in the first place. In the tale the wolf is the sexually aggressive seducer, while in Carter's version the girl is an active participant in the seduction scene. In the company of wolves she hunts as much as, if not more than the wolf, that old melancholic: 'There is a vast melancholy in the canticles of wolves, melancholy infinite as the forest' (Carter 2006: 131 [henceforth BC]). From a patriarchal Christian perspective, she becomes a devouring wolf woman; she does not flinch at the wolf, on the contrary, she desires him, '[his] genitals, ah! Huge' (BC136), to lose her virginity with the beast, and she chases his melancholy away with laughter. As the werewolf is about to devour her, she rips off his shirt and throws it into the fire, thus condemning 'him to wolfishness for the rest of his life', while 'seven years is a werewolf's natural span' (BC132). In the end, the wolf's hunger for her subsides as does the aura of fear surrounding him, and she loves him to the point of wanting to eat his lice, an act that in addition to her loss of virginity with him may render her 'unclean' from a traditional patriarchal and misogynist perspective but serves Carter as an act of liberation. That this purported strategy of liberation has been met with scepticism can be documented by the writing of critics like Kimberley Lau who has argued that Carter's attempts at sexualizing the classic fairy tales may not fully deconstruct their dominant patriarchal agency. Instead, Lau argues, the question remains 'whether such erotic re-imaginings of classic fairy tales exceed patriarchal definitions of the erotic or whether these women are producing a sexual agency that exists alongside, and perhaps operates with and through, a dominant erotic' (Lau 2008: 80).

In much of this gendered writing about wolves the latter are seen as unrealistically and metaphorically as in the patriarchal fairy tales. One of the key elements, however, in feminist *récriture* of the patriarchal wolf myth is the wolf's catalyst function in women walking out of a male-dominated and destructive environment. The wolf becomes a target of female projections of desire for a world that safeguards freedom, wildness, unpredictability, a recovery of instincts and a certain amount of mystery and mysticism. The idea of sanctuary is prevalent in this quest for a world that lies buried under traditional structure, and the wolves' own quest for a sanctuary coincides with that of women trying to escape the patriarchal yoke. The relatively recent migration of wolves from the wilds of Eastern Europe and Asia into Central Europe has offered new artistic forms of exploration for female artists who see the wolf's own quest in gendered terms. One of these artistic products is Nicolette Krebitz's film *Wild* (2016), featuring the young female protagonist Ania who is trying to escape her tyrannical boss Boris and her stultifying job in an IT company of a drab Eastern German town. When one day she encounters a wolf in a city park, she decides to bring him home with her, and in similarity to Angela Carter's *The Company of Wolves*, a love relationship unfolds between the two, resulting in Ania's self-liberation from her social and professional environment, her exploration of new forms of sexuality, and her eventual disappearance with the wolf into wilderness.

Part of the attraction the wolf represents to the young protagonist is its ancient association with lawlessness. As woman running and even – in her imagination – copulating with the wolf she is a contemporary outlaw seeking sanctuary. This idea of sanctuary does exist for wolves in Germany. In an interview, Nicolette Krebitz has mentioned those abandoned sites of old military bases, the so-called *Truppenübungsplatz*, among the spaces that in recent years have offered wolves in Germany sanctuary, and that have inspired her to make this film (http://www.planet-interview.de/interviews/nicolette-krebitz/48770/). Ironically, these are places that had once been used for preparation of war, that is, the very opposite of sanctuaries. Ania's need for a sanctuary arises primarily from the threat emanating from her work environment, and here especially from her boss Boris whose predatory advances contrast sharply with the gentleness of the purportedly predatory animal that then becomes her lover. Krebitz's film about how routine in life is spontaneously given up for an arduous pursuit of one's instincts is a far-fetched but entertaining fantasy, and yet another product of female desire to run with wolves, to unearth buried *Urtriebe* (primordial drives) and to discover the potential to be liberated from a male-centred and in Rousseau's sense diseased civilization. Krebitz takes Carter a step further by placing her story outside of the fairy-tale world, although the notions of migration and the quest for a sanctuary that tie a young woman to the wolf carry over from the folktale. This also happens in another literary text I briefly wish to discuss here.

Misha Defonseca's fictional memoir *Surviving with Wolves* (1998) is another narrative in which the thoroughly negative perception of wolves proffered by the Lycaon myth and patriarchal folktales is brushed against the grain, and in which protective wolves and femininity clash abruptly with the indescribable horrors and cruelty of the male-dominated world. The folktale scenarios of the absent (dead) loving mother, her replacement by a nefarious stepmother or mother substitute, and the young daughter's relationship with wolves are also present here. The book was initially marketed as memoir or autobiography but turned out to be yet another Holocaust survival fraud. It is, however, interesting material in view of its engendered adaptation of the devouring wolf paradigm. In particular, Defonseca's memoir questions the evil folktale wolf, as her wolves offer the errant protagonist girl a peaceful sanctuary while Europe is being torn apart by the Second World War.

The actual wolves in this story are very different from the devouring folktale wolf in that they become benign mother substitutes. We remember that in the Little Red Riding Hood tale the devouring wolf appears the moment the mother has absented herself from the scene. Although he brings about the girl's initiation to adulthood, contributing to her maturation, the fact that he is primarily destructive echoes the prevailing sedentary perception of wolves over millennia. Defonseca deconstructs this view by highlighting the nurturing side of wolves. In search of her missing parents who were deported from Belgium to an Eastern European concentration camp little Misha sets out across continental Europe, living off the grid in forests and finally being taken in by wolves that feed her through the war years. When after returning to Belgium from her adventurous journey around war-torn Europe she hears the story of Little Red Riding Hood, she flies 'into a memorable rage and flung the book across the room calling them [the Grimm Brothers] lunatics'. 'This is rubbish,' she insists, 'it makes no sense at all [...]. There's no such thing as a wolf who eats children' (Defonseca 2005: 206).

Since the memoir turned out to be a fabrication, we can safely assume that although some wolves may indeed eat children, the perception expressed here is meant to destabilize traditional perceptions of wolves as child-devouring monsters. It is a view, however, that also replicates the traditional binary of femininity or nature versus masculinity or culture, the fear of wolves stemming in large part from patriarchal agrarian communities. Defonseca's novel is a classical example for feminist projections and the over-evaluation of animals in comparison with humans. By using the backdrop of the Second World War it goes so far as to glorify animals as the only benign creatures, while condemning humans as malicious beasts: 'Grandpère had no time for human beings in general. I can still hear him saying, "Beasts are better than men. Beasts mean you no harm. They are grateful. You'll never see an animal waging war. An animal kills only for food. Humans kill for any reason, not just for food"' (D 38). Misha internalizes his words, seeing them confirmed on her journey across the woodlands of Eastern Europe and its countless atrocities. Witnessing a German soldier rape and kill a young peasant girl, she goes berserk and stabs him to death. It is one of those moments in the tale in which she reactivates the werewolf myth by stressing that she too has become a wolf. She sees this transformation reflected in the eyes of the pack she travels with, which upon seeing her covered in blood, think, as she points out (always in tune with what her fellow animals think) that she has just killed some prey. Although she consistently tries to re-evaluate wolves as benign creatures, thus debunking the myth of the evil, blood-lusty wolf, she falls into the trap of reviving the myth in this particular scene as well as in others.

Becoming a wolf in this narrative implies the typical parallels with the myth of Lycaon. Misha's abandonment, her migratory exile, her continuing trauma and the gradual loss of speech after years of travelling in the company of wolves ('attempting speech in vain' as the Lycaon myth says) are all reminiscent of the lycanthropy of early Greek myth. One essential difference, however, is that while Lycaon is severely traumatized by his transformation into a wolf, Misha welcomes it, learning that humans cannot be trusted. Echoing her *grandpère* she realizes: 'What men do to animals, they're also prepared to do to humans […]. Man is the despicable predator of the world. He has learned nothing […]. He's full of vice. How can I be a human being? […] I had become a wolf' (D106–7).

Wolves in this text are once again the product of human projections, not projections of fear but of desire. She puts words and thoughts into her wolves, claims that she 'understood much of their language' (D137) as she becomes an integral part of the wolf family, and even makes comments on their emotional life: 'They were happy' (D101). The memoir is far from doing justice to wolves. Instead, it reactivates the one-dimensional myth of it being a nurturing creature, both in a physical and in a psychological sense. Misha's projection into the wolf goes so far that Maman Rita, the first she-wolf she encounters, becomes a mother substitute ('I had become her pup' [D97]), 'a godsend [and] gift from my parents' (D99). Misha tells herself at the end that 'the death of my she-wolf was the death of my mother' (D226). The wolf here becomes a projection of personal loss, but its purported nurturing and even healing qualities ('they gave me the chance to recover' [D138]) are also directly opposed to the cruelty of men and in final analysis of genocide which claims her parents' lives.

The state of nature for Defonseca is a place of refuge from the cruelty of men, a sanctuary where she can survive solely in the company of animals. Her wolves embody a utopian vision, a sort of prelapsarian island of happiness in the middle of war-torn Europe: 'This was the way life was supposed to be, in perfect communion with the animal world' (D133). Unlike in Hobbesian thinking the state of nature here is the very opposite of the state of war, but it is the state of exception. In that sense, her withdrawal from humanity is similar to that of Simplicius in Grimmelshausen's novel about the ravishes of the Thirty Years' War, his withdrawal into the forests, and then to a distant island. Defonseca's fake memoir may be far from being a picaresque novel, but it never sheds certain myths of the early modern period. The myth of the wolf girl as witch remains alive in this tale of survival, of young women walking away from the domestic space, from a war-torn home into wilderness, and while rebelling against the injustice of folktales such as Little Red Riding Hood, the witch paradigm in the context of female migration keeps reverberating through the text.

So does the man-as-wolfish-predator theme. The beast metaphor is appropriated here from the tale, something Emily Fridlund has also recently done in her *History of Wolves* (2017). The novel was shortlisted for the Man Booker Prize in 2017 and is less about wolves than about corrupt men, first and foremost the heroine's paedophile teacher Mr Grierson. 'What do wolves have to do with human history,' fourteen-year-old Linda is asked by one of the judges of her school project on the history of wolves and she says: 'Wolves have nothing at all to do with humans, actually. If they can help it, they avoid them' (Fridlund 2017: 14). The novel is part of a range of texts in which women have expressed their fascination with wolves without, however, staying clear of the kinds of totemic traps we have seen humans walk into over millennia. The wolves in Fridlund's book are ghost wolves, they never make an actual appearance and one might want to argue that that is actually how wolves are. We just never get to see them. Still, like Defonseca's fictional memoir the text engages wolves as an allegorical device in the depiction of male vices. *Little Red Riding Hood* stood model, but the contexts vary from the atrocities of war-torn Europe to the crimes in Minnesotan woods.

Three wolf or gender paradigms have emerged: (1) Man as wolf from whom women run away, (2) women as wolves persecuted by men and (3) women running with wolves. The latter has seen a lot of writing over the years, including Clarissa Pinkola Estés's New Age proto-feminist totemization of wolves in *Women Who Run with the Wolves* (1989), Hélène Grimaud's wolf sonatas in her sanctuary in upstate New York where she combines her love of music with her love of wolves, and Elli Radinger's bestselling *Wisdom of Wolves* (2019) which promises us that wolves can teach us how to be more human. Although admirable in their advocacy of sanctuaries, these and the other narratives I have looked at in this chapter all demonstrate that we inject our gender issues into wolves. Not just wolves, but also bears, even dingoes if we look at a famous Australian law case in which yet another mother has walked away from the domestic sphere and paid a bitter price.

4. Wolves and Wayward Women

Dingo took my baby: Myth, race and gender in the Lindy Chamberlain case

Absent parents and the presence of predatory canines are the stuff not only of fairy tales and fake memoirs. What happens if myth and folktales become a reality reveals itself in the sinister legal case surrounding the disappearance of Azaria Chamberlain in the Australian outback. Few legal cases in Australia have endured the national spotlight as pitilessly as the trial of Lindy Chamberlain, suspected of murdering her baby Azaria despite her claim that a dingo took her. The case is located at the intersection of gender and race politics and myth.

Strangely, the tragedy in which on 17 August 1980 Lindy Chamberlain briefly absented herself from her nine-week-old baby Azaria at a camp site near Uluru which resulted in the baby's disappearance has some uncanny links with the German folktales and the cultural history surrounding wolves and witches. Like in the Red Riding Hood tale here too the mother's absence from her child is closely tied to the presence of the canine predator. Although rather impressionistic, these parallels with myth and folklore have been pointed out now and again in comments on the case. Diane Johnson, for example, argues that the ways in which some of the media portrayed Lindy Chamberlain – a vamp one day and demure the next – were reminiscent of representations of witches in the Middle Ages and in folktales (cited in Cunliffe 2003: 109; Johnson 1982: 100). The media were quite successful in condemning Lindy a long time before she was actually tried and sentenced, disseminating the belief that she had violated the sanctity of motherhood, that she was a 'dangerous woman ... with faraway eyes', that her dress in court was too sexy; even her alleged 'new Mom glow' seems to have been the target of the media's portrayal of her as overly sexualized (Cunliffe 2003: 108). Lindy, the purported witch, a woman between *hold* (fair) and *unhold* (sinister): How does a reading, as the media suggest, of the history of her case through the lens of folktales about predators and witches and their theoretical background inform the underlying ramifications concerning the public's constructions of motherhood in the Chamberlain case?

Azaria's body was never found. Following Lindy Chamberlain's own allegations the first inquest suggested that the baby was taken by a dingo. Her jumpsuit had been found and an Aboriginal tracker had discovered dingo tracks around the tent. The second inquest, however, veered from this initial conviction that the dingo had taken Azaria suggesting that the mother took her child to the family car with the intention of murdering her (cf. Cunliffe 2003: 8). This sudden turn in the case was based partly on the behaviour of the Chamberlains, which was considered to be strange, as both Lindy and Michael had reacted rather coolly and rationally after the disappearance of Azaria, quite possibly assuming too early that she was already dead. All this raised suspicion and led to the fabrication of a mother's murder of her infant, an act in which the husband was deemed complicit. The Crown's second inquest proceeded to contradict eyewitness allegations and those of the indigenous tracker, who, strangely, was never invited to court. A largely science-based case was subsequently built against the mother, and two main factors became the focus of her purported guilt: (1) blood was found in the car, which forensic experts identified as the blood of an infant and (2) the damage on Azaria's jumpsuit indicated to these experts that apparently Azaria's neck had been cut, causing her to bleed to death. The jury ended up accepting scientific evidence over the defence's insistence on Lindy's intact motherhood. On 29 October 1982, the jury found Lindy Chamberlain guilty of murdering her child. She was sentenced to life imprisonment with hard labour. Almost four years later, on 2 February 1986, the baby's matinee jacket was found near Uluru. This was the garment Lindy had insisted Azaria had been dressed in the night she disappeared. It proved the mother's innocence. The verdict against the Chamberlains was reverted, Lindy released from prison, and she and her husband Michael received 1.3 million dollars in compensation.

The duality of the mother archetype is at the heart of this case: the prosecution insisting on the bad mother archetype, the defence focusing on Chamberlain as a good mother. In both inquests, however, the focus lay on images of the bad mother: in the first scenario Chamberlain was absent from the tent and thus neglecting her role of maternal protection; in the second scenario she was actively seeking the destruction of her child. The jury was thus faced only with negative constructions of motherhood, the absent mother or the murderess, while the defence was still trying to build images of her as the loving and protective mother. In addition, these competing constructions of motherhood interfered with Chamberlain's own self-understanding as a mother and her repeated impulse to defend herself during the trial, which in the end may have persuaded the jury to find her guilty. She had been cautioned by her defence lawyer not to appear too smart and aggressive in court so as not to undermine the defence's image of her as a caring mother.

If it holds true that 'the dominant ideology of motherhood presumes a unity of interest between a natural mother and her child' (Cunliffe 2003: 33) then that interest may be missing between a stepmother and her child. Folktales persist in reiterating this absence of love between the stepmother, who is not the natural mother, and her children. Although the text is not clear about this, we may assume that Red Riding Hood's mother is her natural mother, and yet she exposes her daughter to danger. So does Lindy Chamberlain by leaving Azaria unprotected in the tent. It does not make her a murderess. Nonetheless, that moment of neglect is enough to sway a jury to believe that she is not the loving mother that she may undoubtedly have been, because part of the dominant ideology of motherhood is that a mother does not leave her infant alone in a tent in the outback – not for one instant. Red Riding Hood is a teenager, her lonely walk through wilderness a *rite de passage*. The Azaria case is obviously different, and Chamberlain was indeed criticized for taking a nine-week-old child into the Australian wilderness and for forgetting to zip up the tent. To this day, there is a large section of the public who do not forgive her for this failure to protect her child. Moreover, she was criticized for her unusual calmness following the death of her child, for reportedly not taking care of her when she was sick and for subscribing to a religious faith that was aberrant from the norm and included child sacrifice (Bryson 1985: 349; the name Azaria was falsely understood as sacrifice of the desert; it means 'helped by God').

Competing constructions of motherhood concocted with the media's aggressive representation of her as a witch as well as the public's indignation over the fact that the Chamberlains would take a nine-week-old baby camping in inhospitable natural terrain has contributed to Lindy Chamberlain's sentence of life imprisonment with hard labour. The sentence reflects the potential cruelty in patriarchal constructions of motherhood and women's lifestyle that condemn these women if they fail to fit the pattern of the domestic model mother. Such a pattern is offered to us, for example, by the Grimm Brothers' tale of *Mother Hulda* (Frau Holle) which praises domestic diligence and condemns women who fall short of it. On the other hand, we see women such as Red Riding Hood's grandmother and the Hänsel and Gretel witch living far from civilization and being punished for it – one is devoured by the wolf, the other one burns in her oven. To this day, woman venturing into wilderness or absenting herself from civilization challenges conceived patriarchal notions of femininity and motherhood. But it is not until the mother and the canine predator come together and the child gets lost that the media's and the public's association of Lindy with a witch assumes its greatest momentum.

In parallel to the folktales the Chamberlain case reveals a symbiosis between the mother and the predator in that the mother's absence causes the appearance of the predator. From the vantage point of the prosecutors, in absenting herself from her child the mother *becomes* the predator. In the tale of *The Wolf and Seven Kids* this is partly alluded to through the wolf's mimesis of the mother by adopting her voice, a metamorphosis that creates the illusion of an identity between them. Oddly, at one point of the trial the prosecutor Barker Q. C. drew parallels between Lindy and the dingo by cynically questioning the clean cuts in the baby's jumpsuit and the dingo's ability to carry away the child without ripping her clothes, and by calling the animal a tidy dingo adroit at handling a pair of scissors, thereby simultaneously alluding to Lindy's own domestic and maternal role as homemaker (cf. Cunliffe 2003: 49) and thus blurring the line between the mother and the dingo.

The identity between the two also results from their position as potential child murderer. If it wasn't the dingo it was the mother, there is no other alternative. We remember that in folktales wolves, witches and evil mothers form a symbiosis. In *Hänsel and Gretel* the *Doppelgängerin* of the evil stepmother abandoning her children is a child-devouring witch, filling the same position as the wolf in *Little Red Riding Hood*. In the Chamberlain case both the absent mother and the canine were marginalized as purported predators: Lindy as the alleged 'bad' mother, who left her child alone in a tent that was not zipped up, and the dingo, whom European settlers have generally considered to be a pest. The dingo as vermin is an image far removed from his status in Aboriginal myth, where he has predominantly benevolent qualities. King points out that among some tribes the dingo is a totem animal:

> Dingo is said to represent each of us individually as we 'step out' on our own. He supports each of us as we venture out [...] Dingo is the young person setting out into the world [...] the captive released after a long time of forced segregation; the sufferer of depression; the victim of grief [...] Dingo embodies those of us currently 'testing the waters'. Dingo dares us to look at life through the eyes of a child again, to shun all adult, tainted cynicism and to start our journey over as a 'newborn babe' [...]. Be warned though: [...] Dingo often appears blind to the perils that blatantly appear right in front of him [...] like a naïve child. (King 2003: 43–4)

In the Chamberlain case, the Western world's rationalism clashes with the mythological side of indigenous culture to the point that some voices in defence of the mother have pointed out racist attitudes inherent to the trial, especially in view of the tracker who had discovered dingo tracks outside the tent not being admitted to court (Howe 1989: 31–2). As Aboriginal evidence was not disclosed to the jury, scientific evidence was in the end allowed to trump over what was discarded as mere superstition. Ignoring the presence of indigenous culture, their outback experience and mythology was certainly a grave mistake. The disappearance of Azaria took place deep inside Aboriginal sacred space, where for the sake of initiation indigenous youth are still sent to go walk about. White European Australia, however, sees the outback predominantly as a hostile space, a taboo area in many ways to women and white middle-class city dwellers like Lindy Chamberlain, especially to a new mother and her infant. While Aboriginal myth views the dingo as someone who helps people gain a higher level of consciousness and experience, white European Australians, especially stockmen, hound the dingo as vermin. The dingo shares that with the perception of the wolf as vermin and the *homo sacer* who cannot be sacrificed because he is morally 'unclean' but can be killed by anyone. In condemning Lindy Chamberlain as an unnatural, morally unacceptable mother she too is forced into the position of *homo sacer*, hounded by the media and the public and exiled from the community.

The beast stealing our children at night: it is a moment that extends much further back than myth and folktales, those oral narratives that still echo our most ancient fear of the beast that comes at night. 'Could it be,' Bruce Chatwin has wondered, 'that *Dinofelis* [the sabretooth tiger] was Our Beast? A Beast set aside from all the other Avatars of Hell? The Arch-Enemy who stalked us, stealthily and cunningly, wherever we went? But whom, in the end, we got the better of?' (Chatwin 1988: 255). Despite some of these links I have listed between the folktales and the Chamberlain case, the latter contains a grim reality that resists all mythification. On that ill-fated day in August of 1980 at Uluru there was just a dingo that took away the child from her mother. What remains to this day are interminable grief, feelings of loss and the continuing absence of the baby girl.

Chapter 5

THE WOLVES OF WAR: FASCISM, TERRORISM, RESISTANCE

Figure 5.1 Soviet Propaganda Poster by Kukryniksy depicting Nazi Germany as a Wolf, *c.* 1930s.

Figure 5.2 Propaganda poster from the Second World War: 'Der Polnische Wolf begehrt eure Heimat!' 'The Polish wolf covets your country!' © IWM.

In propaganda posters from the 1930s and 1940s Nazi Germany sometimes features as an aggressive wolf attacking and devouring its neighbours, reflecting the Führer's imperialist appetite. In turn, the Third Reich also drew on the wolf image for its own propaganda against its reviled Eastern neighbours. What such posters generally reflect is how quickly a myth could be transformed for changing political scenarios, from, for example, a depiction of Germany as treacherous wolf breaking the Munich agreement of 1938 that had guaranteed Nazi Germany the annexation of the Sudentenland in exchange for promising not to go to war (fig 5.1), to maligning 'the Polish wolf' for the purpose of attacking it (fig 5.2).

Needless to say that wolves are being done extreme injustice in being appropriated for the iconography of bellicose aggression, imperialist invasion, national resistance, or lone wolf activities such as individualist resistance to totalitarian regimes or terrorism. Any of the propaganda during the war that exploited the wolf for its aggressive policies is based on a superficial understanding of the species *canis lupus*. Granted, wolves are aggressive when their territory is being threatened by outsiders, and they will fight to the death to resist such trespassing from other wolves. As for the lone wolves so readily appropriated in recent rhetoric on terrorism of individuals like Anders Breivik but mostly in an anti-Muslim context, in zoology lone wolves have a particularly hard standing, as I will explain below. And yet, myth and false wolf lore are astonishingly persistent when it comes to ultranationalism, immigration perceived as invasion, resistance to immigration and invasion, and the lone wolf activist or even terrorist. What are the cultural roots of this phenomenon of the wolf as aggressor?

Two of the principal human emotions persistently and falsely ascribed to wolves are melancholia and rage. The widespread perception of wolves as melancholic stems no doubt from its lonely nocturnal howl: 'There is a vast melancholy in the canticles of the wolves, melancholy infinite as the forest,' says Angela Carter in one of her rewritings of *Little Red Riding Hood* (Carter 2006: 131). The perception of melancholia and madness as lupine fills early psychoanalytical and medical discourse, above all Robert Burton's seminal study *Anatomy of Melancholy* (1621) about the causes and cures of melancholy. Burton understood this disease to be a veritable epidemic of an age full of religious superstition in which the disease of melancholy was perceived as being stimulated by witchcraft and demonic possession (Gowland 2006: 18). As early as in 1567, Aëtius had called it *melancholia canina*, a condition that was believed to emanate from too much black bile secreted by the spleen – the dog organ, as Walter Benjamin called it in his *Origins of the Bourgeois Tragedy*: 'The spleen rules the organism of the dog' (Benjamin 1991: 329).

The more intense form of this psychic state was the so-called *insania lupina*, lupine madness (Heffernan 1986: 187), Lycaon's rage as he is frothing at the mouth after his transformation as well as the rage of the God Jove. Although closely linked to what we now know as lycanthropy and rabies, to Burton these psychic conditions were caused primarily by idleness, passion and loneliness. Guided by the religious fanaticism of his time, Burton believed that as long as passions were allowed to dominate the soul and body, these sinful humans were essentially like beasts, animals stuck inside human form. The religious comments about wolves in the early modern age are inextricably intertwined with Burton's medical opinions, a hybrid discourse, as it were, that found its way in metaphorical fashion also into literature, above all the picaresque tradition from the seventeenth to the eighteenth century, which featured under-developed humans as stuck inside animal skins.

However, the association of rage or madness and the transformation of man into wolf manifest most saliently in the Germanic Wotan myth. While Jung equated the Germanic God of war and rage (German *Wut* is derived from *Wotan*) with the Greek God of intoxication (*Rausch*) Dionysus (Lewin 2009: 230), seeing *Wotan as the Shadow of Dionysus* (Bishop 1995: 298), Jove the Thunderer turning Lycaon into a wolf strikes us as closer to Wotan than the God of wine, not only in medieval myth but also in its twentieth-century revival in the wolf cult of the Third Reich.

One prominent lycanthropic descendant of Lycaon located between history and the Wotan myth, and for whom rage becomes a central attribute, is the so-called *berserkr*, a variant of the medieval *vargr* or human wolf who was expelled for his crimes. The liminality of the wolf man between sovereignty and abjection shows itself particularly in this ambivalent figure between great prowess and strength on the one hand and immorality, expulsion and persecution on the other. It was customary among such warriors to don the skins of the animals they had slain, especially wolf or bear hide, by dint of which they were able to work themselves into a state of frenzy for the purpose of intimidating their enemies. Theories as to the origin of the word *berserkr* vary. One explanation for this term is that the *serkr* (Old Norse for 'shirt' or 'coat') referred to the bear or wolf hide used by these warriors in Scandinavia, while another theory is that the word could also be derived from 'bare skin', that is, 'without fur', naked (Speidel 2002: 253–90). He was an early example of the so-called *Friedlos*, literally without peace as their task in life was to be in a permanent state of war.

Revered in pagan times as a frenzied warrior subject to diabolical fury the berserkers had certain privileges as long as society still recognized their value. He was, for example, able to 'invite himself to any feast, and contribute his quota to the hilarity of the entertainment, by snapping the back bone, or cleaving the skull, of some merrymaker who incurred his displeasure, or whom he might single out for murder, for no other reason than a desire to keep his hand in practice' (Baring-Gould 2007: 34). With the arrival of Christianity in Scandinavian Europe in the eleventh century (McCone 1987: 102), however, berserkers came to be banned from the community, outlawed for their moral corruption resulting from their privileged position outside the communal agreement of shared laws. He (or she, as Speidel argues, 2002: 271) was an early form of despot who had the right to invite himself onto the property of any farmer, participate in their feasts and even rape the farmer's daughter (Orchard, 19). Berserkers were lycanthropes in the sense of suffering from *insania lupina* as they were able to work themselves into a state of frenzy to the point of appearing demonic. Positioned between history, myth and literature they straddled pre-Christian madness and Christian associations of them with the devil.

As a migrant figure outside the community the berserker is interesting to us because of not only his fury but also his fierce resistance against the community at large, whether as a lone wolf fighter or in groups of frenzied men and women. As ferocious wolf warriors they inspired the idea of resistance in regimes such as National Socialism as well as Ernst Jünger's thoughts expressed in timely fashion after the demise of the Third Reich on the so-called *Waldgänger*, the rebel who takes to the real and metaphorical forests and his resistance against the state. While we have seen that wolves are being associated with migrant ethnic minorities, primarily Jews and Gypsies, and with lawlessness in general throughout the Middle Ages and the early modern age, the berserker as lycanthrope in wolf hide highlights the wolf's qualities of purported aggression, fierceness and strength as metaphors for both invasive aliens or foreigners and resistance to such invasions. In literature and politics this image surfaces especially during times of heightened nationalism.

As a literary image for resisting foreign invasion wolves occur, for example, in Heinrich von Kleist's play *The Battle of the Teutoburg Forest* (Die Hermannschlacht, written in 1808, first published in 1821), a dramatic representation of the famous battle between the Germanic leader Arminius and the Roman troops under Varus (9 AD). The defeat of the Romans in this play refers to Germany's conflict with Napoleon, featuring a dramatic clash between the Germanic partisans and the Tiber wolves, between a colonizing wolf pack and strategically savvy individualists like Arminius. In this drama about Germanic guerrilla warfare against a far superior colonial power, the image of the powerful wolf is accompanied by that of the clever fox. The latter refers to a logic also expressed in Macchiavelli's *The Prince* (1532), namely that the politician who does not have the strength of a lion should make use of the tactics of the fox (Blamberger 2011: 371).

While in Kleist's play the wolf is seen as an invasive creature from abroad, in Hermann Löns's early twentieth-century novel *Der Wehrwolf* (The Werewolf, 1910) the metaphor stands for resistance against invasion by either foreign armies or undesirable migrants and minorities. In this ultranationalist context the image of the wolf is seen as an animal of great strength and courage in defending its territory. As one of the worst literary testaments regarding the treatment of migrants on European soil Löns's novel exploits this image of the resistance wolf. Although Löns is a completely unknown author today, he was hugely popular among Nazi ideologues, and his concept of the self-defence against vagrants displayed by a group of farmers and the protagonist during the Thirty Years' War had a great following for its blood and soil energy. The novel became an instant bestseller in the Third Reich, which celebrated him as a front fighter and was enamoured with the book's hero Wulf, who fights so-called tartars (Gypsies and marauding itinerants) with the ferocity of a wolf:

> Our commander Wulf is a real wolf, for when and where he leaves his bite there are thirty three holes. Hence we call ourselves the werewolves and wherever we see nefarious activity we leave our mark, three cuts with the hatchet, one up, one down, the third one across. (Löns 2007: 78)

The novel introduces a new view of the idea of the werewolf into German literature, that of the so-called *Wehr*wolf, the wolf who defends himself. The spelling is important here as unlike the *Wer*wolf (without -h-) the prefix *Wehr* is derived from 'sich wehren' meaning to defend oneself.

Fascist wolves: Nazi werewolves and Mussolini's children of the she-wolf

To some extent influenced by Löns's novel and its racist, xenophobic messages National Socialism engaged in a national glorification of wolves, of werewolves in particular. Adolf Hitler in particular, sovereign ruler above and beyond the rule of law, saw himself as a wolf leading the German pack (Waite 1993: 166). He took a certain pride in his first name Adolf derived from *Aethalulfr*, the noble wolf in Old Norse, and he was familiar with the Disney movie *Three Little Pigs* from 1933, frequently whistling its theme song 'Who Is Afraid of the Big Bad Wolf'. In his early writing Hitler used the pseudonym 'Herr Wolf' and called his first shepherd dog Wolf (Ahne 2016: 70); and as Shelley Puhak points out, 'Hitler even called his beloved all-male S.S. his pack of wolves and saw himself as their leader'. But, she adds, 'Hitler, like modern day dog trainers and pick up artists, was terribly misinformed. Among actual wolves, the females are usually the specialist hunters. So are the pack alphas' (Puhak 2016: 74).

However, the Nazis' lycanthropic energy went well beyond the Führer himself. In the final months of the war a berserk troop was created, 'trained to engage in clandestine operations behind enemy lines' (Watt 1992: 844), a top secret movement modelled in part on Löns's idea of the werewolf as *Wehrwolf* (resistance or defence wolf). The novel had also revived the image of the *Wolfsangel*, that iconic symbol for a *Männerbund* (band of men) consisting of thirty-three werewolves that rise up against the marauders during the troubled times of the Thirty Years' War, and not being not all that different from the swastika-like symbol of the Nazi Werewolves, to whom Himmler first referred in a speech from 18 October 1944 (Watt 1992: 881). Originally, the *Wolfsangel* was a wolf trap, but both Löns and the Nazis used it as an instrument of intimidation and strength (Watt 1992: 882). The Löns cult even went so far that it led to the exhumation of his remains in France (where he had died in action in 1914) and their reburial in Fallingbostel under a stone with the *Wolfsangel* engraved into it.

Roderick Watt, however, has argued that this Nazi Werewolf movement towards the end of the war, also known as *Operation Werwolf*, owes less to the Löns novel than to the propaganda exploitation of the primitive fear of lycanthropy which is deeply rooted in Germanic myth, legend and the gothic extremes of Romantic literature (Watt 1992: 889). *Operation Werwolf*, which then also went by the name of *Unternehmen Karneval* (Operation Carnival), was not placed under the control of the military but under the SS (Biddescombe 1998: 14). It implied the idea of berserk-style resistance in a so-called *Volkssturm* (an attack involving the entire people) targeted against the enemies of the Reich. Then, on 1 April 1945, Joseph Goebbels made his infamous appeal to these werewolves: 'Hatred is our prayer and revenge is our war whoop' (Watt 1992: 845). It was the moment when the werewolves had gone from an originally clandestine operation to a public terrorist organization, and Goebbels planned to form bands of partisans, even a werewolf radio programme and a newspaper for this organization.

Some of the most detailed scholarship on this phenomenon of the final months of the war has been undertaken by Perry Biddescombe in his books *Werwolf: The History of the National Socialist Guerrilla Movement 1944–1946* (1998) and *The Last Nazis: SS Werewolf Guerrilla Resistance in Europe 1944–1947* (2000). Unlike Watts, Biddescombe supports the idea that the Werwolf movement was hugely inspired by Löns's novel, whose sales during the Third Reich rivalled only those of Hitler's *Mein Kampf*, but he points out also that another very important author for the movement was Karl May with his books on the imagined American Wild West, which May had never visited. It was especially May's description of Native American attack strategies that were envisioned by ideologues as forming a model for the German resistance fighters (Biddescombe 2000: 17). However, this kind of romanticization of resistance, of resilience and of shrewd fighting manoeuvres contrasted starkly with the reality of the *Werwolf* movement. Biddescombe argues that it failed to inspire the intended enthusiasm and grow large-scale, but was in the end rather marginal, consisting of scattered groups of crazed individuals, mostly arsonists, snipers and men armed with explosives.

As loosely organized as they may have been the Nazi Werewolves acted as *Freiheitskämpfer* (freedom fighters), a concept that evokes the terminology associated with *homo sacer* as being *wolfsfrei*, with berserkers as free as wolves to do anything. This is a desperate notion of freedom in the end and one more marked by self-sacrifice than liberation from the enemy. As unpopular as it may have been among the Germans this new terror organization was directed as much at faltering civilians at home as against the Allies, as the *Völkischer Beobachter* (3 April 1945) made clear in no uncertain terms: 'The werewolf justice will strike wherever meek creatures try to abandon their ranks.' The wolf's purported qualities of cunning and aggression thus turning inward upon its own offspring, this strategy is far removed from any nurturing instincts that may be accredited to wolves.

By way of contrast, such nurturing instincts were exploited ideologically by Benito Mussolini and Italian fascism. Mussolini drew on the symbolism of the Roman she-wolf in particular for his so-called *figli della lupa,* six- to eight-year-old boys and girls who in 1935 were admitted to the *Opera Nazionale Balilla*, a fascist youth organization that existed since 1926, had been inspired partly by Robert Baden Powell's boy scout movement and was similar in its ideological education and insistence on athleticism to the Hitler Youth. These very young children, who had previously not been able to join the Balilla, were known as the children of the she-wolf and were a substantial part of Mussolini's politics of establishing Italian identity through Italy's and especially Rome's glorious past and destiny. But as Cristina Mazzoni has so eruditely shown, to most Italians the term *figli della lupa* revealed a strange irony which had the tendency to destabilize the serious intentions of the fascists. As everyone knows in Italy, the word *lupa* not only means she-wolf but also refers to a prostitute. Traditionally, in Italian culture the *lupa* as a woman of ill repute evoked aggressive and exploitative rather than nurturing associations, which meant that the *figli della lupa* implied that 'Mussolini unwittingly questioned every Italian mother's sexual conduct' and their children's legitimacy (Mazzoni 2010: 160).

The other initiative that Italian fascism undertook concerning the Capitoline wolf for the purpose of strengthening a ubiquitous identity of shared *romanità* was to increase the number of wolf statues not only at home but also abroad. A good example for this is the set of bronze statues bestowed during the 1920s on the Romanian cities of Bucharest, Timisoara and Cluj-Napoca. These bronzes symbolized the Latin pact between the two countries sharing a Latin-based language. They stand in for the old concept of the Roman empire, and for Rome's protective, loving and defensive stance vis-à-vis one of her allies. In that sense, they are similar to the way in which Kipling uses the she-wolf in his *Jungle Book*, where Raksha, the defender, protects Mowgli as a child of the empire threatened by the dark and inchoate forces of the jungle as an embodiment of the colony. The Romanian wolf statues, however, are a rather ambiguous gift

Figure 5.3 Capitoline Wolf, Pisa, Italy. Photo by Peter Arnds.

Figure 5.4 Capitoline Wolf, Cluj-Napoca. Photo by Peter Arnds.

considering, as Mazzoni has so convincingly argued (2010: 71), that the love of the wolf mother was lost on her two children, with Romulus killing Remus. Fraternity thus turning to fratricide in the myth, the bronzes of the Capitoline she-wolf may not have been understood as the unambiguous gifts as which they were initially intended.

While Mussolini and the Italian fascists tried to exploit the nurturing instincts of the she-wolf, elevating a national myth for the construction of the state and international brotherhood, an attempt that ultimately failed, the Nazis' appropriation of Germanic myth with its openly aggressive and defiant wolf imagery became even more self-destructive in the end. The metaphorical German wolf with its animal passions that had become suppressed with the Enlightenment and led to national neurosis was at last fully set free in the Nazis' self-devouring, all-consuming final show-down before their complete *Untergang* (downfall). Wagner's *Götterdämmerung* (Twilight of the Gods), modelled on the mythological complex of Odin or Wotan and Ragnarök, the end of the world devoured by the great mythical wolf Fenrir, had suddenly found its grand historical enactment. It embellished the downfall with a strangely perverted aura of glory as Hitler's manic vision of total destruction and of himself as 'a Teutonic God fulfilling ancient myth' (Waite 1993: 425) led to the *Totale Krieg* (total war) in the final days of the war. Tragically also, the path for this wholesale destruction of all Germans considered not worthy of their leader had already been laid through the politics of euthanasia – of the elimination of life not worthy being lived – in the late 1930s and the Holocaust with its objective of eliminating one entire people as a 'final solution'.

Much of this kind of nebulous nationalist appropriation of mythology had already been undertaken in the nineteenth century with its primary interpreter of myth for the purpose of nation building, Jacob Grimm. The wolf, however, is not unique to German- or Italian-style nationalism but also features in other cultures, such as Turkey. With its dual positions of being hunted and hunting, however, its roots in early Germanic thinking are of particular interest, as there were two words for the wolf, *vargr* and *ulfr* expressing the ambivalent perception of the animal, both feared and revered. While *vargr* stands for the expelled human as wolf and his complete loss of peace, *ulfr* is the wolf brother of the sovereign ruler. As Wilhelm Grönbech pointed out in his book *Geist der Germanen*, 'Wolf [ulfr] is the friend of the king and often men bear his name' (Grönbech 1942: 48). Hitler's personal wolf cult is rooted in this kind of thinking, and it is this latter concept of sovereignty as a radical freedom that ignores the prevalent social contract which still determines nationalist wolf cults such as the Grey Wolves, an ultranationalist Turkish group, to this day.

It is a metaphor of tribal thinking, this idea of the pack that resists and invades other places, rather than of the *Weltbürger* in Kant's vision of the earth belonging to everyone. This brotherhood of wolves has more to do with Jack London's law of club and fang. It perceives the pack as a means of consolidation of power for getting organized in larger numbers to resist main stream politics and disseminate a neo-fascist agenda. Unsurprisingly, the appropriation of the wolf metaphor with all its appending symbols like the infamous 'wolf greeting' of the Grey Wolves' or the Nazis' *Wolfsangel* does severe damage to the wolf species. While it may still represent only a few crazed neo-fascists today, however, the danger of what Elias Canetti had once called the *Vermehrungsmeute*, the pack that increases its numbers (Canetti 2011: 126–33), is becoming more and more acute as various nations and their politicians are exploring 'trial runs for fascism' (O'Toole 2018). To what extent an image like the wolf can seize an entire *Volkskörper* is demonstrated by Hitler's and Mussolini's ideological appropriation of the wolf, but also, as we shall see in this chapter, by artists like Rainer Opolka whose wolf sculptures remind us of the power of such images.

Lone wolves: Ernst Jünger's Waldgang, terrorism, Michel Tournier's The Ogre

This pernicious wolf representing the freedom of the sovereign is one kind of *Waldgang* (the act of going to the forest) according to Ernst Jünger. Without explicitly naming the Third Reich he developed this concept in his famous essay from 1951 in memory of the Nazi years. By *Waldgänger* Jünger identifies the individualist who is resisting that type of regime and who, if discovered, will get singled out and destroyed by it. That the abandonment of the early Germanic *vargr* from the community into the forest is not far from his mind becomes clear in sentences such as 'Der Waldgang folgte auf die Ächtung' (the Waldgang followed the ban, Jünger 1980: 40). The *Waldgänger* is, in a broad sense, an anarchist, someone whose mental freedom may offer a maximum of resistance against official governance.

Jünger's concept is steeped in the ancient biopolitical ban of man as wolf, although, as he points out, we have entered a new age in which large masses of people are mobilized in whose 'Bannkreis' (Jünger 1980: 7) the alternative voice of the *Waldgänger* is not tolerated and its bearer will be destroyed. The word *Bannkreis*, the circle of all those who are banned within a certain ideology, is indicative also of the one who bans himself from that circle, who is the *Waldgänger* and therefore the modern-day *homo sacer* who can be destroyed by anyone. 'Nobody knows if he does not belong to a group tomorrow that finds itself outside of law' (Jünger 1980: 40). The old medieval formula still applies in Jünger's thinking, and he is thinking of the *Waldgänger* in terms of wolves, listing a series of words starting on W that the *Waldgänger* is associated with: 'Wachsam, Waffen, Wölfe, Widerstand' (Jünger 1980: 17, alertness, weapons, wolves, resistance). Jünger's wolves are typically lone wolves; lone wolves, however, who like the zoological wolf become stronger in numbers so that joining the pack to Jünger means easier resistance. Following the traditional ambiguity of the wolf metaphor Jünger's *Waldgang* is a twofold concept: it is performed by the one who resists the state but also by those despotic forces that exercise a maximum of authority over the state and draw others into their power:

For wolves are hiding in the grey herd, which means: they are individuals (*Naturen*) who still know what freedom is. And these wolves are not only strong by themselves, but there is the danger that they may, some evil morning, transfer their strength onto the masses, so that the herd (*Herde*) becomes a pack (*Rudel*). (Jünger 1980: 22)

Jünger's wolves are thus both the Derridean beasts as tyrants and despots and those individualists whose resistance can affect the crowd (*Herde*) in such a way that they may recruit others onto their side and form a pack (*Rudel*) of resistance wolves (Wehrwölfe=Waldgänger), for the most important feature of these human wolves is 'dass der Waldgänger Widerstand zu leisten entschlossen ist' (Jünger 1980: 28, that the Waldgänger is determined to practise resistance). The choice, Jünger says, is either to howl with the wolves or to fight against them (Jünger 1980: 47).

A word about lone wolves is necessary at this point. In nature, they are usually two to three years old and decide to leave their packs for a variety of reasons. This happens frequently after losing out on a

Figure 5.5 Alfred von Wierusz-Kowalskim, The Lone Wolf. Date unknown.

fight with another dominant wolf so that the loser has to embark on a journey into exile, for he would otherwise be surely killed. The freedom he thus gains is ambivalent. As the *homo sacer* is free from the social contract, so the wolf no longer needs to submit to the rules of the pack, and yet that freedom comes at a high price, as the protection of the pack is no longer available. Most of these so-called dispersers die during their journeys. Sometimes they are able to join other packs, but this is indeed very rare (Kotrschal 2012: 134). Most of the time they are in danger of losing their lives when trying to be adopted by a new pack, as wolves tend to be highly xenophobic (Kotrschal 2012: 68). Generally, wolves are not nomadic but intensely territorial. There are exceptions, as Kotrschal has shown, like the tundra wolves who travel every year for 2500 miles along with the reindeer herds (Kotrschal 2012: 70). A lone wolf, however, is forced to be a migrant, which makes him extremely vulnerable as he needs to fend for himself without the wisdom of the pack.

Vincent Steiger has recently documented such a journey based on the story of the Romanian wolf Slava who travelled 3000 kilometres all the way to North Western Spain, oblivious to national borders and constantly having to negotiate between human civilization and wilderness ('Die unglaubliche Reise der Wanderwölfe,' Südwest Rundfunk, 30 June 2019). In astonishingly beautiful cinematography, Steiger reconstructs Slava's monumental journey with the help of trained wolves, his hunting symbiosis with a raven (for wolves and ravens are known to put their skills together for survival), his romance with an Italian she-wolf, who will most likely stay with him for the rest of his life (for wolves are monogamous), and their various encounters with shepherds trying to protect their sheep (for in order to preserve energy as they hunt alone, wolves like Slava naturally prefer sheep to animals that run away). Even here, however, in this well-documented story of a migrant wolf we cannot help but surmise that there is much speculation about these elusive creatures. In *The Philosopher and the Wolf* Mark Rowlands puts it like this:

> Sometimes a wolf will leave its pack and head off into the woods, never to return. They have begun a journey and they will never again go home. No one is sure why they do this. Some postulate a genetic longing to breed, coupled with an unwillingness to wait their turn to move up the pack's hierarchy. Some argue that dispersers are especially anti-social wolves who don't enjoy the company of other wolves in the way that normal wolves do [...]. But who knows?

5. The Wolves of War

Perhaps some wolves just think that there is a big old world out there and it would be a shame not to see as much of it as they can. In the end, it does not really matter. Some dispersers die alone. Others, the lucky ones, meet other dispersers and form packs of their own. (Rowlands 2008: 243)

Rowlands's philosophically romanticizing view of the lone wolf is far removed from Ernst Jünger's philosophical politicization. And Jünger's glorification of the lone wolf as anarchist contrasts sharply with its demonization in recent rhetoric on the terrorist. In all cases these solitary dispersers still cannot escape their mythification. Perhaps it is due to their tendency to cross territorial boundaries, their lonesome battles in a hostile environment, their purported fearlessness, their threat to the community at large and, above all their stealth, the secret lives they lead: if packs are elusive how much more so must the dispersing wolf be? Surely all this contributes to their mystique.

As for the so-called lone wolf terrorist, stealth, menace to the community and a propensity to crossing boundaries are key factors. As Raffaello Pantucci has shown in his typology of lone wolf terrorists, mental illness as another variant of Lycaon's rage, his *insania lupina* frothing at the mouth, also plays an important role in this phenomenon: 'This is not to say that all lone wolves are mentally ill, but when one compares the instance of mental health issues amongst the roster of individuals involved in organised terrorism (where it is very low) to that of Lone Wolves (where it is higher than average), it can appear to be a defining factor' (Pantucci 2011: 5).

Pantucci, who sees lone-wolf terrorism entirely in an Islamist context, distinguishes between four types of terrorists: the Loner, the Lone Wolf, the Lone Wolf Pack and the Lone Attacker. 'Lone Wolves,' he says, 'are individuals who, while appearing to carry out their actions alone and without any physical outside instigation, in fact demonstrate some level of contact with operational extremists,' while 'the principle behind the Lone Wolf Pack is [that][…] rather than there being a single individual who becomes ideologically motivated, it is a group of individuals who self-radicalise using the Al Qaeda narrative' (Pantucci 2011: 19, 24–5).

The metaphor of the lone wolf for terrorists is as abstruse as its orientalist limitation to Islamist individuals, as characteristics like mental illness, loner action and the urge to join self-radicalizing groups also apply to other historical phenomena ranging from serial killers like Jack the Ripper via the Red Army Faction to Anders Breivik. Examples are legion and a term that would demythologize the concept of the lone wolf as criminal would be the 'lone actor'. If applied solely to Islamist terrorists the term 'lone wolf' indicates the ancient fear of trespassing, of coming into the nation from outside. On the other hand, in US terminology the 'lone wolf' tends to be applied solely to home-grown, domestic attackers, while 'terrorism' is in the media and legal rhetoric used almost exclusively in the context of Islamism (Bayoumi 2017).

The term 'lone wolf' is in itself a myth, but it also shows us that certain attributes from the Lycaon myth survive into contemporary rhetoric on terrorism, principally Lycaon's rage, his depression and his loneliness. Jünger's *Waldgänger* who works for the benefit of human rights is therefore very different from the 'lone wolf' actor who works to destroy. Such lone actors also appear in the arts. In literature, in the context of National Socialism in which the self-radicalizing pack extended its confines as far as engulfing an entire nation, there is one key post-war text in which these phenomena of the *Waldgänger* and the lone 'wolf' actor who then finds his 'pack' apply, but as parody: Michel Tournier's novel *Le Roi des Aulnes* (1970; translated as *The Ogre*, 1972). I want to discuss this novel in some detail here because it exemplifies the concept of the *Waldgänger* in the double sense of resisting and joining the pack.

Drawing on a blend of German and French myths and folklore as well as the gruesome history of the infamous fifteenth-century serial killer Maréchal Gilles de Rais, whom Sabine Baring Gould described as a werewolf (Baring-Gould 2007: 132–70) and who by dint of Pantucci's typology was one of those lone wolf types who sought 'to express rage through the mass murder of fellow citizens' (Pantucci 2011: 7–8), Tournier's novel is an ironic comment on the international appeal of fascism with its celebration of the Nordic mythical, pagan past. Tournier is 'exploring the psychic, erotic and aesthetic processes which informed mass fascination with, and support for, fascism' (Woodhull 1987: 79). By demonstrating how his French protagonist takes to Eastern European forests where he falls victim to the lure of National Socialism Tournier manages to appeal to his readership to resist the international fascination of fascism, thus also acting as a *Waldgänger* in Jünger's sense.

Tournier's loathsome protagonist Abel Tiffauges is one of those classical literary loners, marginalized by his own people, and densely associated with lycanthropic imagery. This anti-hero embodies the very opposite of Jünger's concept which is based on individualism, resistance and freedom from the state apparatus. Abel Tiffauges is the disperser in the biological sense of the wolf leaving one pack that has expelled him to join another. As we shall see, his *Waldgang* is treated

5. The Wolves of War　　　　　　　　　　　121

with irony, however; it is a parody of Jünger's concept, as Abel does not understand the deeper implications of his partnership in crime, whereas Jünger's *Waldgänger* is a political activist who exercises a maximum of freedom and resistance to the state. He or she is someone who understands politics, who fights against despotism and cannot be drawn – as Jünger puts it – from the crowd into a pack. With his message of anti-fascism the author Tournier is a lot closer to this concept than his character.

Migration features as nomadism in this text. Abel is the classical nomad in the middle of staunch politics advocating sedentariness in search of blood, soil and *Lebensraum* (living space). His name evokes the story of Cain and Abel, of Cain killing Abel, metaphorically the transition in the evolution of humanity from nomadic hunters and gatherers to farming and hence sedentary clans, and the suppression, that is, 'killing' of the nomads by those settling down to till the ground.

> Abel was still a keeper of the sheep, the nomad, while Cain was a tiller of the ground. [...] The quarrel of Cain and Abel has gone on from generation to generation, from the beginning of time down to our own day, as the atavistic opposition between nomads and sedentaries, or more exactly as the persistent persecution of the first by the second. And this hatred is far from extinct. It survives in the infamous and degrading regulations imposed on the gypsies, treated as if they were criminals, and flaunts itself on the outskirts of villages with the sign telling them to 'move on'. (Tournier 1997: 31)

Tournier's novel displays the international appeal that fascism's exclusion of the poor, transients and the Gypsies had and still has for the bourgeois mind. It is, however, also a comment on French collaboration with the Nazis in general, and more specifically on the Nazis' *Operation Werwolf*, the clandestine berserk movement at the end of the war that drew thousands of under-aged recruits into its machinery of destruction. *Operation Werwolf* too was a *Waldgang* in Jünger's sense, one that fed itself on what Canetti called the *Vermehrungsmeute*, the pack that tries to grow stronger by increasing its numbers – an enforced one for sure and consisting of left-over recruits: Germany's juveniles, her wolflings.

Myth and biopolitics conjoin in Tournier's novel which draws densely on motifs of lycanthropy and teratology. The lycanthropic subtexts of the novel metaphorically identify both France and Germany as wolf countries: France with its rich werewolf lore from the fifteenth and sixteenth centuries, its blend of historical werewolf figures such as

Gilles de Rais who then became mythologized in French folklore, and Nazi Germany with its revival of the werewolf myth in its final days of the war. The protagonist unites these myths in himself. He is a monster of a man – the text makes that clear from the beginning – with a wolfish appetite, an admiration for all things Nordic, a devourer of Rabelaisian proportions, wolfing down huge amounts of meat every day. After being imprisoned by the Germans in a 'prisoner-of-war camp' in the remote forests of Eastern Prussia, the area around Kaliningrad today, he discovers his love of Nazi Germany and converts into a passionate defender of their cause without, however, understanding the broader picture of its policies. Then, after finding employment at Hermann Goering's infamous Rominten Forest Reserve, he starts working for the Castle of Kaltenborn, a napola (Nationalpolitische Erziehungsanstalt or National Political Institute of Education) possibly named by Tournier after SS-General Ernst Kaltenbrunner who was closely associated with the Werwolf movement. Here his job is to go out in the surrounding areas and abduct children of suitable age and superior race so that they can be turned into *Jungmannen* (cadets) for the war on the Eastern front.

His new vocation gives him a densely mythological character. Not only is Abel modelled on the French fairy-tale ogre but also the Germanic Erlking, that spirit of the night that whisks away children from their parents, as well as the Pied Piper of Hamelin. The novel makes no secret of its subtexts. It explicitly mentions Charles Perrault's Tom Thumb tale *Le Petit Poucet* and Goethe's famous poem of the Erlking (*Der Erlkönig*), thus blending the French fairy-tale tradition with Germanic literature and myth. However, while densely referential to myth and folklore the novel also has a truly sinister background in a specific historical moment which in turn produced more folk culture, above all the Bluebeard myth. Especially the name Tiffauges, Abel's horse *Barbe Bleue*, and Abel's voracious, wolfish appetite for children allude to the mid-fifteenth-century Maréchal Gilles de Rais, whose murder of hundreds of children from villages like Tiffauges (hence Abel's name) near Nantes fed substantially into the werewolf mania of his time.

The Bluebeard story shows us how history turns into oral folk culture before finding entry into literature. Tournier uses several details from the story of Gilles de Rais: in the trial the Maréchal answered that he knew nothing of the disappearance of the children, arguing that he wasn't their keeper, Cain's words about his brother Abel. Allegedly, Gilles de Rais also bathed in the blood of his victims, a motif that

Tournier adapts by having Abel Tiffauges sleep on a mattress made of the hair of the shorn *Jungmannen* before emptying the content into a fish pool and swimming in it. The Blue Beard tale is said to have its roots in this historical figure because during the trial it was observed that in a certain light his beard assumed a blue hue, earning him the surname of 'Blue Beard' (Baring-Gould 2007: 151). Apparently also, his servant Henriette collected children for his master and was present while he massacred them in a special room at the Chateau de Machecoul before bathing in their blood (Baring-Gould 2007: 157-8). Designating one room to the massacre also corresponds to Bluebeard's chamber in the popular myth and in Charles Perrault's fairy tale by that name.

Tournier's duplicitous Abel is thus a hybrid made up of a mixture of historical and mythical sources. He is also an apt embodiment of the Agambian wolf-man, who appears in a number of guises in the novel, making a first literal appearance in Abel's childhood as he reads and dreams about the wide expanses of the Canadian north:

> The hero of the story was Bram, a huge wild half-breed, part English, part Indian, part Eskimo, who wandered alone over terrible icy wastes drawn by a team of wolves. And to say he howled like a wolf was not just a figure of speech. He had suddenly thrown back his great head, sending up a cavernous roar from his throat and chest [...]. At first it was like a peal of thunder, but it ended in a sharp plaintive wail that could be heard for several miles across the level plain. It was the call of the leader to the pack (*meute*); of the animal-man to his brothers. (T35-6)

Abel is a lone wolf in the double sense of being, on the one hand, expelled from the French community, imprisoned by the Nazis and then roaming the Eastern Prussian forests as Bram, his fictional model, does in Northern Canada. On the other hand, he is a human wolf as tyrant and Nazi werewolf with his newly gained ties to the self-radicalizing pack, and by helping to recruit children for the front he is trying to strengthen *la meute* (pack).

As we have seen, wolves have better chances of survival in packs. In order to facilitate his own survival the human wolf expelled from the community also had to bond with other outlaws. The two principal packs that Elias Canetti distinguishes in his seminal work *Crowds and Power* (Masse und Macht, 1960) are the hunting pack (*Jagdmeute*) and the war pack (*Kriegsmeute*). They are both *Vermehrungsmeuten* in the sense that individuals organize themselves in a process that, as we have seen, Jünger identifies as the *Herde* (flock) turning into a *Rudel* (pack) (Jünger 1980: 22). Outlaws were associated with wolves because they lived like them, in the woods, ready to attack and kill travellers, maraud villages and so on, sometimes working alone but often, for the purpose of being less vulnerable, trying to increase their numbers. Such gangs of outlaws populate myth and reality from the werewolves of Zeus Lykaios to Robin Hood, from the Irish *fianna* and the Old Celtic *koryos* (hence the word *choir*) to the Germanic *Männerbünde* and *haryaz*: all of these are associations of men, a brotherhood of human wolves (cf. McCone 1987: 112). While the *fianna* and *koryos* were limited in number and imply the idea of an initiation rite, a youthful phase of wandering and thievish warfare that evokes the image of the wolf or even dog, the Germanic *haryaz* possibly reflect at their best Canetti's *Vermehrungsmeute* as it etymologically predates the German *Heer*, the army. Canetti sees the army as symbolically connected to the forest, with its trees standing up strong and in resistance to the elements, and which can only be cut down but not otherwise be defeated (Canetti 2011: 98). This symbolism equating the forest with the army, which generally obediently follows orders and the state at large, may contrast with the idea of resistance to the state of expulsion, but it also highlights the wolf man's relationship with war.

Abel Tiffauges is in this position of the wolf man who recruits others for the purpose of resisting foreign invasion. Expelled by his French community, however, a wolf to them in the sense of being the *homo sacer*, he has joined the Nazis as war pack. By running over from the French to the Nazis he switches positions from the wolf as *homo sacer* to Derrida's sovereign wolf. The German translation of the title of the novel *Le Roi des Aulnes* into Volker Schlöndorff's film version *Der Unhold* (1996) captures his dual status of victim of expulsion and sovereign evildoer, anchoring the protagonist at the intersection of myth and biopolitics. While the *roi des aulnes*, literally the Erlking, is a figure rooted entirely in Northern European folklore, the *Unhold* is a more politically charged term in denoting the male equivalent of the *Unholde*, the witch, in whom biopolitical persecution and folklore come together.

In what I would therefore call a novel of 'mythical realism', a genre that in blending myth and folk culture with politics is more focused in its definition than magic realism, Abel is being joined by a range of other ogres. Hitler is the supreme one in this story in comparison with whom Hermann Göring, the 'Ogre of Rominten' and Master of the Wild Hunt, *la chasse Arlequin*, in his expansive game reserve, dwindles to 'the rank of a little, imaginary, picturesque ogre out of an old wives' tale' (T236). Hitler's *Volkssturm* was modelled not only on the myth of Odin's wild hunt with the berserks but historically also on Napoleon's *Landsturm* of 1813. Tournier alludes to this *Volkssturm*, which incorporated every able-bodied man between sixteen and sixty. The Second World War itself takes the role of a mythological ogre with the 'Jungmannen serving and feeding the monstrous idols of steel and fire that raise their monumental jaws amidst the trees' (T291).

Despite the various folklore subtexts, Abel is also modelled on the picaro who runs into trouble and remains naïve for the longest time, but somehow always gets lucky in the end and manages to muddle through. The profane and the sacred uneasily come together in this carnivalesque, neo-picaresque text about the Nazi race crimes forming a sinister backdrop to the events on the Eastern front and the recruitment of innocent children. The children Abel picks from trees and out of their parents' homes are used as cannon fodder but also for the purpose of racial selection. Again myth and biopolitics come together. The folklore motif of a child's abduction, as one encounters it in the Pied Piper legend or Goethe's Erlking, is an element of fantasy that serves the representation of the historical reality of Nazi eugenics. At the Kaltenborn Raciological Centre Commander Professor Doctor Otto Blättchen continuously searches among 'the children they bring me for the grain of gold dust that justifies selective reproduction' (T250). Here is another ogre, whose olfactory sense is so refined (Perrault's ogre can smell human flesh) that he can distinguish between races by their individual smell, 'black, yellow, Semitic and Nordic with his eyes shut, just by the fatty volatile acids and alkalis secreted by their sudoriferous and sebaceous glands' (T252).

Still unaware of the horrible consequences of the Nazis' concern with eugenics Abel expresses his fascination with these ideas, shares with the likes of Josef Mengele – the notorious Nazi doctor known for his experiments on concentration camp inmates – a special attraction for twins, and eagerly participates in a painstaking examination of their bodies, their 'brachycephalic skulls, wide faces with prominent cheekbones, pointed ears, flat noses, widely spaced teeth, green rather slit eyes' (T287). However, everything Abel undertakes in his career as an ogre he does out of love for children. Unaware of his sinister work he carries it out with extreme joy. In the final scenes where he meets the little Jewish boy Ephraim, who has survived Auschwitz, Abel's dream world is suddenly shattered as he realizes the horrible ambiguity of the word

'Canada'. While Abel's life in the Eastern European forests surrounded by the boys of Kaltenborn had been the realization of a childhood dream about the cold expanses of the Canadian north, it had meant to him the 'rejection of the human world of warmth and friendship, and the embrace of a world of ice and abstraction' (Rowlands 2008: 148), 'Canada', Ephraim tells him, was also the name for the treasure house in Auschwitz where the possessions of the dead were stored. All of a sudden Abel understands that as he was euphorically stuffing his mattress with boys' hair; this was indeed a reflection of the grim reality in the death camps where the hair of the victims was recycled for various purposes.

It is in these final scenes that Abel loses his political naiveté and morphs from a fairy-tale monster into a saint, but we need to keep in mind that Tournier parodies the idea of saintliness and professions of innocence in the face of fascism and totalitarianism. Abel quite literally grows an excess of humanity in the hump on his back formed by the messianic child he carries to safety, an act that evokes Saint Christopher, especially as the latter carries Jesus across a body of water. Abel experiences a sort of *Bildung* – and yet this is a parody of the Bildungsroman genre – in the course of his development from a naïve Nazi sympathizer to a figure that resembles Saint Christopher, who like Abel morphs from his initial worship of the devil into a figure of redemption. The earliest Oriental representations of Saint Christopher show him with a dog's head, and the legend goes that it symbolizes his initial worship of the Devil as his Master before being converted by Christ, whom he subsequently follows as the stronger Master. His conversion is thus from a dog-headed sinner, a *cynocephalus*, to a saint, and this shifting of identities underlies the strange transformation of Abel Tiffauges from fairy-tale ogre to the saviour of a Holocaust victim, whom in Saint Christopher fashion he carries across the glacial swamps. We will come across a similar use of Saint Christopher in the context of wolves in David Malouf's novel *An Imaginary Life* discussed in Chapter 8.

In his intertextual relationship with the Pied Piper and Erlking myths Abel is also part of the Wild Hunt, abducting and recruiting youth for the purpose of war. Abel is one of Wotan's wolves, Wotan being Göring, the *Reichsforstminister*, literally the leader of the Wild Hunt for game but also as supreme Nazi ogre, the leader of the wild hunt for soldiers and Jews. Abel becomes a mimic man of sorts in that he mimics Göring, the Great Hunter at the Rominten Reserve. While Göring hunts deer, stags and wild boars, a reflection also of the people he hunts, Abel then ends up hunting children. Both partake of the mythological Wild Hunt complex in these scenes, and are reflections of each other. They seem to recognize and respect each other. Like Wotan who is associated with wolves, Göring is a predator accompanied by two lions. The Wild Hunt thus happens at three levels in this multi-facetted novel, much in the way the figure of the ogre is also located on various levels (Abel, Göring and the moose Abel encounters at one point, named *Ogre*): it happens as a hunt for game and as a hunt for children, which is sinister enough. But the truly sinister backdrop of what Abel perceives as joyful activities is the hunt for Jews and other minorities that goes on behind the scenes. This dimension does not surface until the very end, the Holocaust as a backdrop remains hidden, *heimlich*, until Ephraim brings it to light for Abel. In view of the other two wild hunts for game and boys, however, the hunt for Jews is clad in an aura that is truly *unheimlich*, precisely because of the contrast of terror and joy that it reveals, as, for example, in the motif of Abel taking a bath in the hair of the boys.

Abel strikes us as even more monstrous if we hold his naiveté next to the crimes of humanity that happen while he is enjoying Nazism. Seen in that light, the dog-headedness of Saint Christopher indicating his worship of the Devil is the true nature of Abel. With his passion for everything raw, be it meat, nature, his own manners or fascism, Abel also reminds us of the philosophical tradition of the Cynics, whose name derives from *kunos*, the dog. As Frédéric Gros has shown in his *Philosophy of Walking* (2015: 131–5), Cynics such as Diogenes were vagabonds shuffling about the streets like dogs, human monsters that ate raw meat, barked their abuse rather than spoke, and embraced being perpetually exposed to the elements and the gaze of the public (i.e. monsters in the sense of being *shown*). Tournier, however, adapts these motifs in Abel, especially in view of his uncritical and ultimately monstrous subscription to fascism, and, unlike the Cynics, inability to accuse and denounce political conditions. Precisely this is, in the end, achieved solely by the author himself, through his portrait of Abel.

Abel is thus located between wolf and dog, a mythological proximity that also points to the mythical underworld with its canines like Kerberos being traditionally positioned at the gates to hell (Erler 1940: 307). The Egyptian god of the dead, Anubis, who has the head of a jackal, and Saint Christopher are clearly related to him, although their relationships with the dead are different. Like Hermes in Greece, Anubis was a conductor of souls to the underworld. This idea of the wolf, dog or jackal as being connected to death and the underworld survives in the demonization of the wolf by Christianity as well as in the association of the Wild Hunt with wolves. The mythological proximity of canine creatures to the devil reappears in literary images such as Mephistopheles's first entry in the shape of a poodle in Goethe's *Faust* or in the wolves at the gates of hell in Stoker's *Dracula* (note that Abel's admired wolf man is also called Bram), where just before Van Helsing arrives at Dracula's castle his carriage is being attacked by wolves. *Dracul* means dragon or devil in Romanian, and Dracula's Castle thus functions as Hell, making Van Helsing's trip there one to the underworld.

In what is a typically postmodern parody Abel's metamorphosis from a monster into a saint is reminiscent also of Oskar Matzerath's transformation from a hunchbacked dwarf to his illusion of being Jesus at the end of Günter Grass's *The Tin Drum* (1959). Like Grass's famous novel, this is a parody of professions of innocence, and by extending the hybridity between human and animal from his protagonist to that of the mythological material approximating French and German culture Tournier makes a highly ironic comment on French claims of inculpability after the war. By giving us this ironic portrait of a French collaborator (in German *Mitläufer*, someone running with the pack is an apt expression here) participating in National Socialism's wholesale destruction of Europe, Michel Tournier himself can indeed be seen as a *Waldgänger* in Jünger's sense of 'der Dichter ist Waldgänger' (the poet practises resistance, Jünger 1980: 42). He is a post-war artist who works to destroy the covers of *lethe*, of forgetting and the concealment of truth. Through the art of parody Tournier reveals the falseness of professions of innocence as complicity, but he also shows us to what extent the position of the loner engaged in aesthetic pursuits can naïvely become absorbed by the nefarious activities of the pack. In spite of all parody, however, a portion of humanity, of humaneness in the sense of a deeper comprehension of history and sympathy with its real victims is recovered at the end of his novel. The silhouette of Abel walking through the swamps with the child on his shoulders, this opening of the contours of his body as a token of shared humanity, in final analysis makes him more human, stripping him of his ogrishness, even though the little Jewish boy he saves, Ephraim, insists on calling him *Behemoth*. The burden of history on Abel's back is a burden not limited to Germany, thus Tournier's message, but also extending to France.

The wolves are back: Turkish nationalism and Rainer Opolka's wolf sculptures

Coinciding with their return in the natural world, wolves have had a miraculous comeback in contemporary nationalist appropriations of their iconic mythic qualities. Most prominent among these are the Turkish Grey Wolves, an ultranationalist, neo-fascist group that originated with Alparslan Türkeş's foundation of the Nationalist Movement Party in the late 1960s and has been advocating pan-Turkic unity and such radical agenda items as the denial of the Armenian genocide. With the Grey Wolves we are moving from the lone wolf back to the nationalist wolf pack, the Turkish wolf icon being even more prominent than in National Socialism. In the Third Reich, apart from Hitler's own wolf cult the wolves were largely an end-of-war phenomenon. They were part of the wider context of Nordic myth making and its very own iconography, but the mechanisms of myth making are the same now as they once were.

Mary Fulbrook has argued that myths are 'propagated for their effect rather than their truth value' (Fulbrook 1997: 73). As for the Turkish Grey Wolves, their myth-making symbols, principally their so-called wolf greetings, have at the beginning of the year 2019 been banned in Austria, while Germany at the time of my writing this book is still contemplating whether or not to ban them. This sort of precaution, although vehemently attacked by the Turkish government and diplomatic circles, is perhaps not entirely surprising. The ideology of the Grey Wolves feeds itself from the pan-Turkist myth of national homogeneity founded on a bond of blood and moral integrity. Their rhetoric has since their beginnings in the 1960s resembled that of the Nazis in view of racial purity and hygiene. In their 'Creed of the Grey Wolves', written in 1942, the pan-Turkists even went so far as to claim that 'science has proven that seventy five percent of children born from parents of different races become abnormal, deaf, mute, crippled, prone to tuberculosis, prostitutes, homosexuals, alcoholics, heroin users, kleptomaniacs, epileptic, and insane' (Burris 2007: 614). The term 'Grey Wolves' derives from this document, but in part also from two novels by Huseyin Nihal Atsız, *The Death of the Grey Wolves* (1946) and *The Grey Wolves Come Back to Life* (1949). Their protagonist, commonly evoked in pan-Turkist discourse, is Kiir-Sad who leads a group of pre-Islamic Turkic heroes into war against an imperialist Chinese enemy against whom they ultimately sacrifice their own lives for the nation. Like in Jiang Rong's 2004 novel which I will discuss in Chapter 7 these texts describe the clash between nomadic people from Central Asia worshipping wolves and the sedentary Chinese.

Atsız, who went to a German School in Istanbul and was influenced by the Nazis' racial ideology of purity of blood and nobility of a national character (Landau 2003: 205), plays a key role in pan-Turkist patriotism and ultranationalism directed against enemies abroad (the Chinese in this case) and within (primarily Communists). But the image of the grey wolf is also derived from the myth that all Turks are descended from a Central Asian she-wolf (the myth gave birth to Ataturk's nickname Grey Wolf while Genghis Khan was called the 'Blue Wolf'), a narrative that carries obvious parallels with the Roman one. Much like in ancient Rome the nurturing she-wolf is connected to the idea of the warrior soldier in the pan-Turkist movement with its wolf greeting meant to unite these warriors. Common to the myth of the wolf in Rome, Nazi Germany and the pan-Turkist movement is therefore the idea of turning men into warriors.

The Grey Wolves' traditional glorification of war is reminiscent of Nazi Germany, especially its final years where the wolf image appears in exaggerated form and Goebbels's desperate question to the German *Volk* 'Wollt ihr den totalen Krieg?' was designed to take the whole world into the abyss. The *Creed of the Grey Wolves* too addresses the question of whether war should be embraced at all cost, whether the pursuit of Turkic political unification merited war: 'Yes! War when it is needed! War is a great and blessed law of nature. We are the descendants of warriors. The Grey Wolves believe that war, militarism, and heroism must be brought to a state of respect' (Burris 2007: 618). And the racist rhetoric around this time does not shy away from the kind of animal metaphor that we see in the National Socialist vocabulary of parasitism applied to humans, as Atsız's use of the word 'microbe' demonstrate: 'The best way to get rid of this microbe [foreign elements] is massacre. Only the Turks should have the right to live in Turkey' (Burris 2007: 618). While *Ungeziefer* was the term the Nazis used for Jews and other undesirables, Atsız's microbes are directed against the Kurds and other people considered alien to the idea of pan-Turkism, but primarily against the Left. In addition to this rhetoric of war-mongering and racism the pan-Turkist movement also targeted women, contrasting the vanguard of masculine warriors represented by pan-Turkists with the Turkish left depicted as 'filthy prostitutes whose shameful promiscuity threatened to destroy the moral fibre of the nation' (Burris 2007: 617). That similar processes of debasing undesirable groups through their feminization happened in Nazi Germany has been documented by George Mosse

5. The Wolves of War   131

(1996: 68–70) and Kaltenecker (1995: 91–109) in their analysis of the debasement of the 'effeminate Jew'.

The history of the Grey Wolves is thus blighted with a discourse of race, war and hostility towards ethnic minorities and women. This history is embodied in their central gesture, the wolf greeting, in which the two middle fingers and the thumb form the wolf's muzzle while the index and pinkie form perked-up wolf ears. Given Germany's and Austria's own shared past with the *Sieg-Heil* salute it is not too difficult to see why in a world in which liberal democracies are increasingly threatened these two countries may wish to ban the wolf greeting. As a homogenizing tool this gesture, much like the Hitler salute, is trying to unite individuals into one *Volkskörper* (national body), to turn 'lone wolves' into a nationwide 'wolf pack'. I am placing these terms in single quotes as I am acutely aware that by using them at any point I am in danger of walking into the same trap of doomed metaphorical rhetoric this book is directed against.

The wolf with its mythologized features of aggression, strength, pack mobilization, moral integrity (such as monogamy) and ability to devour large prey thus becomes a representative of a folk body that uncritically heeds the commands of its leaders. At a deeper level the gesture is not as harmless as it may seem but with its erectness of two fingers pointing in the direction of an inflexible political teleology repeats the intolerance of alterity that is also embodied in the Hitler salute whose very own erectness – that classical body posture – contrasts sharply with all images of what the Nazis persecuted as degeneracy. We will see in a minute how post-Third Reich art parodies and carnivalizes this particular gesture.

After Hermann Löns's novel *Der Wehrwolf*, the wolf greeting may also remind us instantly of that other ill-fated lupine image, the *Wolfsangel* (wolf trap) which the North German author uses in the context of unspeakable racism. But the Turkish wolf greeting has yet another connection with the 'German' salute. With its roots in Roman salutation rituals, which were later 'revived in David's "Oath of the Horatii"[…], adopted by d'Annunzio's Legionnaires in Fiume, then by Mussolini's Fascists, and eventually taken over by the Nazi Party at its 1926 party congress in Weimar in symbolic reaction to the KPD's clenched fist' (Korff/Peterson 1992: 77), the imperialist *Heil-Hitler* or *Sieg-Heil* salute is linked to the Turkish wolf greeting via the myths about two she-wolves, one marking the beginning of both the pan-Turkist world, the other nourishing Roman imperialism as a model to the Nazis' vision of the Thousand-Year Reich.

The Grey Wolves Come Back to Life – Atsız's title has a certain relevance for Rainer Opolka's anti-hate exhibit *Die Wölfe sind zurück* of *Sieg-Heil*-saluting wolf sculptures with which he toured Germany in 2016, especially those areas that have been caught in the claws of right-wing movements such as the *Alternative für Deutschland* (AfD) or the *Pegida*. Opolka deliberately appropriates the Nazi iconography of wolves as figures of war, hatred, anti-Semitism and xenophobia. Many of his wolf sculptures made from bronze, cast iron or brass can be seen raising their paws with claws to form the salute, a gesture banned in Germany. One may wonder why a gesture like the *Wolfsgruss* of the Turkish Grey Wolves is on the agenda for being banned in Germany while Opolka's wolf provocations were being tolerated.

Unlike the Turkish wolf greeting Opolka's Nazi-saluting wolves do not promote nationalism but are directed against hate, xenophobia and racism. They specifically serve as a reminder also of Third Reich ideology with its wolf imagery. As a so-called *Wanderausstellung* (migratory exhibit) travelling from Berlin to Potsdam, Dresden and Chemnitz

Figure 5.6 Rainer Opolka's Wolf Statue 'Anführer'. Courtesy of Rainer Opolka.

5. The Wolves of War

the idea of promoting immigration and warning against hatred and xenophobia towards immigrants is worked into the very marrow of this flexible installation of sixty-six lycanthropic sculptures. In Berlin they were provocatively placed right across from the Reichstag, where they posed with pistols or the Hitler salute, their hybridity of wolf heads and human bodies evoking the Nazi werewolf movement. Visitors are meant to mingle with them to come to understand what it feels like to become part of the pack and thus experience a sort of Brechtian *Entfremdungseffekt* (alienation or distancing effect) that will make them reflect upon current trends of populism and right-wing extremism and thus critically distance themselves from these.

Opolka has been criticized by members of the right-wing *AfD* for being a left-wing fascist, by others for breaking the German taboo of displaying the Nazi salute and also for his lack of subtlety, as – in Chemnitz at least – large posters behind the wolves tried to explain what they stand for, almost as if the audience were too ignorant to figure this out by themselves. The other criticism one could level at the artist is that he falls into the usual trap of mythologizing wolves, as once did those he rallies against.

As we have seen throughout this book, wolves suffer from their mythologization and politicization, with politics exploiting the myth and ignoring the reality of zoology. The ghost wolf always clashes with the corporeal wolf. In Opolka's defence, however, it needs to be pointed out that although he aggressively draws on wolf lore his installations re-appropriate the Nazis' wolf iconography for the purpose of revealing and destabilizing it. In their public display his Nazi-saluting wolves are meant to shake people who seem to have forgotten about the past out of their lethargy. There is always the danger of the return of fascism, thus goes his message accompanied by the motto *The wolves are back*. Ultimately, Opolka's wolf imagery is a parody of the deadly seriousness with which it was applied in the Third Reich, a re-appropriation for a good purpose. Although parody, they contain a new sense of seriousness, one that is diametrically opposed to its antecedent but also different from the kinds of carnivalizations the Nazi iconography has been represented with by artists around the world.

Displaying the symbols of National Socialism is in itself extremely controversial, but since Charlie Chaplin's *The Great Dictator* in 1940 they have repeatedly been used in the arts as a form of iconoclasm to point to the dangers of fascism. The Nazi salute in particular has been parodied in literature (Günter Grass), film (Agniezska Holland), painting (Albert Bloch) and photography (Anselm Kiefer). It is one thing for non-German artists to parody National Socialist body gestures and iconography. Examples range from Mel Brooks's *The Producers* (1968) with its famous musical number 'Springtime for Hitler' where the Nazi salute is performed as a Can Can dance, to Roberto Benigni's *Life Is Beautiful* (1998) which turns the Holocaust into a game between father and son, and Agniezska Holland's *Europa, Europa* (1991) where Soli, the protagonist, performs a dance in front of the mirror saluting himself. It is, however, an altogether different challenge for German artists to tamper with Nazi symbols and the salute, and such provocations contain varying degrees of intensity. In his world classic *The Tin Drum* (1959), Günter Grass, for example, carnivalizes the crowd's salute at a Nazi Party rally by turning marching music and the stiffly stretched-out arms into the fluidity of a waltz (in the film) and jazz (in the book), a scene that Volker Schlöndorff has marvellously rendered in his film adaptation of 1979.

Time is certainly a determining factor in responses to such carnivalizations of a gesture that is still taboo in Germany. Possibly the most controversial parody of the salute came from the artist Anselm Kiefer who in his photo series *Occupations* (1969) and *To Genet* (1969) posed with a *Sieg-Heil* salute in various locations – in front of the Colosseum or in drag in his own bath tub – in order to point to a fascist and imperialist past Germany in the 1960s had not come to terms with, and that was not being adequately remembered, but also by reminding us that the phallic gesture in its bluntest symbolism implies the idea of imperialism linked to an aggressive male sexuality and drive for power.

It is to be noted that Germany's engagement with the Nazi past took an extremely sluggish start in the Federal Republic where the general public did not engage with the Nazi crimes until the late 1970s. Seeing as in their tampering with a taboo gesture Kiefer and Opolka are fifty years apart, they obviously differ with regard to the intent and effect of their performances. While Kiefer attempts to break through the shame covers of repression, Opolka uses the wolf salute as a warning that the fascist past can easily return. *Nichts ist vorbei, alles kommt wieder*, nothing is over, everything comes back, Grass notes clairvoyantly in *The Tin Drum* (Grass 1986: 392). By re-enacting the Hitler salute Kiefer is pointing out to his German audience that the Nazi past has not yet been worked through if such working through is at all possible. His salutes are a form of 'acting out' in order to start the process of *Vergangenheitsarbeit*, working with the past to work through it. One needs to be sceptical about such projects, however, as *Vergangenheitsbewältigung* is an unfortunate term implying that in being 'mastered' the past is meant to disappear. Opolka's Nazi-saluting wolf sculptures are aimed directly against such a process, as they try to engage their audience with a past that after over seventy years may all too easily be forgotten, as working through the past may entail forgetting about it.

Perhaps not surprisingly, reactions to Kiefer's and Opolka's provocations are similar in spite of the fifty years that lie between them. Both have been criticized for being neo-fascist and both had to defend themselves against such claims. Kiefer pointed out that he identified 'neither with Nero nor Hitler', conceding, however, that he had to 'sympathize with them just a little bit so as to understand their madness' (Winter 1988: 70), and in an interview with *Deutschlandfunk* in September 2018, Opolka stated:

> When I recently saw the images from Chemnitz of people doing the Hitler salute I thought: 'Get the truck ready and go there'. At the moment there is a situation in Germany where people think they need to express their frustration by chasing foreigners through the cities, attacking Jewish restaurants or set refugee houses on fire. At the same time, there are some politicians who deem the Hitler salute insignificant, although it was the gesture of a society that in the end produced 50 million dead, and among these 6 million gassed Jews. (https://www.deutschlandfunkkultur.de/kunstaktion-in-chemnitz-wenn-der-wolf-den-hitler-gruesst.1008.de.html?dram:article_id=427965)

It is this important merit of artists like Kiefer and Opolka in their solitary creative *Waldgänge* that they are ready to break with taboos and the shame covers of a society in order to either awaken that society from the slumber of repression, as in the case of Kiefer, or, as does Opolka, attempt to stifle neo-fascism on the rise while defending pro-immigration policies in precarious areas where the appearance of immigrants raises the hackles of the locals. In either case, their work does not attempt to master the past, but it continues to stimulate what one may call *Vergangenheitsreflexion*, reflecting upon the past, especially at critical times.

Chapter 6

NO TRESPASSING: WOLVES, BORDERS AND IMMIGRANTS

Hospitality means the right of a stranger as long as he behaves peaceably not to be treated as an enemy upon arrival in another country. This right of a visitor is common to all people due to their shared ownership of the surface of the planet, upon which, owing to its spherical shape they cannot disperse *ad infinitum*. They are consequently forced to tolerate each other's presence. (Kant [1795] 1923: 21; my translation)

It is worth repeating Kant's thoughts in view of potential human rights violations, of contemporary political moves such as the Danish Parliament's consideration in 2018 of a proposal to isolate 'unwanted' immigrants on the uninhabited island of Lindholm, site of a former research station for contagious animals. The island is associated with infectious disease, one of the ferries crossing over to it even bearing the name of *Virus*. The island's soil still holds traces of swine flu and rabies and would require decontamination before it can be used to house immigrants with criminal records who cannot be repatriated, often for fear of torture and death should they be returned to their home countries. The proposal by the anti-immigrant Danish People's Party was designed to further isolate and stigmatize immigrants in the hopes that they would want to leave the country of their own accord, as was made clear in a post by Denmark's immigration minister at the time, Inger Støberg: 'They are undesirable in Denmark, and they must feel it' (Sorensen 2018).

This idea of literally isolating undesirables and alleged intruders is of course not new, and it is not limited to Denmark. Nor is the discourse of contagion and the strategy of quarantining immigrants and refugees compared to infectious animals which the Danish case evokes and which has been so pervasive in recent populist rhetoric in immigration politics denigrating migrants or so-called undocumented aliens as 'animals' breaking through borders and 'infesting' the nation states of the global North. While the president of the United States persistently calls migrants trying to cross the southern border 'animals', a former British prime minister once famously invoked Kafka's story *Metamorphosis* (1915) and the insect world by labelling refugees as '*swarms* of people coming across the Mediterranean' (http://www.bbc.com/news/uk-politics-33716501); and his foreign secretary used the word 'marauders' (Shariatmadari 2015), a term that, as we have seen, has stuck around at least since the Thirty Years' War when it was used in the context of denigrating rootless 'Gypsies' and dispersed soldiers having deserted their regiments.

These are just a few among a variety of other dehumanizing metaphors currently in use in the context of immigration. Crediting Jane Zavisca's sociological research on metaphors describing migrants crossing the US–Mexican border, in his 2018 memoir *The Line Becomes a River* Francisco Cantú points out that these metaphors fall into several categories:

> Economic metaphors were predominant, characterizing migrant deaths as a 'cost', 'calculation' or 'gamble.'[…] Violent metaphors were the second largest category, depicting death as the vengeful punishment of an angry desert or the casualty of a war waged along the border[…]. Dehumanizing metaphors constituted Zavisca's third category. Here migrants were depicted as animals, something hunted, the persecuted prey of smugglers, law enforcement agents, and militant vigilantes. 'Lured' to the border by the prospect of well-paying jobs, migrants engage Border Patrol 'trackers' in a 'cat-and-mouse' game with deadly consequences. "A related metaphor," writes Zavisca, "depicts enforcement agents as humane shepherds tending to a flock." This allusion "reinforces the humanity of the Border Patrol as 'saviors.'" An associated livestock metaphor, widespread in Mexico, casts migrants as chickens and smugglers as chicken ranchers – pollos at the mercy of their polleros. (Cantú 2018: 109–10)

The Mexican chicken is a rather unusual metaphor for migrants, suggesting confusion and a lack of power and determination. In the history of animal metaphors used for migrants these tend to be described more in terms of their perception as trespassers, as criminals and as parasites. As a metaphor the purportedly vagrant and marauding wolf is intimately connected to this representation of human exile, migration as an act of trespassing, criminal behaviour and human qualities such as aggression, greed and violence. It seems that the time-worn human fear of wolves, of their purported hunger, greed and cunning, metaphorically of a trespasser and predator attacking the nation's very own body, offers itself as a suitable image to reflect fears of foreigners invading our nation state fortresses.

In areas where wolves have been stigmatized for centuries, if not millennia, especially in Central Europe with the bad reputation they have received in particular since the Grimm Brothers and where they have now reappeared coinciding with the arrival of large numbers of migrants, the political rhetoric likening migrants to trespassing wolves has been on the rise. As wolf debates loom large in the United States and Central Europe, with wolves entering new territories that had so far been wolf-free, this metaphor too has experienced increased media coverage in the context of fears relating to immigration and terrorism, from headlines, as we have seen, such as 'Donald Trump Supporters Tell Immigrants "The Wolves Are Coming, You Are the Hunted" as Race Hate Fears Rise' (Adam Lusher, *The Independent*, 9 Nov 2016) to the persistent use of the wolf metaphor in the context of Islamist terror: 'We Must Track and Trap Lone Wolf Terrorists' (Micah Halpern, *The Observer*, 25 Nov 2014).

While the wolf mostly stands for aggressive intrusion from outsiders as well as a home-grown metaphor for resistance to such intruders, its medieval association with the moral uncleanness of the outlaw who infects the community has shifted to related metaphors of parasitism. As for the rhetoric on borders and immigration in the UK, for example, Andreas Musolff points out in a study on media sources in that country – in press, online forums and blogs – that metaphors of parasitism loom large. As one of the categories of metaphors for immigrants Musolff identifies the 'scrounger', who 'sucks, bleeds and drains the country dry, aims for freebies and lives off or sponges from Britain, thus exploiting it as a treasure island. Its references to immigrants range from relatively moderate depictions as welfare tourists to their dehumanizing stigmatization as leeches, bloodsuckers and other parasites' (Musolff 2015: 46–7).

Such fears of the nation being sucked dry to its ultimate demise are nothing new, whether in political rhetoric or literature as a reflection of the phobias of an era. National Socialism already labelled Jews as parasites thriving on the substance of other nations and as vampires draining Germany of its life blood (Bernatzky 1991: 393), and Victorian England's fear of being invaded and vampirically drained by foreigners is nowhere better described than in Bram Stoker's *Dracula*, as we have seen in Chapter 2. Dracula as wolf man, bat man and bloodsucking vampire surreptitiously entering England in Whitby – traditional territory of Viking invasions – offers new readings in light of UK immigration paranoia and Brexit as does a more recent text, one in which the wolf becomes a key metaphor in the context of British identity and isolationism.

First and last wolves in contemporary European novels

That national borders are demarcation lines in which environmental politics and the politics of migration are inextricably intertwined has recently been documented in reports on border fences aimed at refugees but also threatening migratory animals. When in 2015 Hungary closed its border to refugees from Africa and the Middle East, Slovenia promptly erected a razor-wire security fence along its 400-odd-mile border with Croatia, 'giving little if any consideration of the environmental impacts on the wildlife' (O'Donnell 2016). It affects mostly deer but also bears, wolves and lynx, a scenario that is not limited to Europe. O'Donnell goes on to explain that 'the fence along the U.S.-Mexico border blocks 16 key species from about 75 percent of their habitat. The U.S. Fish and Wildlife Service has said that a fence proposed by [...] Donald Trump would impact 111 endangered species and 108 migratory birds.'

In Sarah Hall's novel *Wolf Border* (2015), which expresses national anxieties when it comes to wolves entering the UK, this connection between environmental politics, borders and migrants is a central topic. It is the story of Rachel Caine who returns from Idaho, where she has studied the local wolves, to her native Cumbria, where she is put in charge of reintroducing the animal to the vast estate of the ecologically minded Earl of Annerdale. As the first (completely fictional) attempt after hundreds of years of rewilding the cultural landscape of England with a set of wolves imported from Romania – of all places, classical wolf country in literature and in the context of negatively perceived migration if we think of Stoker's famous novel – this project is described as being of key significance to British identity. On a metafictional level it parallels the impact the reintroduction of wolves has in Idaho on the indigenous population whose cultural self-understanding is inextricably interwoven with the presence of wolves in that area (covered in depth in Chapter 7 of this book). But like in Idaho, where 'it's not a good time to be a wolf' (WB 32), the presence of wolves in England causes a great deal of tension. In spite of its lakes and fells, Cumbria is a cultural landscape, 'a kempt place, cultivated [...] [while] true wilderness lay elsewhere' (WB 29), and the idea of a full reintroduction is deemed utopian rather than realistic: 'In thirty years maybe, and not in England [...]. This country isn't ready for an apex predator yet' (WB 146).

In Hall's novel, too, the wolves are an intensely complex metaphor. The so-called wolf border, the title of the book, refers to the boundaries between several paradigms: between myth and fact ('Sometimes a country just needs to be presented with the fact of an animal, not its myth' [WB 35]), between medieval wilderness and the great British Empire with its vast colonial extensions, between nature and culture, between wilderness and the city, the border between the less tamed landscape of Scotland and the garden landscape of its southern neighbour, the rift between the defenders and the opponents of the rewilding project. Rachel 'would like to believe there will be a place again where the street lights end and wilderness begins' (WB 234), yet like in many other parts of the world where wolves reappear the Cumbrian farmers are worried about their livestock, and parents about their children. By many their reintroduction is perceived as invasion, as foreign intrusion, paralleling isolationist views of the immigration of people from the former colonies as the empire is striking back.

Their reintroduction 'is historic, [Rachel] thinks. It's five hundred years since their extermination on the island. They are a distant memory, a mythical thing. Britain has altered radically, as has her iconography of wilderness, her totems. Once *in situ*, she knows, they will divide the country, just as they will quarter the imagination again' (WB 146). As the wolves emerge from the depths of myth to reality they become a catalyst for the crisis of identity of a crumbling island nation whose last vestiges of empire threaten to break away. 'They will divide the country' (WB 146), Rachel argues. And while they could mark a new beginning for the nation as it is being rewilded, by that very quality they also signify the end of empire, a vision of returning to pre-imperial medieval times before their extermination by King Edward I – Britain's return to an unfettered wilderness, the wolves' centuries-old 'unbelonging reversed. Nothing of history will matter to them: land is land' (WB 248).

Although they officially 'immigrate' to England, where after an initial period of quarantine they are eventually released to the Lake District, the wolves have a particular relationship with Scotland. Their migration across the border into Scotland as the more suited environment for them reflects a series of human qualities these animals are once again associated with, such as wildness, ferocity, rebelliousness and independence from the social contract. That social contract has since the Act of Union in 1707 been a colonial one, interestingly only a few years after the last Scottish wolf was killed: 'Perthshire, 1680: the date of the last reported wolf killed in the old kingdom' (WB 248). The alleged freedom of wolves here stands for the Scottish thrust for independence from the UK, the defenders of rewilding even heralding the animal's role in creating a national icon: 'I wouldn't be surprised if the wolf ends up on the Scottish flag' (WB 248).

The metaphor, however, transcends the notion of wilderness, political freedom and rebelliousness against empire, and also refers to social strata. While the wolves signify Scottish independence from a class that had once colonized Scotland, it is that class also that is associated with the purported 'nobility' of the wolf, an apex predator as the private toy and joy of the 'apex class, the financial raiders in charge' (WB 152). Derrida's sovereign as wolf comes to mind in the association of the Earl of Annerdale with his wolves, the territory they are being given identical with the territory owned by the Earl. These wolves' freedom is indeed ambivalent. They are free to roam in a landscape that conveys the semblance of a borderless, classless, non-national wilderness, while at the same time their habitat is closely linked to the land ownership of one of the wealthiest members of society. They are thus part of the hierarchy that constitutes the imperial polity of Britain, while paradoxically also representing a possibility for those colonized by that class to break away from Britain. At the same time, the anti-wolf league consisting of the lower and middle classes is adamantly opposed to rewilding Britain with this 'noble' animal, as opposed to it as to the idea of porous borders open to immigration from abroad.

Sarah Hall's novel is part of a range of texts that have recently been published in the UK expressing profound concerns about the state of nature in British isles tied to the desire to rediscover British identity through its landscapes and hidden wildernesses. The possibility of rewilding Britain, which has largely been destroyed through monocultures, is part and parcel of this search for a new identity, without, however, letting go of its deeper roots tied to ancient lands. We can observe this trend in Robert Macfarlane's books *The Wild Places* (2007), *The Old Ways: A Journey on Foot* (2012), *Landmarks* (2015), *The Lost Words* (2017), in Paul Readman's *Storied Ground: Landscape and the Shaping of English Identity* (2018) or George Monbiot's *Feral: Rewilding the Land, Sea and Human Life* (2013). Monbiot laments the fact that nature in the UK has been largely destroyed by sheep grazing, while advocating the idea of rewilding, that is, letting nature run its own course after introducing more biodiversity. Unlike Hall's fictional view of a rewilding by wolves at the hands of landowners and the aristocracy, however, he argues that those few in the UK who own most of the land would, together with the farmers, be adamantly opposed to the idea of rewilding, especially when it comes to top predators such as wolves. As we shall see in the discussion of Robert Winder's *The Last Wolf: The Hidden Springs of Englishness* (2017) in Chapter 7, when it comes to the presence of wolves in Britain little may have changed since the Middle Ages.

The associative link in Sarah Hall's novel between the rewilding of a cultural landscape such as that of England and current nationalist politics has as a more extreme version recently been made by some voices on the far right. The Danish People's Party, for example, in line with their proposal to isolate unwanted migrants was recently trying to outlaw 'burqas and wolves' (Nors), urging the Danish government to fortify the southern border with Germany and blaming the EU for the presence of immigrants and wolves, as the debates surrounding a recent appearance of one wolf in Denmark reflected. In Germany, too, right-wing groups – AfD (Alternative für Deutschland) politicians and their followers – show predictably similar reactions to Islamization in the context of wolves on German soil. In his blog bürgerstimme.com of May 2015 Marko Wild has claimed that

> the wolf and foreigner are both unreformable robbers. The wolf belongs to the zoological order of predators. The so-called 'refugees' steal Germany's social systems. They are asylum swindlers, depriving the Germans of their peace, their property, living space, health, security or even life itself. The wolf and the refugee generally go for the weakest, most defenceless member of society. […] The craft of refugees has a lot to do with professionalized robbery. Where the numbers of refugees are high the quota of burglaries is also very high. (Wild 2015)

In view of such statements, the need of sanctuaries for wolves and immigrants, of a shared space in which multiculturalism and ecological diversity can thrive is a contemporary issue of urgency. There are lessons to be learned about the rights of others from animal sanctuaries such as the Wolf Science Centre in Ernstbrunn near Vienna, or, indeed, from contemporary literary texts such as László Krasnahorkai's one-sentence novella *The Last Wolf* (2015) and Roland Schimmelpfennig's novel *One Clear, Ice-Cold January Morning at the Beginning of the Twenty-Frist Century* (2016), both written in reaction to the heated debates surrounding the presence of wolves and their impact on ecology, immigration and culture.

Unlike Sarah Hall's vision of hope for wolves and humanity Krasznahorkai's story about the last wolves of Extremadura is extremely sinister and alerts us to planetary decline. The wolves here are on the brink of extermination in an impoverished part of Spain, a landscape reflecting the abysses of the human soul. Like in Hall's novel, however, they are also a border phenomenon as they metaphorically bridge Berlin with Extremadura and Extremadura with the world outside. Berlin's cultural diversity is contrasted with the monoculture of a forgotten region where tensions are ripe among locals and Arab immigrants, and the ecology is threatened by the rapid disappearance of wolves. In a half-drunken stupor the narrator tells a barman in Berlin of his assignment to travel to this distant part of Spain to report on the plight of last wolves, how he met the warden José Miguel who then told him about the *lobero*, the wolf hunter who tracked down the last pack but managed to kill only seven out of nine animals, leaving alive a young male and pregnant female, the hope of a future for wolves in Extremadura. Too slow, however, to cross the road the pregnant female is run over by a truck so that only one wolf is left in Extremadura. And he vanishes completely.

The story contains little in the way of optimism or hope, and yet it is interesting to us primarily for its contextualization of wolves with the concept of territory and porous, moving borders. While forming a vanishing presence in Extremadura, whose very own name implies extraterritoriality, these wolves are, due to the narrative situation, also omnipresent in Berlin where their vanishing presence casts a ghost-like shadow. Like the Arab immigrants mentioned several times with whom they are closely associated, the wolves instil fear and prejudice in the local population. It is a historical fear of course grounded in Spain's colonization by the Arabic world, so that the wolves become an orientalizing allegory, a species breaking into Extremadura from the world outside. Although tension with the Arabic *Gastarbeiter* (guest workers) has developed in Andalusia to the southeast of Extremadura, there is the danger of it spreading in similarity to the way in which wolves keep crossing boundaries, challenging the territorialism of other populations. Being from Kreuzberg the Berlin barman is well aware of the phenomenon of *Gastarbeiter*, the issues of ethnic divides and immigration thus waxing borderless in this novel, in addition to being strangely tied to ecological concerns, as these Arabs on Spanish turf are mentioned in a journal on ecology that contextualizes them with the last wolf killed south of the River Duero in 1983 (LK 22). The collapse of the fragile ecosystem through the wolves' gradual disappearance coincides with the arrival of an altogether different culture into Extremadura, the sort of post-species phenomena that the anthropologist Marc Augé once identified as non-places, a world full of highways and ugly shopping malls. Globalization has thus reached Extremadura as the world of the wolf has disappeared, and it turns out, the narrator assures us, that while obsessed with the possible danger of wolves and superstitions about their unbelonging, nobody in Extremadura had actually been aware of the real dangers 'presented by the proximity of the world' (LK 34).

Krasznahorkai's story is a sad tale of the end of a species in a forgotten part of Europe, a metaphor for the hatred and superstitions of local people towards what is perceived as the trespassing outsider, whether human or non-human animal. In his typically absurd style somewhat reminiscent of Kafka the Hungarian author demonstrates what happens to an area that loses its biodiversity alongside with its own cultural identity and all hope for cultural diversity. As Extremadura is slowly becoming industrialized it contrasts somewhat with Berlin, likewise described as a bleak place, and yet one in which cultural diversity is the norm, 'a mixed neighbourhood, or rather a neighbourhood that was preponderantly Turkish, but not entirely Turkish, the few bars serving alcohol at that time being crowded with Germans, Poles, Russians, Serbs, Romanians, Vietnamese, and God knows who else' (LK 47). In the end, the last wolf in its obliviousness to all borders is perhaps more present in the drab Berlin bar than it ever is in Extremadura.

Unlike this ghost-like presence of wolves in a Berlin bar, in Robert Schimmelpfennig's *One Clear, Ice-Cold January Morning at the Beginning of the Twenty-Frist Century* (2016) a real wolf is sighted one day approaching the German capital. The characters of the novel quickly agree that 'a wolf in the city or near the city was dangerous' (RS 66), a statement that may remind us of the medieval *vargr i veum*, the maligned wolf who threatens to break into the sanctuary. The vagrant creature in this conglomerate of small episodes, overlapping snippets from people's lives, has a similar function of bridging borders as in Krasnahorkai's and Hall's texts. This solitary wolf physically moves between Poland and Germany, inside and outside of the city, between what used to be East and West Berlin, between individual lives and ethnic groups. As such a border crosser who awakens old folktale fears among the Berliners he is a catalyst for each character's own life, their crisis situations, their personal losses and decisions. He is also a sort of multicultural wolf that looms in most scenes, expressive of the characters' fears, their xenophobia and neuroses (cf. Mika Provata Carlone), an animal that unites Germans, Turks, Poles, a Chilean and many more in their existential angst. He is a wolf on the threshold, a position he has held over time in myth and science, trotting along seemingly aimlessly but generally in a northwesterly direction, facing and gazing at various characters, some of whom are hell-bent on killing him. When one of these elusive, merely faintly sketched-in characters, a young man named Charly, finally shoots at him the wolf loses his paw but keeps on migrating on three legs. He is sighted one more time, in bad shape and hiding in the labyrinth of Berlin's train track and tunnel system, and then 'the wolf had vanished' (RS 233). With his spectral exit the novel ends.

Schimmelpfennig positions his wolf between myth and reality. While the novel intertextually plays with the German folktale tradition – there are faint echoes of *Hänsel and Gretel*, *The Wolf and the Seven Kids* and *Little Red Riding Hood* – the wolf also faces the harsh reality of having to navigate through a hostile cultural landscape consisting of an endless web of motorways ('A wolf in the traffic jam', RS 21) and a city landscape that although known for tolerating all sorts of wildlife from foxes to wild boars feels extremely uncomfortable about having a wolf on its doorstep. The Berliners' reactions reflect very real contemporary anxieties about the presence of wolves in Germany fed by myth and the folktale tradition. One of these tales alluded to is that of *The Three Pigs* included by Joseph Jacobs in his *English Fairy Tales* (1890): 'The children had asked if the wolf could come to their house. No, he'd said, the house is made of stone. [...] He thought of houses made of straw and houses made of wood and houses made of stone' (RS 48). In the folktale the wolf finally tries to enter the brick house of the cleverest little pig but gets his hide singed in a cauldron of hot water. The detail, however, is significant, as it identifies the wolf as the kind of threshold figure that is typical for the folktale tradition, the wolf at the door of Little Red Riding Hood's grandmother or in the chimney, in both cases between nature and culture. Schimmelpfennig is playful with such details as he is with Kennedy's famous words 'Ich bin ein Berliner', which he ironically applies to his wolf: 'This wolf is a Berliner' (RS 203).

In spite of the irony, his novel contains a great deal of sadness about the plight of the wolf, who throughout his precarious journey stirs the murderous fantasies of various characters. He seems doomed from the start having come in from the East – even a Polish immigrant is at one point believed to have brought him in – and travelling through places like the 'no-man's land [...] where the wall and the death strip once were' and where now in reminiscence of GDR border forces shooting their own country's refugees 'armed police with dogs combed the area, thereby unwittingly driving the wolf eastwards' (RS 91). As an animal that unites various cultures through their shared fear of the beast he points to multiculturalism in a state of crisis. Kennedy's great invocation of Berlin's freedom fails as the wolf prompts reactions among its observers ranging from the media's vilification and speculation as to whether he has rabies to the public's increasing obsessiveness over his threatening presence. The aggression and xenophobia the wolf inspires are possibly most evident in Charly's quest that fills a large part of the loose plot. He dreams about killing the wolf, feeling humiliated by its stare (RS 94–5), that trans-species stare that for a moment strips him of his humanity and becomes as unforgettable to him as the famous gaze of Derrida's cat once did to the French philosopher. In Peter and the Wolf fashion Charly sets out to kill the wolf, and it is this hunt that I would argue becomes indicative of the crisis of multiculturalism inscribed into this text, based on the xenophobic aggression and violence triggered by the gaze of the Other. In Schimmelpfennig's somewhat sinister and pessimistic novel that gaze does not set the Berliners free but it imprisons them within their stifling personal boundaries.

The three novels by Hall, Krasznahorkai and Schimmelpfennig constitute a new type of text in contemporary European literature in which border-crossing wolves feature as catalysts in the discourse on migration and biological and cultural diversity. In all three texts the wolf is a metaphor that blurs the borders and makes them ebb and flow. And yet, the animal occupies a different position in each narrative. We have seen that Sarah Hall's optimistic vision of an entrenched world full of class hierarchies and anti-Europe, anti-trespassing sentiment quickly fading in view of the economically beneficial and environmentally curative results of wolf conservation and protection is a far howl from Krasznahorkai's and Schimmelpfenning's sad end of first and last wolves. This difference notwithstanding, these are timely narratives in an age in which multiculturalism continues to be in crisis and the global ecology is more threatened than ever before. All three authors look beyond national space at the idea of shared space, shared between cultures and species, and yet such shared territory for which migrating wolves have become a metaphor is as fragile as the lives of these animals.

Cormac McCarthy's she-wolf in The Crossing

Going beyond Europe we hear similar voices in North America where the discourse on immigration both in politics and in literature draws on the wolf metaphor. Along the US–Mexican border *el lobo* is only one of a series of metaphors that describe human traffickers, others are 'coyote' and *el pollero*, the chicken farmer. These are human smugglers who take women and especially children across the border, a business that has been taken over by the Mexican Cartels and is, as one can imagine, extremely risky.

> Some may never make it across the U.S. border or face violence when they finally arrive at their drop houses. Wolves are being taken over by the Cartels because they have better communication devices and transportation as well as relationships with corrupt Border Patrol officers. They are able to smuggle humans and drugs simultaneously. With the rising instance of the Cartels intervening on good Lobos, kidnapping and deaths are on the rise. Although having a guide greatly increases the chances of survival, now that the Cartels have taken over the business, people from Central America could be better off getting a visa and going through the legal immigration process. (Gallagher 2014)

The wolf and coyote metaphors point to a purported slyness of these animals, their knowledge of the terrain, but also their complete disregard for international borders. As long as there is no wall or fence to stop them they will cross, and there has been many a time when even a fence could not stop these animals from crossing the border, although as Jim O'Donnell has shown fences that are aimed at refugees are often threatening migratory animals as well.

Although animals crossing international borders are rarely in the news, in artistic representations of these borders the animals' journeys can feature as allegories for human journeys. One American novel in which this is the case and where the wolf metaphor is used very differently from the way the Mexican Cartels use it is Cormac McCarthy's *The Crossing* (1994). That McCarthy's she-wolf is an allegory for free migration in a landscape divided by one of the toughest international borders on the planet goes to show that the wolf metaphor, in spite of never really escaping its mythification, can have nurturing qualities in representations of the grim reality that exists in this area. She seems to be far more than just a wolf, a mythical being rather who represents some kind of world order:

> He said that 'the wolf is a being of great order and that it knows what men do not. […] The wolf is like the copo de nieve. Snowflake.' […] 'Escuchame, joven. […] The wolf is made the way the world is made. You cannot touch the world.' (MC 45-6)

As such a mythical creature she comes to embody a balance between all species sharing this planet, and her back-and-forth journey can be read as signalling a mission for the ideal of world peace. In the end, however, in McCarthy too that mission fails.

When sixteen-year-old Billy Parham traps the errant pregnant wolf near his home in New Mexico he decides to take her back to Mexico from where she has entered the United States. By returning her, Billy is himself trespassing onto foreign ground and is being accused by various locals of treating Mexico as if it were a dumping ground for wild animals. This first out of three journeys into Mexico ends with the wolf's death after having to fight several packs of dogs the locals pit her against, with Billy ending up having to shoot her. Alienated and disillusioned he returns to his home in New Mexico where he finds his parents murdered. The only family tie left to him is his younger brother Boyd with whom he then sets out on his second journey to Mexico to find their parents' murderers and retrieve the horses they have stolen. After Boyd is shot through the chest and nursed back to health he disappears with a local girl. Billy returns once again to the United States, now at war with Germany. He wants to join the army but fails to be recruited because of a heart murmur. Failing to fit in, he runs away to Mexico for the third time, where he learns of his brother's death. He exhumes his remains and returns them to their home soil across the border.

McCarthy's she-wolf is a metaphor at multiple levels, expressive of violence between humans and animals, for inequality between different social and ethnic groups, the inequality of a region spreading into two countries known for its harshness and potential for violence, and for the boy himself. She becomes a catalyst for Billy's development over his three journeys to Mexico, his increasing loneliness and loss of a place in the world. McCarthy in his unique kind of *Anti-Bildungsroman* thus explores the premature disillusionment of a young man who has not even come of age – by way of a series of episodes highlighting man's cruelty towards creatures, human and animal alike.

The Crossing deserves renewed attention in light of the politics of (im)migration, especially of undocumented individuals. The wolf is a border phenomenon, a border crosser and oblivious to borders – the border in a political, personal and metaphysical sense. It is the border that blurs and disappears, between species and regions, between youth and adulthood, between life and death, the dead being ever present during the journeys of the living. In crossing the US–Mexican border several times the wolf straddles several binaries: the two countries and their socio-economic differences, colonization versus indigeneity and the gender binary: femininity in a region known for its male cruelty – no country for old men or women. Moreover, she bridges abstract binaries such as myth versus culture, community versus loneliness, home and its loss, the protagonist's wanderings through nation states striated by fences and other boundaries, encroaching upon the wide open spaces of nomads and the indigenous. Ultimately, her own lonely wanderings reflect the deep loneliness experienced by Billy Parham.

To ranchers on both sides of the border and those trying to establish law and order in a country perceived as lawless she is nothing but the usual pest. Their hatred of wolves (*lycophobia*), however, clashes with the deeper understanding and respect (*lycophilia*) for this creature held by several of McCarthy's typical spectral characters – indigenous people, nomads, Gypsies and other travellers on the margins of society.

The early colonists of North America viewed the wolf as a metaphor for the frontier between a purportedly civilized European world and the unknown wilderness populated by 'savages', a frontier that in the minds of populists and neo-colonists seems to have shifted to the divide between the so-called North and the South. The wanderings of McCarthy's wolf reveal the continuity of such colonial power structures at the seam of North or South, and Europeanness and indigeneity, especially between the Mexican descendants of the *conquistadores* in the state of Sonora and the local native tribe of the Yaqui, whose bloody history of oppression (cf. Folsom 2014) reflects the wolf's own long history of persecution. Those owning the land and holding the reins of power tend to see the wolf, indigenous people, those 'last free remnants [...] like shadowfolk of the nation' (MC 104) and itinerants in the same light. They see her crossing the international boundary and agrarian land as acts of trespassing.

While in Texas and New Mexico, where agrarian culture has even more intensely displaced wilderness and forced it into domestication, the she-wolf is even more out-of-place than in her native Mexico, her wanderings have a strange metaphorical significance for Mexico as a whole. The country's reputation in the United States is described as that of wild wolf country, a place of exile also for outlaws escaping persecution north of the border: 'There ain't no law in Mexico. It's just a pack of rogues' (MC 176). These rogues also refer to McCarthy's Mexico in the throes of neo-colonial structures revealing what Homi Bhabha has described as mimicry (Bhabha 1994: 85–92). While sentient of the colonizing pressures of the United States, Mexico also colonizes its own indigenous populations within, as the dominant culture sees itself contaminated by the linguistic and racial differences of the native self. The wolf as a reflection of indigeneity embodies this threat to those in power in Mexico, who are torn between being colonized by the United States and their mimicry of US culture. This tension between Mexico's image as outlaw terrain and its mimicry of US-style law and order is thrown into stark relief by the wolf's return to Mexican soil.

She symbolically divides Mexican society, a rift also revealed in the so-called *corridos*, the Mexican ballads. They are a reflection of Billy's and the wolf's wandering through the desert landscape, tied to his heroic journeys forever under threat of losing themselves. As the songlines running through Mexico the *corridos* are as divisive as they are unifying, separating the rich from the poor and uniting the latter against those in power. As 'the ballad of the country side that mythologizes the deep economic divide and political struggle between rich and poor in Mexico' the corrido, according to Vince Brewton, links 'Billy Parham's quest to find his brother and bring him home [...] with the larger narrative of class struggle and national identity in Mexico' (Brewton 2004: 137). The corridos indict the American government as an ally to Mexico's rich and powerful in this class struggle. But to a large extent, they embody also what is still untamed about Mexico, as does the wolf. Travelling between the powerful and the oppressed, between dominant European culture and indigenous culture, she is seen as forever threatening dominant power and its domesticizing mission. We see this reflected in some of the characters' reactions to her migrations, for example, the rancher's view that the wolves brutalize 'the cattle in a way they did not the wild game. As if the cows evoked in them some anger. As if they were offended by some violation of an old order. Old ceremonies. Old protocols' (MC 25), or in various Mexicans' subconscious denial of the wolf's true nature, reducing her to a dog: 'He looked at the wolf. 'Es buena cazadora su perra?' (MC 75). In both cases wilderness clashes with domestication, outlawry with law and order, a boundary that runs deep across McCarthy's relentless landscape on both sides of the international border, a land 'undifferentiated in its terrain [...] wholly alien and wholly strange' (MC 74).

McCarthy distinguishes between those who show no sympathy for the wolf and those who identify with her migratory and homeless nature. Her time-worn position of outlaw culminates in her Sisyphean fight against a consistently renewable pack of dogs, a fight to the death between her own untamed nature and the forces of domesticity, reflecting her position of *lupus sacer*. Repeatedly, McCarthy seems to wonder where the real Mexican wolves are, in the stereotypical, superstitious sense of the metaphor. It is those who suppress nature and indigeneity: the colonizers and their sovereign power. Their bond with the she-wolf is as intimate as Billy Parham's, but in a different way. While Billy Parham identifies with the wolf as *lupus sacer*, those with sovereign power are at its opposite end but tied to it through lawlessness. As we have seen, in being expelled to a life outside of communal law the *homo sacer* is uniquely tied to the sovereign whose power to abandon individuals equally positions him outside of the law. Sovereignty is inextricably linked to abjection, a fact Derrida emphasizes in his lecture series *Séminaire: La bête et le souverain* (*The Beast & the Sovereign*), equating the sovereign above the law with the wolf. *El lobo es una cosa incogniscible* (MC 46) and, yet in the end, when Billy Parham watches her die she stands in for the forces of inequality, violence and injustice in the world's power systems – Mexico as a *pars pro toto* for the world at large.

In such a hostile world Billy and the wolf form a symbiosis that is primarily defined through their shared migration. One of the differences, however, between human wandering and animal wandering is that humans need to travel with some kind of ID in order to cross international boundaries. Without it they are classified as undocumented migrants, the position Billy finds himself in as he enters Mexico:

> 'De donde viene?' he said.
> 'America.'
> He nodded. He looked out across the river. He leaned and spat. 'Sus documentos,' he said.
> 'Documentos?'
> 'Si. Documentos.'
> 'No tengo ningunos documentos.'
> The man watched him for a while.
> 'Que es su nombre,' he said.
> 'Billy Parham' ....
> 'Pasaporte?'
> 'Nada.' (MC 95)

This scene in particular approximates the novel with the current debates about undocumented immigrants. What is different, however, is the direction of travel. While the debate is generally about undocumented

Mexicans entering the United States, here a US citizen illegally enters Mexico, and with a wolf in tow at that. American literature and film have often romanticized the escape across the border into Mexico, in the popular imagination a land of unfettered freedom and a sanctuary for all kinds of outlaws. McCarthy plays with this myth, but quickly also debunks it by pointing out that trespassing is an act that affects crossing the border in both directions:

> 'You think that this country is some country you can come here and do what you like.' 'I never thought that. I never thought about this country one way or another. [...] We was just passin through, the boy said. We wasn't botherin nobody. Queríamos pasar. No más.' 'Pasar or traspasar?' The boy turned and spat into the dirt. He could feel the wolf lean against his leg. He said that the tracks of the wolf had led out of Mexico. He said the wolf knew nothing of boundaries. (MC 119)

Both Billy and the wolf are trespassing, but they share a great deal more than that. She is a creature that finds no place in this world, her loneliness reflecting that of the boy and his Lycaon-like journey into wilderness, exile and deracination in the 'silent fields' (Ovid 2004: 13). And she may know nothing of boundaries, but she crosses them all the time. One divide she straddles is that between the two genders. As a mythical of the nurturing she-wolf she stands in sharp contrast to the violent male world. Metaphorically she represents the archetypal Mexican mother, 'this old woman of Mexico, her sons long dead in that blood and violence which her prayers and her prostrations seemed powerless to appease. Her frail form was a constant in that land, her silent anguishings' (MC 390).

Billy stands between both, the wolf as nurturer – 'He tried to see the world the wolf saw' (MC 51) – and the harsh male destructive world he comes from, which sees her as vermin. The nurturing side of the pregnant wolf is that element that has gone missing in Billy's life, orphaned and thrust into the world as lone wolf. 'He told the boy that although he was huérfano still he must cease his wanderings and make for himself some place in the world because to wander in this way would become for him a passion and by this passion he would become estranged from men and so ultimately from himself' (MC 134).

He is the classical *homo sacer* as lone wolf, located outside the community of men, as well as outside his national community, which has no place for him in its army but looks upon his wolfish freedom with traditional feelings of hatred and reverence: 'Ragged, dirty, hungry in eye and belly. Totally unspoken for. In that outlandish figure they beheld what they envied most and what they most reviled. If their hearts went out to him it was yet true that for very small cause they might also have killed him' (MC 170). In this ambivalence of reverence and hate lies his identity as a 'lone wolf' and true inner bond with the she-wolf.

In the end, McCarthy's wolf embodies the idea of levelling all differences, of straddling all boundaries. Her dismal end, however, depletes the book of any hope for the end of social violence. She is being killed by dogs, an interesting detail, as the wolf representing wilderness and freedom from all boundaries is getting killed by an animal standing in for the idea of domestication. Ownership of land, human territorialism, conquest and colonialism are the forces she is pitted against. As she is being crushed by them so is her human double Billy Parham, whose inability to fit into the domesticated world reaches its climax in a finale so typical of McCarthy, filled with despair, disillusionment and the destruction of youth. His final reluctance to help a dying dog, that creature expressing *par excellence* the success of domestication, reflects Billy's regression rather than progress in this coming-of-age story, much in contrast with his initial eagerness to help the wolf.

Although alive, and holding new life inside herself, the wolf embodies death. Her presence and wandering point to the oppressed strata of Mexican society, to all those undocumented migrants traversing, like the mythical Lycaon, the fields of *lethe*, of concealment, forgetting, death. On a deeply personal level she also points to a symbolic bond with the brother whose remains Billy Parham brings home, as her death in Mexico is followed by Boyd's. The wolf is that shadow creature, condemned by humanity to the night side of life, the shadow of Boyd and ultimately of Billy. But while Boyd dies physically, Billy dies spiritually. His final reaction to the dog seeking help from him reflects this death of his spirit, and as once again the 'godmade sun' rises over the American South West there seems to exist no more difference in the struggles and plights of all creatures, as 'for all and without distinction' (MC 426) death, that great equalizer, reigns supreme.

Brother Wolf in Francisco Cantú's The Line Becomes a River

To live in the city of El Paso in those days was to hover at the edge of a crushing cruelty, to safely fill the lungs with air steeped in horror. As I ran and drove through the city, oscillating from work to home, the insecurity of Juárez drifted through the air like the memory of a shattering dream […]. This narrative, of a city fractured by its looming border, saddled with broken institutions and a terrorized populace, had become part and parcel of its legacy, the subconscious inheritance of all those who came within the city's orbit. To comfortably exist at its periphery, I found myself suspending knowledge and concern about what happened there, just as one sets aside images from a nightmare in order to move steadily through the new day. (Cantú 2018: 130-1)

This area with its twin cities is possibly one of the most prominent examples for the precarity of contemporary cities with a large intake of migrants. Francisco Cantú's memoir *The Line Becomes a River* (2018) is the account of the experiences of the author, a third-generation Mexican American, during his four years as a border patrol agent and the horrors he encounters faced by the border crossers. In many ways, the text is reminiscent of McCarthy, in its muscular prose that includes untranslated Spanish passages and dialogues, but also in the appearance of the wolf as a border phenomenon. When it comes to the US-Mexican border the wolf is not the only metaphor in the context of migration. The 'mule' and 'coyote' are two others, mules being those whose migration is facilitated by guides from the Cartel and coyotes, in exchange for their willingness to transport drugs across the border. These metaphors are all border phenomena, the wolf in particular in his ambivalence between the *homo sacer* and the sovereign, in this case between the migrant refugees for whom he stands as much as the violence emanating from the Cartel and from various US forces defending the border against undocumented aliens.

It is a wolf of migration, of death and of wisdom whom the narrator, reminiscent of Freud's wolf man, encounters several times in his dreams, a wolf who embodies the author's demons that visit him at night but who also teaches him about his own identity in relation to the border and immigration, and how to come to terms with his own past. Largely a psychoanalytical paradigm the wolf is a blend of the Jungian shadow, the legend of the wolf of Gubbio and the wolf of Native American cultures. There is a close synergy between the Ojibwe or Pawnee tribes and wolves, not only in view of their myths but also in their understanding of shared experience of social life, hunting and suffering under the yoke of the colonizers. In her multi-voice novel *The Painted Drum* Louise Erdrich puts it like this:

> I spoke to the wolf, asking my own question: Wolf, I said, your people are hunted from the air and poisoned from the earth and killed on sight and you are outbred and stuffed in cages and almost wiped out. How is it that you go on living with such sorrow? How do you go on without turning around and destroying yourselves, as so many of us Anishinaabeg have done under similar circumstances? (Erdrich 2019: 120)

Like the character in Erdrich's novel, Cantú also faces the wolf of his own past – 'something is being communicated' (C 13) by this wolf – and his experiences with the violence riddling the landscape around him: 'I dreamed of a cave littered with body parts, a landscape devoid of color and light. I saw a wolf circling in the darkness and felt its paws heavy on my chest, its breath hot on my face' (C 117). Drawing on Jungian paradigms he identifies the wolf with the shadow in need of being integrated in his personality to avoid repression. In order to begin a true reckoning with our inner situation, 'we have to expose ourselves to the animal impulses of the unconscious without identifying with them and without running away.' (C 165) Jung, who was acutely aware of the psychological damage of borders, the Iron Curtain during the Cold War in particular, stresses the human inclination to condemn the other as devil rather than looking at individual life within, urging 'us to recognize the selfsame nature of the other.' (C 163) The wolf, however, keeps haunting the author over time and makes him understand that he cannot really split off his totem animal from himself, for if he did, 'the urge of what had been split off to unite with you becomes all the stronger (C 165); [...] maybe you wish to be rid of it, to wash yourself of it.' (C 231) But surely, we learn, that is the wrong way to face the wolf.

The wolf, thus the message goes, has to become a 'Brother Wolf'. The Jungian message of personality integration – what Nietzsche before him had discussed in *The Birth of Tragedy* as the integration of Dionysian impulses in the *principium individuationis* – replicates indigenous philosophy of terrestrial harmony and the religious teleology of the legend of St Francis of Assisi who tames the wolf of Gubbio, and by bringing him from the wilderness with its perpetual state of war into the city tames the human shadow. Here too, we recognize the time-worn binary of the wolf and the city, the *vargr i veum* who breaks into the city as a sanctuary. The legend illuminates this binary, as the citizens of Gubbio fear him and 'dare[d] not go beyond the city walls' (C 81). The city and its inherent peace are dissolved as the wolf enters it and carries with him the state of nature as state of war, identified by Deleuze and Guattari as the war machine extraneous to the *polis* or state (Deleuze/Guattari

1987: 351). The migrant is treated as wolf, seen as bringing the state of war into the *polis* as fortified nation state, hence the current climate of paranoia in border politics in places around the globe, a paranoia rooted in ancient fears of the beast breaking into the clan's dwelling place.

'Thou shalt no longer suffer hunger,' says Saint Francis to the wolf, 'as it is hunger which has made thee do so much evil' (C 82). Like Saint Francis, after whom the author was named, Cantú faces the 'wolf' as *xenos*, the foreigner at the border. The medieval image of the voracious wolf becomes an allegory here for the migrant in search of a better life, his hunger driven by economic despair, Cartel violence and other forms of persecution. 'Thou shalt no longer suffer hunger' (C 82), promises the saint to the wolf, and so, in some small part, does Cantú with his hope for more porous borders and the idea of 'Brother Wolf'. One can easily discern how Cantú's vision is more optimistic than McCarthy's whose corporeal wolf as border crosser and negotiator between the global North and South finds a dismal end. Although the protagonist of Cantú's nightmares, his imaginary ('ghost') wolf seems to hold an ideal, perhaps utopian vision. Dreams, according to Freud, are expressions of desires, and the narrator's dream would be such a dream of desire. 'All men cry out against thee [...], all the inhabitants of the city are thy enemies, but I will make peace between them and thee, O brother Wolf' (C 82).

Although Cantú engages the nurturing qualities of the wolf metaphor for his humanitarian mission, the traditional evil stigma attached to this animal prevails in its association with the act of trespassing and crime. The metaphor extends to the Cartel as it does to the migrants, hunted like wolves by men north of the border buying land alongside it, not to ranch on it but to be able to hunt those crossing over (C 90), recalling Lusher's headline 'Donald Trump Supporters Tell Immigrants "The Wolves Are Coming, You Are the Hunted" as Race Hate Fears Rise' (Adam Lusher, *The Independent*, 9 Nov 2016). All this happens in an area that has tried to re-wolf its wilderness: 'I was aware, too, of the animal's tentative reintroduction to the landscape –small, carefully bred packs released into closely monitored pockets of wilderness to slowly reinhabit a terrain that had once been their own' (C 119). The tentative nature of this attempt reflects the frailty of animal and human survival in these parts. But it is a detail that also addresses questions of ownership of a land that according to the indigenous world view, that is of those who were there first, cannot be owned.

The wolf is hunting and hunted, here too, the narrator h(a)unted by the wolf of his past, ranchers hunting immigrants, US citizens arming themselves in defence against the caravan, Cartel members exploiting the migrant situation and committing atrocious acts of violence on the underprivileged in their own country and *polis* of Ciudad Juarez; all this is part and parcel of the wolf in this memoir. Once again the animal has to stand in for a stereotypical view of its purported negative qualities. That the city is a fragile concept becomes evident in the representation of Ciudad Juarez and El Paso in this memoir, with CJ's various Cartel-related scenarios of organized crime and violence, but also the cruelty of the US immigration system endured by those arriving from the south as well as those who have lived in the United States for decades and are facing expulsion. The border seems to blur due to the presence of violence on both sides, and it makes the narrator or author wonder 'if the border is a place for me to understand myself' (C 23). Its presence, however, leads to the 'wolfing', that is, the criminalization of migrants from without and those who have lived within the United States and suddenly find themselves separated from their families and expelled back across the border, as in the case of José, a friend of the narrator, who gets separated from his family and whose expulsion back to Mexico shows how the United States is making criminals out of its best citizens.

Cantú keeps seeking both the border and the wolf as liminal sites for self-introspection, wondering if it is the desert, its closeness of life and death, or the 'tension between the two cultures we carry inside us' (C 23) that induces him to do so. That tension created by the twin cities: on the one side Ciudad Juarez, 'murder capital of the world' and 'no longer the city where women died, it was the city where everyone died' (C 138), offers absolutely no sanctuary, while on the other side El Paso was named 'the safest city in the United States' (C 138) in 2008, holding promises of law and order, of respite and sanctuary from the hardships of crossing the desert, *el malpais* (C 35), a landscape of 'sterile waste' (C 59), where migrants are 'lost and wandering without food or water, dying slowly as they look for some road, some village, some way out' (C 34). But given the expulsion of Mexican citizens, the separation from their families and the criminalization of new arrivals for trying to find a home, the reality of a sanctuary on the US side is just as fragile, although in the minds of 'those residing at a distance [it] is imagined to be a perfect paradise' (C 59).

These illusions of a paradise north of the border are sharply contrasted with visions of hell to the south of it, for the crossers in general and especially women. Among Cantú's textual sources that he lists to document this inferno of Dantean proportions is Mexican poet Sara Uribe's poem *Antígona González*. The story of Antigone set in contemporary northern Mexico addresses the disappearance of the *homo sacer*, the absence of the dead that are never found, preventing their families from gaining closure. Much like Billy Parham in McCarthy's *The Crossing*, Antígona González searches for the body of her missing brother and 'in doing so inhabits the consciousness of all those who suffer disappearance, [...] a loss incomplete and unending' (C 115). The poem aims at breaking the silence surrounding these crimes, of those sent like Lycaon to the 'silent fields', and it voices the resistance of those relatives 'to the silence to which they have been relegated' (C 115). This poem too partakes of the wolf paradigm and its mythological blueprint of Lycaon banished from the human community, his relegation to silence in the sense of a loss of speech, reduced to mere howling. As Deleuze/Guattari once put it: 'This exteriority [of the war machine] is first attested to in mythology' (Deleuze/Guattari 1987: 351).

Another document Cantú recruits in highlighting the cruelty on the Mexican side as one of the most violent emanations of the evil wolf is Sergio Gonzalez Rodriguez's book *The Femicide Machine*, a text that describes the complete loss of any sanctuary for women in the border region. The very idea of the sanctuary is perverted in that these women are abducted to so-called safe houses where they are raped, tortured, murdered and then dumped in garbage containers, acts of indescribable horror negating their humanity and resignifying 'the body with indifference and abjection' (C 135) and fetishizing them as 'a kind of sacrificial host' (C 136).

We can see to what extent in Cantú's memoir, too, the wolf metaphor features in the context of outlawry, of sovereign power on both sides of the border, in the twin cities on the Rio Grande, vis-à-vis the abandonment, criminalization and violation of the *homo sacer*. One can observe the traditional juxtaposition of city versus wilderness, although there is no clear dividing line between the two, which turns the cities described here into highly precarious locations. Deleuze's and Guattari's distinction between the field, *nomos*, the traditional territory of nomads and vagabonds carrying with them the war machine versus the policing that happens only in the *polis* or the state extraneous to which stays the war machine does indeed collapse here, as we have seen in the various ways in which it breaks into the city with its ancient concept of *Umfriedung*, the city walls keeping peace inside. In this context of the politics of isolating the migrant *homo sacer* from the *polis* as nation state, the recent debate in the United States about what constitutes a concentration camp after congresswoman Alexandria Ocasio-

Cortez used that term to refer to detention centres on the southern border is of particular interest. It links back to the historians' debate in Germany in 1986 about the question whether the Holocaust was a unique form of genocide. As LaCapra put it, 'The crux of the debate on a popular level was the extent to which certain interpretive procedures, notably the comparison of Nazi crimes with other modern genocidal phenomena (particularly Stalin's Gulags), tended to relativize, normalize or even "air brush" Auschwitz in order to make it fade into larger historical contexts and out of conscious focus' (LaCapra 1997: 85). It is this sort of relativization that Ocasio-Cortez has been accused with.

Cantú also suggests certain links between the migrant situation along the southern border and the Holocaust. Places of rape, torture and murder disguised as safe houses recall the Nazis' strategies of obscuring their horrific crimes against humanity in locations camouflaged as sanctuaries: Birkenau (Birch Grove), the grove being the traditional ancient Greek sanctuary, and Theresienstadt, the camp that once underwent a process of beatification to fool the Red Cross. The narrator tells us that those who have disappeared in the field of *lethe*, the forgotten and destroyed, need to be remembered like the victims of the death camps: 'No one deserves to be just a number […]. The idea is to figure out who they are, and give them their name back' (C 107). Such passages are salient messages at a time when far-right commentators keep referring to migrants as 'cockroaches' and 'feral humans' or – as did European People's Party leader Manfred Weber – calling for a *finale Lösung* to the migrant situation, a choice of words that sounds uncomfortably close to the Nazis' final solution (*Endlösung*) to eliminate all Jews.

Moreover, to say that detention camps for migrants are not concentration camps as the latter only refer to the camps under National Socialism ignores the fact that both operate on the principle of creating a *polis*, that is, a policed and enclosed area, away from the *polis* that denies sanctuary to the metaphorical and 'undesirable' wolf who wants to break into the city. They are camps in which in concentrated form migrants are cut off from any community outside of these centres, places in the sense of Marc Augé's *non-lieux*, non-places, where the trauma of complete homelessness and an uncertain future quickly gathers momentum. In one of its most extreme manifestations the migrant's traumatization has emerged from the sovereign declaration of the state of exception condemning immigrant children to being separated from their families. This is an act by which the children themselves were turned into *homines sacri* as much as their parents, the only difference being that the latter were declared criminals for not only trespassing but also exposing their children to the state of nature they had chosen to walk into. The US government was thus shrewdly able to hide its own criminal behaviour in locking up children in cages by blaming the parents for it. On the one hand, this expulsion of refugee children into a Hobbesian state of nature results in the fracturing of the United States as a nation state that has traditionally defined itself as united and intact through its celebrated ideals and reality of pluralism and multiculturalism, welcoming everyone upon its shores. More importantly, however, this action has resulted in the children's loss of the most intimate and peaceful sanctuary possible, that of the family. One should never tire of pointing to the consummate cruelty of this sovereign act of dehumanization based on fears of 'infestation' attributed to the immigrants, and the severe psychological damage this has caused.

'My boys are not dogs to be abandoned in the street' (C 242), says José, whom the US government sends back after thirty years, breaking apart his family and 'making criminals out of those who could become its best citizens' (C 237). José is one of the personal demons Cantú grapples with at night, one of his ghost wolves, and his mother suggests that maybe he ought 'to visit him [...] go to him and listen' (C 231). She is right, of course. In the end, listening and engaging in dialogue certainly mark a beginning in turning the line into a river, rendering fluid and porous a border that increasingly closes these days. 'Puede ser muy fea la frontera' (C 39); yes, an ugly border indeed, but unlike McCarthy's grim vision Cantú's memoir leaves us with a note of hope:

> As the horse approached the border I questioned my guide about the crossing. Aren't there cameras? I asked. Sensors? No, he said. Està tranquilo. [...] I stood to walk along the adjacent shorelines, crossing the river time and again as each bank came to an end, until finally, for one brief moment, I forgot in which country I stood. All around me the landscape trembled and breathed as one. (C 246–7)

Chapter 7

WOLF TRAILS: REWILDING THE WORLD IN THE AGE OF MIGRATION

> Darkness grew and there was no end to the army of wolves. How long would it take them to move past? How many of them were there? It would take hours. All the wolves of Siberia. […] The commander spoke first. He said: The wolves are coming back. They sense the peace. (Hans Bender 1980: *Die Wölfe kommen zurück*, 189)

Sensing peace and the rejuvenation of the world Hans Bender's wolves are a metaphor for the soldiers returning from the Second World War. In that way they differ markedly from the hosts of negatively portrayed wolves associated with the loss of peace, aggression, destruction, expulsion and exile. Bender's wolves sense a peace that affects both humans and the natural world, for the devastation of the world through the politics of violence always affects both. By evoking some of the gruesome images of the destruction of the Berlin Zoo caused by the carpet bombings in November 1943 W. G. Sebald has shown in *Luftkrieg und Literatur* (Air Raids and Literature 2002: 97–8) how the Second World War in particular left not only millions of humans in its wake but also countless animals.

Bender's story about the migration of wolves contains a moment of ecocriticism, and like Misha Defonseca's fictionalized memoir it inverts the positions of humans and beasts by showing war-mongering humanity as the true wolves in the prejudicial sense of the metaphor. This short story is one of the few pieces in literature in which wolves are not perceived as a threat, and which is therefore much closer to zoological fact than myth. With its concept of peace-loving wolves *Die Wölfe kommen zurück* also offers us a unique perspective on the *Friedlos*, man without peace. While humanity is by nature *friedlos*, the wolves traditionally associated in myth with war and crime yearn for peace, thus posing as a model to humanity. They are wanderers repopulating areas that world politics has depleted of them. This phenomenon is currently either happening – as in the case of Central Europe where after the end of the Cold War and the disappearance of walls and nation dividing fences wolves have returned – or being discussed in various places in Europe and North America as a possibility of rewilding nature, whether in the form of isolated sanctuaries for wolves or in areas where wolves and humans need to co-exist.

Rewolfing and dewolfing: From the UK to Inner Mongolia

In this chapter I will focus on fictional and non-fictional responses to the presence versus absence of wolves in order to gain a deeper understanding of the impact of wolf politics on nature and culture. What are the links between biodiversity and cultural diversity, and what effects do wolf politics take on human populations in terms of cultural losses and gains, identity and migration in precarious parts of the world? I will look at three locations: Inner Mongolia, Germany, especially the German–Polish borderlands, and the Northwest of the United States – Yellowstone National Park and Idaho.

The prominent literary critic Lawrence Buell has pointed out that literature's contemporary responses to the current global crises have activated our 'environmental unconscious', awakening us to a 'fuller apprehension of the physical environment and one's interdependence with it' (Buell 2001: 22). Rewilding, specifically re-wolfing at the intersection between nature and culture, has become a politically volatile topic that has found its way into diverse forms of cultural and scientific representations, including such books as Nate Blakeslee's non-fictional account of O6, a well-known Yellowstone wolf, in *The Wolf: A True Story of Survival and Obsession in the West* (2017) or novels such as Sarah Hall's *The Wolf Border* (2015), which, as we have seen, imagines the rewilding of the British Lake District in the context of questions of British identities, above all Scottish attempts at independence, an impending Brexit and the contemporary migrant situation.

Visions of rewilding countries like the UK for the sake of biodiversity and as a way to build a new national identity contrast sharply with theories of *de*-wilding or de-wolfing such countries that are firmly in the grip of economically rather than ecologically driven lobbies. Books about nations thriving after they have lost all their wolves are rare, but for the UK such a theory does exist. In *The Last Wolf: The Hidden Springs of Englishness* (2017) Robert Winder has analysed the effects of the complete annihilation of all wolves, specifically of Peter Corbett's killing of the last wolf in 1290, on English identity, the economy and migration. According to Winder, England's landscape no doubt shaped the nation's cultural character (Winder 2017: 365), but the initial thrust towards changing the British landscape was done by *de*-wolfing it. One interesting detail, among many, that Winder offers us is that 1290 marks the year in which not only the last wolf was killed but also when, following 200 years of Crusading and anti-Semitic riots in London, York and Norwich, England's entire Jewish population was deported after being 'herded into ghettos, obliged to wear a cloth patch as a badge of their heritage, and taxed almost to the bone' (Winder 2017: 38). The killing of the last wolf was a metaphor for matters of identity, for a new force that dominated England, that of Englishness. Two centuries of Norman and Angevin rule, thus Winder's argument, had merged into a single national consciousness that considered Jews, Scots and all other foreigners as different.

Winder's central argument, however, is that the early extermination of wolves led to Britain becoming a gigantic sheep farm, a country where sheep were happy and able to multiply, causing the nation's great prosperity, while for centuries also dividing it into what Benjamin Disraeli in his novel *Sybil* (1845) once called the two nations, rich and poor: 'The terrific wealth that flowed from wool [...] would eventually give England the flood of capital that allowed it to dominate first the British Isles and then an immense overseas empire' (Winder 2017: 22).

The advantage of course of keeping England wolf-free is that as an island it is a natural fortress with a persistent fear of invasion and trespassing that shows itself as much in a novel like *Dracula* as in fears of rabies and current anti-immigration phobias. Given this ancient fear of invasion combined with a long tradition of wolflessness, a novel such as Sarah Hall's *Wolf Border* which suggests re-wolfing the island is a rather provocative gesture that challenges current politics of separation and anti-immigration as much as more than 700 years of sheepish allegiance to what Michel Houellebecq in one of his novels once called *la possibilité d'une île*.

Wool, Winder argues, is the founding father of British prosperity; it changed the British countryside and set Britain apart from its continental neighbours who were economically lagging far behind due to the persistent presence of wolves on the continent threatening livestock. To Winder natural history is a part of political science, British identity a product of its natural history, while 'vast sheep ranges were inconceivable in Central Europe, thanks to the wolf' (Winder 2017: 66). In Central Europe, the continuing presence of wolves led not only to fewer sheep but also to a different cultural identity with its ominous biopolitical scenarios, such as the persecution of women as witches thought to be riding wolves. In Britain, on the other hand, the absence of wolves went hand in hand with major changes to the landscape, and it had a massive impact on migration. As land was turned into giant sheep pastures owned by only a few, such changes to the British landscape meant the end of feudalism, turning vast numbers of dispossessed people who had been working the land upon which they lived into destitute vagrants. Winder thus adds to George Monbiot's argument in *Feral* about the natural devastation of the land through sheep and the social devastation through monoculture. These changes, however, also led to expulsion and immigration. The year 1290 not only marks the year of Jewish deportation, but the new booming economy then over the centuries also triggered immigration, to wit that of foreign guest workers. Immigration was therefore, according to Winder, a direct consequence of the killing of the last wolf, as it created a prosperity with an urgent need for itinerant workers such as stone masons and weavers from the continent. 'England,' Winder says, 'was built by foreigners,' and this is linked to the disappearance of its wolves, an interesting argument in light of Brexit and its closing borders.

Regardless of whether or not we subscribe to Winder's theory of the last wolf, in most places around the world de-wolfing, the killing of the last wolf, has led to environmental and cultural perdition. The consequences of de-wolfing are perhaps nowhere better visualized than in Jiang Rong's fictionalization of the impact of the environmental devastation of Inner Mongolia on the nomadic cultures of that region. His novel *Wolf Totem* (2004) has been somewhat controversial. Decried by some as written in a fascist spirit it nonetheless carries an important message of what happens to both nature and culture after a species disappears that has for millennia played a pivotal role in the region's ecosystem and cultural identity.

Drawing on the author's own experiences *Wolf Totem* is the story of Chen Zhen, a Beijing-based intellectual who volunteers to live among the nomads of the grasslands of Inner Mongolia, an autonomous region of Northern China. Through his own observations but also in numerous dialogues with the respected elder Bilgee (the Wise One) Chen becomes intimately acquainted with local culture, above all the Mongols' close relationship with the wolf as their totem animal. Wolves form a substantial part of their religion and history of warfare, Genghis Khan's success as a warrior being a result of the close emulation of wolf-hunting strategies. In the course of his sojourn Chen Zhen then decides to capture and raise a wolf cub, an endeavour that turns out to be fraught with problems, since wolves resist domestication, and the attempt to tame one is seen by the locals as messing with the spiritual core of their ancient culture. Chen's own failure with his wolf experiment parallels the increasing destruction of nature and culture in Inner Mongolia. Returning to the area many years later he witnesses the full extent of this devastation:

> Standing alone by his window, Chen looked off to the north with a sense of desolation. The wolves had receded into legend, and the grassland was a distant memory. A nomadic herding society was now extinct; even the last trace left by the wolves on the Inner Mongolian grassland – the ancient cave of the wolf cub – would be buried in yellow sand. (Rong 2009: 524)

Although the novel may not reveal any complexity of plot let alone lyrical quality, as Jerry Varsava has so cogently pointed out, its immense success, having sold over 4 million copies in China alone, goes to show that it

> obviously speaks poignantly to certain yearnings on the part of a broad populace for respect for cultural heritage, for individual rights, and for environmental integrity. Its rhetorico-stylistic imperfections notwithstanding, its place within contemporary global environmental fiction is assured, even as the potency of its political critique continues to be written on the minds of engaged citizens within, but also far beyond, the People's Republic of China. There is much at stake here, both for China and the world. (Varsava 2011: 297)

Wolf Totem, however, has been criticized for what the German literary critic Wolfgang Kubin saw as its inherently fascist message (Clifford), primarily for its glorification of 'the lupine art of war' (Rong 2019: 99) that may echo the ways in which the Nazis and nowadays the Turkish Grey Wolves have appropriated the wolf metaphor. What is different, however, from the blood and soil energy in the Third Reich and pan-Turkic ultranationalism is the association of alleged wolf qualities such as nobility, rebelliousness, freedom, pride, belligerence, passion and fierce strength with a trans-national(ist) nomadic ethnic minority and their traditional culture. The book's hypothesis of the racial superiority of nomadic cultures in view of their success in matters of war, conquest and expansionism differs radically from other theories of nomadism, such as Bruce Chatwin's idea that as a migratory species nomads are less aggressive than sedentary ones since 'migration itself [...] is the hard journey, a leveller in which the fit survive and stragglers fall by the wayside', thus pre-empting 'the need for hierarchies and shows of dominance' (Chatwin 1988: 273). Chatwin extrapolates from migratory animal species to his idealized nomads, their rhizomatic travel being one big songline reminding him of those mythical trails in Australian Aboriginal culture, that 'spaghetti of Iliads and Odysseys writhing this way and that' (Chatwin 1988: 13).

An obvious counter-argument to Chatwin's idealization of peaceful nomads would be to point to Genghis Khan's aggressive expansionism, in Rong's view a manifestation of the wolf spirit that governs the nomadic culture of Mongols. He assures us that they live under the wolf totem, which means they think and feel like wolves, and worship them like a religion to the point of never even daring to sleep on a wolf pelt. Their vigorous wolf culture is set into sharp relief against the Han Chinese way of life, described as weak, its people resembling stupid sheep that unthinkingly follow their leaders without any kind of resistance. To live under the wolf totem, Rong demonstrates, holds a promise of environmental and cultural health in addition to the kind of political rebelliousness that the author himself had once displayed in Tiananmen Square (1989), his 'counter-revolutionary activities' for which he was imprisoned for eighteen months (Hill 2008).

The book was written in memory of the years of the Cultural Revolution with its inherent ideological warfare, its tension with the Soviet Union and the United States over the war in South East Asia. This caused massive militarization, the mobilization of masses of people and environmental havoc, a concatenation of causes and effects about which Janet Shapiro in her excellent study *Mao's War against Nature: Politics and the Environment in Revolutionary China* has said:

> The war preparation campaign of the late 1960s and early 1970s is the best Mao-era example of the unintended environmental consequences of human migration. [...] Coercive and semivoluntary relocations of people to inhospitable regions and pristine wilderness areas damaged or destroyed ecosystems even as they created enormous human hardships. [...] War preparations brought new intensity to the effort to conquer nature, as the "battlefront" shifted to the mountains of Guizhou and Sichuan, the rainforests of Yunnan, the forests and wetlands of Heilongjiang's Great Northern Wilderness, the grassland of Inner Mongolia, and the forests and deserts of Xinjiang. (Shapiro 2001: 142)

It is surprising that given its vehement criticism of Chinese culture, the Communist Party and even Confucianism the novel escaped censorship. In Rong's somewhat simplistic binary of yet another Cain and Abel version – the shackled farming Chinese, dominant colonizers but whose 'small-scale peasant economy and Confucian culture have weakened the people's nature' (Rong 2009: 304) versus the free-spirited nomadic wolves or Mongols – the wolf metaphor is even taken so far as once again being associated with race. This too feeds into the critique of its alleged fascism:

> The wolf totem has a much longer history than Han Confucianism [...] with greater natural continuity and vitality. In the Confucian thought system, the main ideas, such as the three cardinal guides and the five constant virtues, are outdated and decayed, but the central spirit of the wolf totem remains vibrant and young, since it's been passed down by the most advanced races of the world. It should be considered one of the truly valuable spiritual heritages of all humanity. (Rong 2009: 377)

We have seen how in Europe and North America the wolf became a defining metaphor for racial marginalization, especially for nomads, vagrants, indigenous hunters and gatherers, Gypsies and the 'Wandering', cosmopolitan Jew. In Rong's book, by contrast, the wolf is clearly a trope for racial superiority ('the most advanced people today are descendants of nomadic races' [Rong 303]), a hyperbole that echoes the distant literary voice of Bram Stoker, Count Dracula's perception of his noble and ancient lineage. Dracula's understanding of his race, his identification with the allegedly superior Nordic race and his insistence on his family's origins in the berserks, aligns him with the Viking threat of invasion that is similar to Rong's evocations of the superiority of Genghis Khan and Oriental, nomadic and expansionist races waging war under the totem of the wolf.

> We Szekelys [says Dracula] have a right to be proud, for in our veins flows the blood of many brave races who fought as the lion fights, for lordship. Here in the whirlpool of European races, the Ugric tribe bore down from Iceland the fighting spirit which Thor and Wodin gave them, which their berserkers displayed to such fell intent on the seaboards of Europe, aye, and of Asia and Africa, till the peoples thought the were-wolves themselves had come. (Stoker 2000: 25–6)

In view of such distant literary echoes Rong's very similar incantations of the nomadic war spirit and racial superiority seem rather archaic, which means that in spite of its politically correct message about the environment I have read this novel with a good dose of scepticism:

> In world history, Chen continued the thought, nomads have been the only Easterners capable of taking the fight to the Europeans, and the three peoples that really shook the West to its foundations were the Huns, the Turks, and the Mongols. The Westerners who fought their way back to the East were all descendants of nomads. The builders of ancient Rome were a pair of brothers raised by a wolf. [...] The later Teutons, Germans, and Anglo-Saxons grew increasingly powerful, and the blood of wolves ran in their veins. The Chinese with their weak dispositions, are in desperate need of a transfusion of that vigorous, unrestrained blood. Had there been no wolves, the history of the world would have been written much differently. (Rong 2009: 217–8)

It is passages such as this one that may make us wonder how much, if at all, authorial ironic distance the novel may contain and which move it into the arena of magical realism, thus undermining its critical impact and important ecological message.

The wolf metaphor divides sedentary farming from nomadic cultures. Once again we can observe the metaphor's ambivalence of abjection versus veneration. By contrast to Mongolian wolf worship the Chinese Communist ideologues, Rong assures us, consider as wolves all those deemed malicious and greedy, a metaphor also for American capitalists. As Xu Xinjian informs us, to the Chinese 'introducing the wolf into history' (*yin lang ru shi*) is as dangerous as 'letting wolves into the house' (*yin lang ru shi*).

> For centuries, Chinese historiography has linked the wolf with notions of atrocity, brutality and stupidity; Chinese idioms in particular abound with negative words about the wolf, arousing people's antipathy and vigilance. This cultural influence was even extended to the modern revolutionary discourse, so that slogans such as 'We will never withdraw from the battlefield unless all the wolves are killed' (*Da bu jin chai lang jue bu xia zhanchang*) became a typical pledge of fighting uncompromisingly with one's enemies. Accordingly, the narration of the wolf totem not only challenges the 'descendants of the dragon' and the centuries-long Han-centered

discourse, but also suggests a reversal of the value between honor and lowliness, beauty and ugliness, and even kindness and malice. (Xinjian 2011: 100)

In 2008, the Communist Party chief in Tibet even went so far as to call the Dalai Lama a 'wolf in monk's clothes' (Varsava 2011: quoting Claude Arpy 2008: 288). The wolves in this novel thus take centre stage in a discussion of colonial politics, issues of race and ecology. Most of all, however, Rong develops what he calls a wolfology (Rong 215), a kind of wolf philosophy: 'His view of life had altered' (Rong 267).

As Mongolian totem animal and wolf godhead the animal corresponds to Derrida's sovereign beast. Wolves are being elevated in this novel to a sort of super animal, their 'wisdom unfathomable, almost a magical beast' (Rong 318). Pivotal to the politics of friend and foe, their presence separates what Daniel Quinn's philosophical novel *Ishmael* called the agrarian Takers from the indigenous Leavers. Quinn's Ishmael has singled out all the people of so-called developed cultures and calls them Takers. They are the ones who have destroyed the world – the environment, the other life forms and precious resources. Whereas, Ishmael tells the reader, there have been other cultures, those the Takers deem as uncivilized and savage, whom Ishmael calls Leavers, but they are the ones who live in harmony with their surroundings.

In view of this distinction to which Rong's book obviously also subscribes Mongol culture is deemed superior in spite of an absence of print culture. The dominant agrarian culture, however, is that of the Han Chinese due to sheer superiority in numbers of people blotting out the ethnic minority and its way of life. The culture of Inner Mongolia may serve as a *pars pro toto*, reminding us that other ethnic minorities and their cultures are being threatened alongside with their unique environment, be it Inner Mongolia or the Tibetan plateau. The close relationship of migratory cultures with their natural habitat and their peaceful coexistence with other creatures, in this case the Mongols and their grassland, witnessed by Rong in the 1960s and 1970s but rapidly disappearing since then, repeats the destruction of the environment, disappearance of wolves and the demise of indigenous cultures also in other parts of the world, North America being a foremost example. To all appearances, Varsava (2011) points out, *Wolf Totem* contains

> extremely powerful socio-political commentary and arguably effective social science […] [that] through its imaginative scenario […] presents a detailed, first-hand portrayal of how uninformed

developmental and heritage policies and practices were felt at the level of the lived-world in one environmentally sensitive area of China, and how their tragic legacy persists today in the lives of tens of millions of Chinese citizens. (Varsava 296)

The grassland, the novel itself states, 'is a complex place. Everything is linked and the wolves are the major link, tied to all the others' (Rong 238). Wolves are its primary sanitation workers (Rong 313). If it were not for them the grassland would be destroyed by gazelles and mice. This is precisely what happens after all the wolves have been killed: the rodents and gazelles get out of control, turning the grassland into a desert, while the indigenous Mongols have known for millennia how to preserve the land, and like the wolves have always left the grassland as they had found it (Rong 314). Gilles Deleuze and Felix Guattari would have argued that due to the shallow rhizomatic roots of the nomads of the grassland theirs is a culture that does not appropriate the land as would sedentary, arborescent cultures. Reading Rong's book, however, one cannot help but wonder which roots in the end go deeper, the easily eradicable ones of the nomads who are intimately acquainted with their environment or those of colonizing sedentary farming communities.

The irony of Chen's life among the nomads is that he becomes complicit in their destruction. He is a strange hybrid among them, Chinese in origin but becoming increasingly immersed in their culture. His own cultural hybridity is reflected by that of the wolfhound he is trying to raise, a domesticated wolf that negates the idea of cultural purity embodied by wild wolves. Domestication in the face of environmental integrity – of leaving things as they are – turns out to be impossible. Rong shows this kind of domestication on two levels, in the wolf cub Chen raises and in the changes of environmental details such as Swan Lake, which in an attempt to turn it into a water hole for domestic animals becomes a 'graveyard for swans, wild geese, wild ducks, and wolves' (Rong 470). In the end all domestication fails in Inner Mongolia, the grasslands turning into deserts and the wolves having to escape to one of the last bastions of freedom, Outer Mongolia, the 'real Mongolia' (Rong 491). Not all is lost there for Chen's Little Wolf:

> I've become a dentist and have given the cub four sharp steel teeth. Next spring, when he's fully grown I'll secretly take him to the border and free him in the mountains of Outer Mongolia, where there are still wolf packs [...] where few people inhabit a vast territory. There are only twenty million people in the real Mongolia, which is a

spiritual paradise that venerates the wolf totem; it is free of a farming population that hates wolves and wants only to kill them. (Rong 491)

Domestication, which also implies a displacement or colonization of migratory (here nomadic) culture through sedentary culture happened and is happening elsewhere. A classical example is the disappearance of the triadic relationship between Native Americans, buffalo and wolves on the great prairies of the American West. Although this area is now the bread basket of the United States, China, Rong's novel whispers into its readers' ears, could learn a lesson or two from the American history of colonization and species extermination.

Of wolves and migrants in Germany: Right-wing politics and bio-cultural diversity

Jiang Rong's wolves are a border phenomenon defining ethnic boundaries for which the Great Wall stands as a bastion constructed in the Ming Dynasty (1368–1644) for the purpose of keeping the Northern wolves, raiding parties of nomadic tribes such as the Mongol, Turic and Xiongnu, from invading the Chinese Empire. In view of borders, migration and the presence versus absence of wolves and their subsequent impact on nature and culture, Rong's discussion is relevant not only for Inner Mongolia but for other parts of the world. The question of re-wolfing versus de-wolfing has affected both North America and Europe in recent years; it has triggered heated debates and is closely tied to immigration, cultural and ecological diversity. Such debates show that unlike the nomadic cultures as depicted in Rong's novel the conservative territorialists with their sedentary attitudes to land ownership, be it the ranch or the nation, see wolves and immigration as invasive. Such attitudes are steeped in time-worn fears and prejudices and can then shape political preferences that affect the local treatment of the environment and relationships between ethnic groups, resulting in an overall loss of sanctuaries for human and non-human animals.

One such sensitive area where wolf politics, environmental concerns and immigration across national borders come together is the so-called *Lausitz* (Lusatia) in Eastern Saxony. This region along the German–Polish border has been witness to migrations of animals and humans for centuries. It has also seen its share of right-wing extremism. Incidentally, wolves reappeared in the mid-1990s, a time that also saw numerous attacks on asylum seekers in the wake of unification and for reasons of envy about resources. The area has remained fertile ground for far-right political movements such as the *Alternative für Deutschland* party (AfD) or the *Pegida* (Patriotic Europeans against the Islamization of the Occident), which have been able to recruit massively in these parts. According to journalist Katrin Bennhold, AfD politicians talk about wolves in the same way as they talk about immigrants, demanding *Obergrenzen*, 'ceilings' or literally 'upper limits' on the numbers of both. Such politicians insist that wolves and immigrants (especially of Islamic faith) are foreign to the German cultural landscape, that they share a rapacious, criminal nature and that while one allegedly has a negative impact on the natural environment the other equally negatively impacts on the cultural, that is, Christian environment. This type of racist invective draws on ancient prejudices towards both wolves and outsiders in addition to feeding into a national psyche under the spell of what can be summarized by the term 'Little Red Riding Hood Syndrome', a cultural baggage that has left its mark on the national subconscious, more so in Germany than in other countries where evil wolves do not feature in children's bedtime stories.

Lusatia and other parts of East Germany close to Berlin are particularly sensitive due to their proximity to the border that once separated the Eastern from the Western world with their two ideologies that like the wolf were subject to certain mythifications. This region went from the myths that came especially with the closed borders during the Cold War to a completely open border that now admits both apex predators and migrants coming from the East, a direction that has for centuries been perceived as a threat to the West, and has been mythologized, as we have seen, in novels like *Dracula*. Wolves entering Germany across the ghost line of the Iron Curtain are still surrounded by a mystique that has been fed by these perceptions. Berlin, the cosmopolitan centre, unites in itself the former East and West. At the crossroads between these two worlds it has always been intensely multicultural, but is nonetheless in the mind of current populism still exposed to the threats coming from the East. We have seen how Roland Schimmelpfennig exploits this fear of the roaming wolf 'coming from the East' (36) in his novel *One Clear, Ice-Cold January Morning at the Beginning of the Twenty-Frist Century* (2016), which captures the *Zeitgeist* of the current wolf mania holding Germany in its grip, not just Germany but other central European countries as well. Tyrol in Austria, for example, has in August 2019 legalized the free killing of all wolves within its boundaries (Arora).

Such decisions are based on stereotypes and exaggerated fears by farmers about their livestock. It cannot be denied that wolves do pose a certain threat to livestock, a danger that could be diminished by higher fences, which, however, may cost too much. The other fear often voiced comes from parents, although there have been very few documented cases in which wolves have actually attacked or devoured children. Other than to the occasional sheep or calf what is the wolf's actual threat to the cultural landscape in Germany where nature could hardly be more rigorously monitored than it already is? Do they pose a menace to the deer population to a point that the environmental balance could be thrown off? Surely not, as Germany like many other places also suffers from deer overgrazing in its forests. Although it has been able to live without wolves for more than a century, suggesting that wolves may not be necessary to the environment as foresters in Germany have also been very good at keeping numbers of deer under control, the definitive ecological benefits of wolves in that country and other cultural landscapes of Europe will still need to be assessed after a more prolonged presence of the predator.

And yet, wolves seem to be a natural fertilizer to the environment, as is reflected by Rong's sanitation workers. They contribute actively to the vitalization of deer populations, inducing them to be more migratory, thus no longer grazing exclusively on young trees and shoots in certain areas. This reduces damage to the forest and other vegetation, which has more time to recover, allowing protected forests to remain undisturbed. Their rejuvenation in turn prevents erosion, landslides, avalanches and flooding in a natural way from which insects, fish, birds, beavers and in the end also humans can profit. Moreover, unlike the human hunter, who always takes the entire animal from the forest so that no other species will profit from the kill, the wolf usually does not eat a cadaver in one go, its scattered body parts subsequently forming an important source of nourishment for carrion feeders in addition to offering ecological niches to many organisms. Bacteria, fungi and worms contribute to finishing off the cadaver leaving behind nutrient-rich soil which in turn benefits plant life. We need to distinguish, however, between areas in which humans have turned wilderness into a cultural landscape and vast expanses of wilderness where wolves are left undisturbed. Since Central Europe does not have the sort of wilderness that can be found in North America, the presence of wolf sanctuaries, of wolf zoning as David Mech (1995) has suggested, may be an absolute necessity to get a more detailed picture of *canis lupus*' impact on the environment.

Wolves have had a difficult comeback in Germany. In the decades following the Second World War, those migrating there from Poland were always shot as soon as they managed to trespass across the Iron Curtain. According to biologist and wolf expert Ilka Reinhardt, who together with Gesa Kluth founded *Lupus*, an institute dedicated to monitoring and researching wolves in Germany, at least nineteen wolves were killed between 1945 and 1990. Preventing recolonization by wolves was the policy of the German Democratic Republic, while in the Federal Republic the wolf had been strictly protected albeit absent since 1980 (Reinhardt et al. 2013: 14). When Germany was unified, the wolf became a protected species throughout the entire country, although several wolves were still killed by poachers in the 1990s.

Now the wolves have become a symbol for transboundary collaboration between Poland and Germany, an enrichment for both nature and culture, the latter in the sense of a cultural approximation and friendship similar to the US–Canadian initiative for Yellowstone, of which I will say more further down. It demonstrates how migrating wolves can bring different cultures together, something that at a symbolic level Schimmelpfennig has also achieved in his novel. The wolves' international migration and their obvious obliviousness to borders are reflected also in the term 'Central European wolf population' applied by Reinhardt et al. in their 2013 report and subsuming all wolves from Poland and Germany and their impending migration into the Czech Republic and further afield. This terminology is interesting, as it clearly ignores the borders of nation states, the migratory wolf thus offering us a model for a politics of hospitality with its dissolution of ethnic and national divides. The concept of the stranger, which used to be one of the meanings of the medieval *vargr* as human wolf, is inseparable from the phenomenon of the border, and the more closely staked borders are, the more defined the *xenos*, stranger or foreigner, becomes. Needless to say but I will do so again, ultimately there are no borders other than those of our own bodies, and any stranger or foreigner (in French one word, *étranger*) is no other than the foreigner within us, as Julia Kristeva (1991: 191) has taught us and Francisco Cantú has demonstrated with his concept of Brother Wolf.

In environmental studies and conservation parlance wolves are divided into genetic groups called populations, which makes their migration a topic of critical concern as it implies fluctuations in the gene pool of wolves. As Reinhardt et al. point out:

> The term 'metapopulation' refers on a large scale to the entirety of individuals that share a broadly similar genetic structure. The

> distribution of the metapopulation may be spatially discontinuous, but there should be sufficient (potential) connectivity to permit the dispersal of individuals that ensures gene flow and some degree of demographic stabilisation. [...] Boitani and Ciucci (2009) propose to consider European wolves as one large metapopulation. This clearly makes sense for the continental conservation approach the authors ask for. It is also reasonable in relation to the population concept. On an evolutionary scale, isolation of the single European wolf populations is very short termed. Considering the overall positive population trends and the dispersal abilities of wolves, it is reasonable to propose that most populations will be to some degree connected to neighbouring populations within the next decades. (Reinhardt et al. 2013: 15)

Despite their territorialism, wolves are thus not all that different from humans when it comes to a sense of belonging, mobility and willingness to mix with other groups. The biggest challenge, however, will be to make people give up their time-worn fears. As Luigi Boitani wrote in 1995, 'the most important issue in wolf conservation is public opinion,' and ten years later Salvatori and Linnell (2005) stated: 'Human acceptance of wolves appears to be a major problem in many areas, especially in areas where wolves have returned after an absence. This lack of acceptance is linked to many different conflicts, including livestock depredation, competition with hunters, predation on domestic dogs, fear and wider social conflicts for which wolves become symbols' (Reinhardt et al. 2013: 26).

Strangely, wolves have made a comeback at a time that sees the planet's last hunter or gatherer cultures disappear, and with them our ability to share the environment with all creatures. The challenges of cohabitation with wolves in the cultural landscapes of Europe will be at least threefold: (1) Europe will need to create more sanctuaries for wolves in areas designated as pure wilderness so that collisions with farming communities can be reduced; (2) the protection of livestock needs to be rethought on a large scale, the presence of better fences and guard dogs playing significant roles in this; and (3) the challenges of integrating both wolves and migrants will include an increased education to change public opinion fed by the wolf myth and draw attention to the interface of biological and cultural diversity. When it comes to wolves and migrants in their shared *nuda vita*, to lean on Derridean thinking in his seminal *The Animal That Therefore I Am*, we need to learn to return their gaze without judgement, without prejudice. They may see us more than we see them, there may be fear connected to their gaze, but there is not the kind of prejudice of all our mythologizations and symbolism with which we gaze at them. What goes for Derrida's cat also holds true for the way in which we perceive wolves as the alien Other. Our mythologization of animals and humans seen as 'alien' is a false gaze, one that does not truly recognize. Can we indeed learn from animals in this regard for the ways in which we regard both them and humans from other cultures?

> No, no, my cat, the cat that looks at me in my bedroom or bathroom [...] does not appear here to represent, like an ambassador, the immense symbolic responsibility with which our culture has always charged the feline [lupine] race, from La Fontaine to Tieck (author of 'Puss in Boots'), from Baudelaire to Rilke, Buber, and many others. (Derrida 2008: 9)

Most prominently, the tendency to mythologize and create symbols and metaphors pervades some of the media. We need not look far in newspapers in Germany and Austria today until we come across demonizing images of the sort expressed in headlines like *Der Wolf erobert Lebensräume zurück* (Reinhard Bingener in *Frankfurter Allgemeine Zeitung*, 14 Feb 2018). The animal that conquers back its *Lebensraum* (living space), a word forever blighted by the National Socialist past, this is a language of belligerence, accusatory of the crime of trespassing, both a perception and dramatization of imminent danger while exploiting the myth of the ominous East.

Recently, a man got bitten by what was most likely a wolf or dog hybrid, and the tabloid *Bild* was quick to balloon the incident into a full-blown attack coming from Germany's most politicized animal. The myth making continues, from the evil wolf myth of the Grimm Brothers to the master animal of the Nazis, to a kind of hybrid myth based in equal shares on biophilia and biophobia: the wolf as victim in the eyes of environmentalists but a vicious beast to the wolf opponents and an unwanted alien werewolf to the far right, which asks for restricted numbers thus reminding us that the wolf will always remain a border phenomenon, an animal on the threshold. That the wolf's metaphorical link with war continues to remain part of this wolf mythology in Germany is also evident in the fact that many of these newly arrived wolves flourish in particular in decommissioned military zones, simply for the reason that they have figured out that survival here is easier because poaching is more difficult in these areas closed to the public. These zones, however, while perpetuating the wolf or war link, also offer a sort of sanctuary for wolves where they can hunt and multiply undisturbed.

What is the impact of nature on culture, that is the big question here: how does the renewed presence of wolves impact on culture? What happens when myths become a reality? We have seen how the Lycaon myth about expulsion and exile became a sinister biopolitical reality in the Middle Ages. Cultural heritage may, however, also negatively influence the management of nature (such as the Little Red Riding Hood syndrome), and in turn natural change also effects culture. It has the potential to demythologize cultural baggage once science tells us about the definitive benefits of wolves in our ecosystem. On the other hand, natural changes like the entry of wolves currently happening during waves of increased human migration can remythologize biopolitics and thwart the possibility of multiculturalism and thus impoverish culture, as the example of the AfD's use of the wolf metaphor for immigrants perceived as trespassing criminals demonstrates. It is a moment in which biodiversity and cultural diversity merge, when a political party contends that the 'invasion' of a foreign species may impact on the ecosystem in similar ways as the 'invasion' of a foreign culture inevitably impacts on the host culture. This is one of the great fears of the AfD and other territorialist parties and groups, and why the AfD in particular likens the appearance of wolves in Germany with that of migrants, especially of Muslim provenance.

There are obvious links between biodiversity and cultural diversity. As Heyd has shown in one of the few articles that discuss this interface, biodiversity depends on the protection of traditional cultures who know how to maintain the environment balance (Heyd 2010: 159–79). It depends on respect for the past, both in an ecological and in a cultural sense. Rong's defence of nomadic culture is a pertinent example for this. He shows us how biodiversity depends on monoculture, and that the invasion of another culture threatens that biodiversity. In Rong's vision therefore biodiversity and cultural diversity completely rule each other out. The two may indeed not go together smoothly, in spite of arguments such as John Stuart Mill's that Europe's cultural pluralism has created a thriving 'habitat' that will never go stagnant in the way, as he claims, China will do with its monoculture (Mill 1968: 129–30). Differences between biodiversity and cultural diversity also depend on the rights of non-human animal versus humans, as the collective rights of a non-human animal species cannot be reduced to an individual the way it can be for humans. This is an area in animal rights that will still need much attention in future. While human rights are, at least on paper, universal, we live in an era of controlled species conservation, which means that we preserve some species while caring less about others. Wolves enjoy the benefit of being preserved, while the *Ungeziefer*, the parasite that causes diseases and epidemics, is not. The species that tend to be preserved tend to be the ones we have sinned against. Paradoxically in light of this, the wolf myth does wolves a huge favour, as by preserving them the environmentalists among us are trying to redeem ourselves for the way wolves have been maligned over millennia.

No doubt, the discussion of biodiversity and cultural diversity takes different directions. We may want to ask if the reduction of cultural diversity poses the same dangers as the reduction of biodiversity? Is globalization as dangerous for the planet as the loss of ecological diversity? I do not have definitive answers here, but one thing is certain: the age of great migrations in which we currently live is a part of the current trend of globalization, and migration is an ambivalent phenomenon that reduces cultural singularity while also enriching cultures by creating a plurality within them.

What's the matter with Yellowstone? Towards a politics of hospitality

Parties like the German AfD are emphasizing biological and cultural impoverishment and are blind to the possibility of natural and cultural enrichment, the notion that wolves are a natural fertilizer as immigrants are a cultural one. These attitudes so obviously lacking in cosmopolitanism are not limited to Germany but tend to affect other global areas where wolf hunting and xenophobia may well go together, all springing from the same entrenched conservative spirit, from people who have colonized the land, claim it as their own and are reluctant to share it with new arrivals.

On the other hand, research has shown that wolf rewilding, the presence of sanctuaries for wolves, has had a hugely positive impact on biodiversity and cultural diversity. This can be illustrated by the recent controversial history of wolf reintroduction in the lower forty-eight states in the United States, specifically in the North Western Rocky Mountain states of Idaho, Montana and Wyoming with Yellowstone National Park at its centre.

As we have seen, in North America the extermination of wolves in the nineteenth and early twentieth century paralleled the genocide of the indigenous population, as the negative European wolf metaphor came to be deported to the New World. In Yellowstone National Park, the disappearance of wolves coincided with that of the indigenous population in the 1870s. Founded in 1872, this national park is a good example to demonstrate how the European cultural legacy of the maligned wolf displaced a culture that revered the wolf, thus decimating both biodiversity and cultural diversity. As Karin Jones has shown in her work on the wolves of the Rocky Mountains, the local Blackfeet celebrated the wolf in their myths and stories as the animal that would guide them to the spirit world along the so-called Wolf Trail (the Milky Way). They identified with the migrations of the wolf, and storytellers described how lost travellers would find comfort among wolves. The Blackfeet 'Legend of the Friendly Medicine Wolf', for example, features a young woman who got disoriented after escaping enemy captors, but was assisted to find her way back home by a pack of friendly lupines (Jones, 'Fighting Outlaws', 39). The Blackfeet belong to those tribes – as do the Pawnee of Kansas, the Comanche of the southern Great Plains and the Ojibwe of Minnesota – to whom the wolf is either the creator of the world or who from the dawn of their spiritual and psychological being have seen their deeper connectedness with what they consider their closest relative in the wild – Makuyi (wolf; Pierotti/Wildcat 1999: 196). These are cultures that are based on emulation of and cooperation with wolves.

As Pierotti and Wildcat point out, the indigenous people understand their connectedness with other species and the deeper connectedness between animal species (such as the one between wolves and ravens) much better than Euro Americans. Some Western scientists studying wolves have even realized that native people have far greater knowledge of the behaviour and ecology of wolves than Western science, and have turned to native people to help them in their study of these animals (Stephenson 1982: 434–9). For one thing, both Blackfeet culture and the migrations of wolves can teach us a way of thinking that transcends national boundaries. For the Blackfeet the Rockies in their length from their home in the Northern US Rockies up into Canada present the 'backbone of the world', irrespective of national boundaries. It is a cultural way of thinking that at the level of nature tallies with the migration of wolves across national borders – culture and nature as territory rather than striated national space.

This transnational migration of wolves with the benefit of rejuvenating nature and replenishing a culture that had once included wolves as key players experienced a pivotal moment in the 'immigration' of a set of

Canadian wolves to the United States for the purpose of reintroducing them to Yellowstone Park in the mid-1990s. The national park had not seen wolves since the 1920s, but given the increase of tourism, policy makers as early as in the mid-twentieth century were starting to wonder what was America's foremost natural icon without the presence of one of its foremost apex predators–no more really than the Serengeti without lions (Jones 2010: 344). Because of the absence of wolves in the lower forty-eight states, however, the United States decided to import wolves from nearby Alberta. These 'immigrant wolves' have come to stimulate our thinking in multiple ways: as an emblem of US–Canadian friendship they not only regenerated the nature of the park but were also instrumental to transnational politics. Although wolves are oblivious to national boundaries, their deliberate immigration from Canada to the United States presented a unique moment that now shines new light on the current migration scenario at the southern border, highlighting the politics of hospitality in the face of ongoing politics of hostility. At the time these immigrant wolves already prompted a 'satirical discourse on North American relations, migration, Americanization, and cultural difference' (Jones 2010: 345), including comments on how balmy their new life was in the United States compared to Canada, considering they now enjoyed Endangered Species protection (introduced in 1973), a cult status as ecological prodigal sons, and great abundance of elk. The paper *High Country News* even went so far as to include a fictional letter by one of the imported wolves writing home to his Canadian family: 'Mom you ought to come down here, and bring the triplets. There's room here, we're talking lots […]. Besides, it's nice country' (Jones 2010: 345). Other commentators seemed more serious about the entire project, suggesting, for example, 'that the migrant wolves had better be on their best behaviour for the U.S. immigration service and not act like welfare scroungers. Editorials also expressed fear that the naïve Canadian wolves […] would suffer the full force of the U.S. gun culture' (Jones 2010: 345).

Jones persuasively argues, however, that in conjunction with Aldo Leopold's famous dictum that humanity needs to think like a mountain, we ought to think more like wolves when it comes to national boundaries, an idea that not only echoes Kant's notion of world peace but is of high value to our present political climate which sees borders reconstructed and fortified to keep migrants outside.

> Replacing a traditional North American nation-state attitude with the Blackfeet's Backbone of the World points to an alternative way

of seeing the West and offers a fresh perspective on issues relating to environmental and cultural exigencies. Such an approach illuminates the Rocky Mountain landscape from Jasper to Yellowstone as a fluid, vibrant, and liminal space. Borders – whether surrounding national parks or dividing nations – are fictive, arbitrary lines that run counter to ecological realities. (Jones 2010: 348)

The wolves of Yellowstone are thus a densely politicized phenomenon. They were and still are a catalyst for cross-cultural politics, but their primary benefit for the national park, it was argued in the 1990s and early 2000s, was their contribution to the regeneration of nature. The main argument of some environmentalists was that the renewed presence of wolves in Yellowstone reduced the number of elk in addition to changing their feeding patterns. Elk had for the many decades of wolf absence been overgrazing on young aspen and willow trees, and now, the argument ran, the wolves made them avoid certain riparian areas where they could be easily ambushed, allowing the vegetation, mostly young aspens and willows, to recover. This in turn led to a recovery and greater diversity of bird life, and a return of beavers who were then regulating the rivers which, undammed, had been cutting too deep into the terrain. All of this suggests that wolves may have had a top-down effect on the ecosystem. In a word, many wolf defenders believed that the case of the Yellowstone wolf presents what is known as a trophic cascade.

As was to be expected, the views of these environmentalists clashed vehemently with those of ranching communities who like anywhere else in the Western world reacted passionately against the presence of wolves for fear of livestock loss. In the case of Yellowstone, what these ranchers may not have realized was the added benefit of wolves taking out elk diseased with Chronic Wasting Disease (CWD) and buffalo infected with brucellosis, which, if these diseases were to spread to cattle and livestock in the states neighbouring Yellowstone, would be highly detrimental to the sale of beef.

Opposition, however, also came from within the field of environmental studies. In his seminal *New York Times* article 'Is the Wolf a Real American Hero?' Arthur Middleton demonstrated how the Yellowstone wolf story might have been yet another brick in the construction of the wolf myth, one, however, that presents the animal as an ecological hero rather than the traditional villain of folklore: 'By retelling the same old story about Yellowstone wolves, we distract attention from bigger problems, mislead ourselves about the true challenges of managing ecosystems, and add to the mythology surrounding wolves at the expense of scientific understanding' (Middleton 2014). For one thing, Middleton argues, elk are not that easy to kill, as living in herds helps them detect and respond to incoming wolves, and of course elk can 'kick like hell'. The strongest counter-argument, however, was that the whole story about the recovery of the ecosystem due to renewed growth of willows and aspens was refuted by a study from Colorado State University. Middleton concludes that it does not really matter whether the story of the Yellowstone wolf was true or not, what mattered in the end was that it bolstered the case for conserving large carnivores in Yellowstone and elsewhere, which is important for an overall ecological awareness as well as for ethical reasons.

Although the regeneration of nature due to wolves may be questionable, the reintroduction of wolves into the ecosystem of the North Western Rockies has had an impact also on cultural regeneration in the wake of colonization and the stifling of culture that had come with it. Not far from Yellowstone, in bordering Idaho, the 1990s showed a different kind of experiment that involved the reintroduction of wolves into an area that had not seen them for nearly a hundred years.

It is the cultural memory of the persecution and extermination of the indigenous people alongside with wolves that also resurfaces in the wolf recovery initiatives taken in the mid-1990s by the state of Idaho in conjunction with the Nez Perce tribe, whose name refers to the wolf bone with which their warriors once used to pierce the septum of their noses (Lopez 1978: 105). As Patrick Impero Wilson has shown in detail, the wolves of central Idaho became a catalyst for the cultural politics over natural resource management in the American West. Because of state resistance the federal government decided to seek the help of the native Nez Perce in managing the wolf recovery programme, a move that in the end may have had more to do with the cultural politics of decolonization and granting sovereignty to the Nez Perce on land that had been ceded from them but over which they had retained certain rights of usage. One of the principal challenges facing the tribe, Wilson argues, was 'to overcome a bias towards federal and state agencies as managers of land and wildlife resources – an area where native tribes have not generally been recognized as a primary actor' (Wilson 1999: 554). Nonetheless, this act of obvious decolonization was an important step in rethinking land use, its shift from traditional utilitarian values to considerations of plurality of cultures, biodiversity going hand in hand with multiculturalism in opposition to a restriction of species under white American governance. Although the project presented certain challenges to the Nez Perce, it also afforded them a number of opportunities, as Wilson points out. For as with many native tribes the wolf is also part of the spiritual centre of the Nez Perce, so that re-wolfing the state of Idaho has had a massive impact not only on the regeneration of nature but also on reshaping cultural identity.

> First, the tribe, similar to many environmental organizations, was eager to restore the biodiversity and ecological balance of the Northern Rocky Mountain ecosystem. The return of the wolf would be a major step in achieving a more natural balance between predator and large ungulate populations in central Idaho. Second, the Nez Perce saw a chance to recapture an element of tribal cultural heritage that was diminished, if not lost, by the extermination of the wolf. Like many Native Americans, the Nez Perce have a special affinity with the wolf with which they share a similar history of being persecuted and being forced into ever smaller habitats. Restoring the gray wolf to its historic range would allow the tribe to rekindle its cultural ties to the wolf. For the Nez Perce having the wolf back in the spiritual places of their ancestors would lead to a tremendous uplift in cultural and spiritual values. (Wilson 558–9)

The case of the Nez Perce is consequently a good example to demonstrate how biodiversity and cultural diversity influence each other. It also demonstrates to us the extent to which a benign wolf mythology in conjunction with re-wolfing can contribute to restoring a cultural identity that had been lost, whereas in Germany – in the minds of some – the presence of wolves in conjunction with a mythology that has traditionally maligned the wolf fuels a political discourse that, with its comparison of wolves and Muslim immigrants, aims at stifling cultural diversification. One can see by way of these two examples how biodiversity and cultural diversity interact, and how mythologization plays a major role in this interaction. While Idaho reflects the potential of cultural healing and enrichment, given the opportunities recognized in wolf management granted to the indigenous population, which with its longer historical presence, its sense of permanence and cultural respect for the environment has traditionally been more in tune with straddling the divide between the extraction of natural resources and ecological preservation of nature (Wilson 563), the case of Lusatia reflects a volatile situation in which the presence of wolves has the potential of cultural stigmatization and impoverishment, if a party like the *AfD* were ever to come to power.

Unfortunately, the benign Native American wolf mythology is a phenomenon that is in itself jeopardized as we proceed from one generation to the next, with the Little Red Riding Hood syndrome and its much-maligned wolf also taking hold of indigenous cultures as what could be considered a form of recolonization in which the value system of the dominant white culture threatens to obliterate the indigenous cosmology and wisdom. While Kaisa Lappalainen has recently given us a very detailed analysis of the impact of the Grimm tale on North American wolf wars, Pierotti and Wildcat have shown that a study among native people indicated that elders (over sixty years of age) did not fear wolves and viewed them as brothers, while the middle-aged were somewhat indifferent about wolves, and the young between fifteen and thirty were ready to shoot them, 'a classic example of native people being poisoned by the attitudes of the dominant culture' (Pierotti/Wildcat 1999: 199). As Lappalainen points out, it is especially the hunter of the fairy tale whom, given the madness of gun culture in North America, wolf-phobics generally valorize 'as the protector necessary in safeguarding domestic space against a predatory intrusion, be it the government, a criminalized trespasser, or a wolf' (Lappalainen 2019: 762).

Books such as Nate Blakeslee's *The Wolf: A True Story of Survival* (2017) on Yellowstone wolf O-Six named after the year she was born create awareness for the plight of wolves. Embodying the cultural war between those who try to preserve the vanishing Western way of life and those eager to create an ecological balance in the United States' most iconic national park O-Six is the most famous female wolf in the Lamar valley, her story a sort of Bildungsroman or romance, setting out from her natal pack in search of a mate and her encounter with two male wolves of which she chooses the smaller one. Thus begins the love triangle between the three wolves all based on three years of close observation and diary notes the author was given by wolf watcher Laurie Lyman and renowned wolf researcher Rich McIntyre. The unique angle of this book is that it is written from the perspective of the wolf. Although non-fiction it reads like fiction, and is now being considered for a movie by Leonardo di Caprio's company, geared to acquaint a large audience with wolves who are to a certain extent still being mythologized. Although I readily agree with scholars such as Luigi Boitani and Kaisa Lappalainen that imagined wolves have massive influence over biological ones, it is a welcome development to see such books on the rise, as there is a vital need for educating the public about attempts at understanding the reality of wolves.

7. Rewilding the World

The story in Germany is very different from the United States, but both cases demonstrate how nature impacts culture and how in turn culture (the wolf myth) impacts our treatment of nature, how wolf politics are closely intertwined with the politics of human migration and perceptions and uses of the land, of a cultural landscape in terms of its agricultural use but also in the sense of a landscape shaping the culture of its inhabitants. These perceptions are being challenged by the presence of wolves and beg rethinking, in Inner Mongolia and Idaho as much as in Lusatia. It has therefore been the aim of my book to create awareness about how the wolf myth has shaped our treatment of this species and humans compared with them. Chapters 6 and 7 in particular have engaged with fictional and non-fictional responses to the presence versus absence of wolves in our environment in order to gain a deeper understanding of the links between wolf politics and their effects on human populations in terms of their destitution or healing, their identity and questions of migration in precarious parts of the world. Although written in English, my book would be very important also for audiences in Germany and Austria, where the presence of wolves has created heated debates.

Chapter 8

EPILOGUE
DREAMING OF WOLVES: THE CHILDREN OF LYCAON IN THE AGE OF PSYCHOANALYSIS

Then out across open ground trying to scream. As he tried he retched howls. His screams were vomited howls. Trying to shout to his people he heard only his own howls. (Ted Hughes, *Tales from Ovid*, 18)

Ted Hughes's poetic version of Lycaon's exile in wolf shape is rather close to Ovid's *Metamorphoses*, where the tyrant of Arcadia makes a run for 'the silent fields', howling aloud, attempting speech in vain, foam gathering at the corners of his mouth (Ovid 2004: 13). The myth gives us two key ingredients of trauma: the inability to speak and the loss of humanity. Trauma is characterized by a repression of emotions which are too overwhelming to be faced. In their readings of the Holocaust Cathy Caruth and others have characterized trauma as 'a punctual blow to the psyche that overwhelms its functioning, disables its defences, and absents it from direct contact with the brutalizing event itself' (Forter 2007: 259). Representing trauma in literature seems to be impossible according to Cathy Caruth, as 'such an act of narration risks betraying the truth of the trauma, defined as an incomprehensible event that defies all representations' (Leys 1995: 269). The Holocaust survivor Primo Levi had expressed a similar thought in his memoir *If This Is a Man*, claiming that 'our language lacks words to express this offense, the demolition of a man' (Levi 2007: 32).

Yet myths have the capacity to express universal trauma, an experience not linked to time or place, as Hughes and Ovid demonstrate. In *Mythologies* (1957), Roland Barthes approached myth from the perspective of semiology, addressing its capacity to translate into different times and cultures. By applying Saussurean structuralism to myth Barthes concludes that 'it has at its disposal an unlimited mass of signifiers' and that 'there is no fixity in mythical concepts: they can come into being, alter, disintegrate, disappear completely,' in fact myth 'often does nothing but re-present itself' (Barthes 1972: 120). Barthes's concept of unstable myths demonstrates that they are indeed open to 'translation' in the sense of a re-interpretation. It is especially Lycaon's failure after transforming into a wolf to use human language, the fact that his trauma remains hidden in bestial form and unheard by humanity that accompanies the experience of exile through time and space. The Lycaon myth, like many others, may thus contain a blueprint for a more profound understanding of trauma of the migrant, who remains unheard, dehumanized, and whose exodus and exile trigger times of despair. Myth as a precursor of psychoanalysis: both offer an understanding of trauma in the context of enforced migration and exile, one in poetic terms, the other through rationalization, but both engaging with the image of the wolf.

Especially in the years from 1915 to 1930 the sensation of repressed *logos* as we see it in this myth and the metaphor of the wolf is deeply intertwined with psychoanalysis and its reaction to increasing fears of homelessness. Some narratives at the beginning of the twentieth century show us to what extent the medieval outlaw as wolf has morphed from a paradigm of race to an internal form of exile. Specifically C. G. Jung, Sigmund Freud and Hermann Hesse involve dreams and fantasies about wolves and attempts at integrating the wolf as shadow, of turning the demonized wolf into a Brother Wolf. This idea of Brother Wolf, in which we can observe an approximation between psychoanalysis and indigenous culture, is engaged for its potential to come to terms with exile, its enforced peregrinations (a word derived from *peregrinus*, stranger, foreigner or exile) and the subsequent transformation of identity.

As one of the most prominent modernist variants of Lycaon's exile as a wolf embodying the terror of solitude and neurosis in dark urban forests Hermann Hesse's *Steppenwolf* (Der Steppenwolf, 1927) reflects the author's own interest in psychoanalysis. An accumulation of distressing events in his life – the First World War, his youngest son's illness, the death of his father, Hesse's marital crisis and the mental illness of his wife Mia – plunged him into such depression in the mid-1910s that he decided to undergo psychotherapy at a private clinic in Lucerne with one of C. G. Jung's assistants, Josef Bernhard Lang. It was an experience that found literary expression in his novel *Demian* (1919), but lingers on in the story of the Steppenwolf. It also makes clear how resorting to mythical structures and paradigms can aid the process of coming to terms with neurosis, especially in view of the detail in myth of a human turning into a wolf, undoubtedly a metaphor for times of psychic strain and emotional hardship.

For his wolf allegory Hesse drew heavily on Jung's concept of the 'shadow', which the Swiss psychoanalyst had attributed to the collective unconscious of a whole people, the German *Volk* seized by the spirit of

Wotan. Jung's theory in his famous 'Wotan' essay from 1936 where he equates the mythical God of storm, war and rage (note that the German word *Wut*, rage, is derived from him) with the Germans in the grip of National Socialism is a barely concealed reference to Hitler as the shadow of the *Volk*, as the political personification of Wotan by whom the national psyche has become *ergriffen* (seized).

I noticed peculiar disturbances in the unconscious of my German patients which could not be ascribed to their personal psychology. Such non-personal phenomena always manifest themselves in dreams as mythological motifs that are also to be found in legends and fairy tales throughout the world. I have called these mythological motifs archetypes: that is, typical modes or forms in which these collective phenomena are experienced. There was a disturbance of the collective unconscious in every single one of my patients. The archetypes I had observed expressed primitivity, violence and cruelty. I suggested that the 'blonde beast' was stirring in an uneasy slumber and that an outburst was not impossible (Jung 1989: 2).

There is a lycanthropic moment in this psychoanalytical theory, Wotan being densely associated with wolves. The blonde beast, however, that Jung is referring to is a concept derived from Nietzsche's *On the Genealogy of Morals* (Zur Genealogie der Moral, 1887), Nietzsche's argument that the unconscious in the European psyche cannot be suppressed by the artificial morality imposed upon it through Christianity. Jung saw the blonde beast not only as a threat that could seize Germany and other nations at any moment but also as a potential for spiritual renewal. Despite Jung's highly contested equation of Nazism and the *furor teutonicus* of the Wotan myth with its berserkers appropriated to incite the masses at the end of the war, he conceded in a later radio programme with the BBC (Introduction: The fight with the shadow, 3 Nov 1946) that this 'condition was not by any means a purely Teutonic phenomenon [...] [but] the onslaught of primitive forces was more or less universal. The only difference lay in the German mentality itself, which proved to be more susceptible because of the marked proneness of the Germans to mass psychology' (Jung 1989: 2).

In line with Jung's argument in the Wotan essay, Haller's struggle with his own shadow, his repressed subconscious drives, is a literary example for Nietzsche's blonde beast lurking underneath bourgeoisie layers of culture and civility. Following Jung's argument that the shadow needs to be integrated for the psyche to heal, Hesse's story displays a sense of hope for psychic healing, an optimism reflected in Haller's attempt to integrate his wolf side in his overall personality. This is achieved with the help of Hermine and Pablo, his Magic Theatre, where Haller learns to separate from his wolf nature. In a way, based on his own experience with Jungian psychoanalysis, Hesse is rewriting the Lycaon myth by offering an ending in which Lycaon is able to return from wolf form to human shape. His *Steppenwolf* thus complements those Arcadian rituals and tales that exist to this day which express the possibility of escaping permanent exile. This happens, for example, in the Zeus Lykaios rites whose devotees leave their shadow at the gate of the underworld (Buxton 1987: 72), or in the descriptions by second-century Greek geographer Pausanias and Pliny, according to whom Arcadian youth regained human form after abstaining from human flesh for nine years (Pausanias 1918: 8.2.6).

In Freudian psychoanalysis, too, wolves form the shadow of a distant past in the famous case study (1918) of another lonely lycanthrope in the wake of Lycaon, Wolf Man Sergei Pankeiev:

> I dreamed that it is night and I am lying in bed (the foot of my bed was under the window, and outside there was a row of old walnut trees. I know that it was winter in my dream, and night-time). Suddenly the window opens of its own accord and terrified, I see that there are a number of white wolves sitting in the big walnut tree outside the window. There were six or seven of them. The wolves were white all over and looked more like foxes or sheepdogs because they had big tails like foxes and their ears were pricked up like dogs watching something. Obviously fearful that the wolves were going to gobble me up I screamed and woke up. (Freud 2002: 227)

The wolves in Sergei Pankeiev's repetitive dreams are repressed psychic material, Freud's foreign object within the self or the Jungian shadow. They evoke the 'stranger' as one of the meanings of the *vargr*, and they may point to the father in his role as sovereign, as Freud says, as psychoanalyst himself sovereign ruler over the neuroses of his patients, with his responsibility to undo the permanent exile of myth and transform the animal into a human being, to give his patient a voice, relieve him from anger and pent-up frustration, and undo the trauma of being a wolf. I am saying this with a sense of irony and by adopting the metaphor that should not be applied, for who are we to talk about the reduction to the status of an animal?

8. Epilogue

To Freud the dream signifies the trauma of Pankeiev the child at the age of about a year and a half after witnessing his parents during an *a tergum* act, doing the 'beast with two backs' so to speak. The wolves in the dream are completely quiet, they do not emit any sounds, all they do is watch intently. Their silence reflects the Lycaon myth, the boy Sergei also who cannot speak, exiled in 'the silent field' of his childhood and all the neuroses emerging from it. However, beyond the Greek myth with its notion of exile and exclusion the world of Russian folklore also seems to have a presence in this dream. Carlo Ginzburg has emphasized the links between Pankeiev's dream and certain beliefs of Slavic folklore in which people born 'with a shirt' (i.e. wrapped in the amniotic sack), or born in the days between Christmas and Epiphany (the famous Twelve Nights), supposedly had special shamanic characteristics, including the power to transform into werewolves. In this context, the dream of Pankeiev (according to Freud he was born 'with the shirt' on Christmas day) assumes the character of an initiatory dream, perhaps induced by the stories told to little Pankeiev by his nanny. Ginzburg thought that the lack of knowledge of Slavic folklore prevented Freud from realizing the existence of such elements in the dream of the wolf man (Ginzburg 1990: 147–9). Freud, however, had alluded to the folklore content of his patient's dream, the six or seven white wolves in the trees pointing specifically to 'The Wolf and the Seven Young Kids' (005 Grimm Brothers) as well as to a tale Pankeiev's grandfather had told him about a tailor cutting off the wolf's tail and subsequently hiding from that wolf up in a tree (Gardiner 1973: 205).

In Freud's case study, Lycaon's crime of cannibalism may correspond to the crime of incest, for Nicholas Abraham and Maria Torok's study *The Wolf Man's Magic Word: A Cryptonomy* (1976) tells us the wolves in Freud's Wolf Man case do not only signal the act between father and mother but also the father's desire for his daughter. Sergei, Abraham and Torok argue, is haunted by a set of repressed 'pleasure words' encrypted into his subconscious, words such as the number six in Russian, *shiest*, the number of wolves Pankeiev initially remembers from his dream. *Shiest* signifies the phallic 'mast' as much as to *siestorka*, the Russian diminutive for sister, and the German *Schwester* (Vine, 146), so that the six-pack of wolves seen on the tree could be a hidden reference to his sister. By way of revealing several of these cryptonyms – words that hide in the patient's subconscious – Abraham and Torok conclude that rather than having witnessed an *Urszene* (primal scene), as Freud claims, the boy's sister 'makes *buka* to Father' (Vine 2005: 154), *buka* being a

Russian word for *wolf*. This interpretation is in line with traditional, especially medieval, images of the wolf as a creature driven by sexual lust, a motif Dante still uses for his she-wolf but that also takes us to another modernist narrative about the loneliness of exile combined with metempsychosis and the taboo of incest: Franz Kafka's *Metamorphosis* (Die Verwandlung, 1915).

Kafka's story is completely void of wolves, and yet, it is the wolf itself as metaphor of expulsion that has undergone transformation in this tale. Like Hesse, who in 1927 foresaw another war, Kafka wrote about exile, loneliness and neurosis tied to an acute intuition about the terror lying in wait for Europe and the world in the 1930s and 1940s. While Hesse shows us the wolf in his full modernist fatigue and despair, Kafka gives us the old Germanic *vargr* (wolf and outlaw) stripped of all lupine strength and fearsomeness, reduced to the lowliest of vermin, a loathsome *Ungeziefer*. Although far from a wolf in shape, Gregor Samsa is still in the position of the medieval *vargr* and the Roman *homo sacer*, who due to his parasitic nature became outlawed by their communities. The lycanthropic outcast reappears as a psycho-somatic paradigm in which his impurity is deeply embedded in both racial and oedipal structures.

As Katja Garloff has shown, Kafka's writing is deeply tied to his Jewishness and the racial melancholy that determines Jewish culture in the years before the Holocaust (2007: 123–40). His language of abjection anticipates almost prophetically the Nazis' treatment of humans as animals of the lowest order. It is primarily the word *Ungeziefer* of the first sentence with its meaning of an unclean animal not suited for sacrifice – precisely the definition of the *homo sacer* – that makes this story herald the dehumanizing language and atrocities experienced by the victims of 'racial hygiene' during the Third Reich. That Gregor is 'ein ungeheures Ungeziefer', a monstrous vermin, means that he has no place in the family or in God's order, an existence Agamben has seen as the fundamental condition for the camps:

> The wish to lend a sacrificial aura to the extermination of the Jews by means of the term 'Holocaust' was [...] an irresponsible historiographical blindness. The Jew living under Nazism is the privileged negative referent of the new biopolitical sovereignty and is, as such, a flagrant case of a homo sacer in the sense of a life that may be killed but not sacrificed. His killing constitutes neither capital punishment nor a sacrifice, but simply the actualization of a mere 'capacity to be killed inherent to the condition of the Jew as such.

8. Epilogue 195

[...] Jews were exterminated not in a mad and giant holocaust but exactly as Hitler had announced, as 'lice', which is to say, as bare life. (Agamben 1995: 114)

Gregor experiences the same silent fields as Lycaon. As with the king of Arcadia, his humanity is permanently trapped in animal shape and no longer perceptible to other humans. Full of complex emotion and thought, qualities that are primarily human, he desperately wants to express himself but ends up producing only animal sounds in the same way as Lycaon emits nothing but howls. Gregor displays no anger, unlike Lycaon; there is only melancholy and finally his self-sacrifice of almost Christ-like proportions to make room for his family to prosper.

The story clearly reveals the symmetry of *homo sacer* and sovereign, Gregor as the former, his father the latter, Derrida's despot as Wolf Man, but not until Gregor has been abased to the level of vermin. His 'silent field' is his room, his place of exile, accompanied by the paternal violence hidden to the eyes of the world. Every time Gregor leaves his room he experiences the terror of his family, his father's in particular, who throws apples at his son, but also from his sister who in the end craves her brother's death more than the others. *Weg muss es*, she says (Kafka 1989: 100), 'it must disappear', stripping him entirely of a human soul by using the impersonal *es*.

If we compare Kafka's story with Freud's Wolf Man, we can see how Lycaon's crime of breaking the taboo of cannibalism takes the form of incest. Both narratives share a complex triangular family situation in which the exiled protagonist competes with his father not only for his mother but also for his sister. Gregor's desire for his sister is aesthetically and erotically motivated, the pleasure of her violin play feeding his sexual desire but making him wonder whether he truly is an animal considering that music moves him so ('War er ein Tier, da ihn Musik so ergriff?' Kafka 98). When he has perished, his sister places her hand around her father's neck, a scene that shows all the symptoms of the Neo-Freudian Electra complex.

Parallels abound between the Freudian Wolf Man and Kafka's story, based on their shared racial melancholy that informs German Jewish culture before the Holocaust, their oedipal neurosis, and the link between the sovereign father as agent of expulsion and the exiled neurotic son as his victim. The position of the Wolf Man in the sense in which Derrida and Agamben have used this concept is complex in both narratives. He certainly appears first and foremost in Pankeiev as an exiled *vargr* and neurotic son, but perhaps even in Freud as a

Jew. Thus Freud can be seen to unite the two positions of sovereign and *homo sacer* in himself: sovereign psychoanalyst, 'Father Freud' (as Arnold Zweig used to call him), and 'godless Jew' (as Freud once called himself), forced into exile at the end of his life. In a way, the Wolf Man case became a sinister personal harbinger for Freud twenty years prior to his own expulsion, in similarity to the ominous significance Kafka's *Ungeziefer* has in view of the Holocaust.

In the end, the fate of Lycaon is also that of Ovid himself, his trauma after being banned from Rome by Augustus for the crime, most likely, of *carmen et error*, his erotic poetry and a personal indiscretion. We know almost nothing of his exile, but there is one literary text that provides us with a poetic reading of his final years in Tomis: David Malouf's *An Imaginary Life* (1978). This novel about the strange relationship between Ovid and a child raised by wolves, an allusion to the ever-present Roman myth in his life, is an exploration of the trauma and, strangely, pleasures of exile: not only Ovid's exile among the Thracian tribe of the Getae in the Danube delta, but also of Europeans in Malouf's native Australia.

At the beginning it seems to Ovid as if he had been banned to a land full of savages outside of Roman law, 'another order of beings [...] not yet [...] fully human' (M 13). His most acute trauma is his loss of language accompanying his expulsion from the Latin tongue, 'that perfect tongue in which all things can be spoken, even pronouncements of exile' (M 13). It feels to him as if he has died, in line with the *homo sacer* as the one banished to the night side of life, death, his fate eerily resembling that of Lycaon who features prominently at the beginning of his *Metamorphoses*: 'I am dead. I am relegated to the region of silence. All I can do is shout' (M 20). Ovid's loss of speech, however, initiates his transformation. Unlike Lycaon, who is condemned to permanent dehumanization, Ovid is beginning to thrive in his exile, reflecting Malouf's belief that cultural transformation is necessary for survival. Scholars have often asked themselves and the author if *An Imaginary Life* addresses the topic of European exile in Australia. As Avis McDonald has argued, Malouf has confirmed in an interview with Julie Copeland (1982) that Ovid's exile from Rome can be read in the context of Australia as the colonial edge in relation to the European centre, although he warns us against a simple equation of Tomis with Brisbane (McDonald 1988: 52). It is more than that, however. In spite of its persistent use of the wolf metaphor poised between perdition and fruition, Malouf's novel is a rare hymn played to a solitary existence in exile and the possibilities of reconciliation with it.

8. Epilogue

When one day a feral child appears in Tomis who has been raised by wolves, he becomes a catalyst for their shared metamorphosis as the child's becoming human parallels the poet's strange transcendence to a sort of post-human state of being eventually taking him from life to death. The child teaches the poet the value of all life and the necessity to transform: 'He has no notion of the otherness of things. [...] I must drive out my old self and let the universe in. The creatures will come creeping back' (M 92). Despite his loss of language, speech in all this is essential, the poet tells us. He learns to love the Gaetic language and decides to teach it to the child rather than his own native Latin, realizing that Gaetic is a language of harmony and reconciliation, the way he himself once used to speak as a child, while Latin is full of distinctions and delineations. In 'learning the sounds made by men he [the child] is making himself man (M 88). And Ovid slowly comes to realize that his place of exile is the true destination he has always been seeking.

Although animals are part of a benign universe that the poet embraces and although he acknowledges that 'indeed there is some part of our nature that we share with wolves and something of their nature that is in us' (M 2), the wolf is still a metaphor of fear and ultimately of the poet's death. Here too, like in Freud's Wolf Man case, there is much dreaming of wolves.

> Sometimes wolves come. [...] Howling. We dig together, and they pay no more attention to me than they would to a ghost. But I know that whatever it is they are scratching after, I must discover before them, or I am lost. So I dig harder, faster, sweating, with the moonlight greasy upon me. Unable to tell myself: this is a dream. I know what it is we are looking for. It is the grave of the poet Ovid – Publius Ovidius Naso. [...] In all this desolation no one knows where he lies. (M 10)

The wolf signifies his fear of dying unremembered, unloved in exile. At least these are his initial fears, for he will learn to transcend these anxieties and embrace his life and death on the margins of civilization. As he transforms more and more beyond his own humanity, the contours between him and the animal world become increasingly blurred, his own lycanthropy pervading his dreams:

> I fall asleep almost immediately, and dream. [...] We have all been transformed, the whole group of us, and become part of the woods. We are mushrooms, we are stones. [...] I am a pool of water. [...]

And softly nearby, there are footsteps. A deer. The animal's face leans toward me. I am filled with tenderness for it. [...] Part of me enters the deer. [...] What if a wolf came, I suddenly ask myself? What if the next tongue that touched me were the wolf's tongue, rough, greedy, drinking me down to the last drop and leaving me dry? That too is possible. I imagine it, being drawn up into the wolf's belly. I prepare for it. (M 55–6)

It is the moment Lycaon becomes a wolf that is captured here and, yet, it lacks the same trauma but displays a rather pleasant, almost erotic experience similar to the one Cantù describes in his wolf dreams in *The Line Becomes a River* with its Jungian vision of integrating the wolf as shadow in his personality. Malouf imagines Lycaon's transformation into a wolf as his human essence merging with the creaturely world, as a deconstruction of European logocentrism, and a transcendence that liberates the soul. For this too the wolf can stand.

From human to animal, from life to death. In Malouf's version the poet dies after crossing the Danube near its delta, the River Ister, so central to the thought of Heidegger and Hölderlin, Heidegger thinking about Hölderlin. It is the mythical river that flows through the field of *lethe*, a silent field in itself separating life from death, human consciousness from the unconscious. *Lethe*, as Heidegger has shown, in his Parmenides lectures appears in its three functions of (1) concealment, (2) forgetting and (3) destruction. Heidegger wrote of these things in the winter semester of 1942/43 in Freiburg, at a time when millions were sentenced to *lethe* in the concentration camps. These too are a salient example of the silent fields in which the myth is linked to biopolitics and where the screams of the *homo sacer* remain unheard. It is that silent field of *lethe* that ultimately reveals the light of truth, the Greek *aletheia*, and that lies at the base of the myth of Lycaon and all the massacres of the world.

We have encountered these silent fields where trauma reigns supreme for migrants caught in limbo between their loss of home and an uncertain future, between life and death. They are the metaphorical wolf-lands where the *homo sacer* is perceived as *vargr*, wolf and outlaw, be they refugees in the US–Mexican borderlands or Muslim or African asylum seekers in Lusatia. The most extreme version of these silent fields, however, is the extermination camps where, having abandoned themselves, the so-called *Muselmänner* are caught in limbo between life and death.

8. Epilogue

Malouf draws a very different picture of these silent fields. Here the poet's moments just before his death, *lethe*, are painted in positive and poetic hues, as a beautiful form of transcendence that liberates him from an exile he no longer suffers from. On the contrary, his exile has become a place of healing. It prepares him for a journey to absolute freedom that inevitably leads to death, described here as a moment of bliss more reminiscent of Heidegger's harmony in the fourfold (of sky, earth, mortals and gods) than of Paul Celan's harrowing words *in den Lüften da liegt man nicht eng* (a grave in the clouds where it won't feel so tight). 'We are continuous with earth in all the particles of our physical being, as in our breathing we are continuous with sky. Between our bodies and the world there is unity and commerce' (M 147). And thus he finally arrives in the place he has 'dreamed of so often [...] but could never find in all my wanderings in sleep – the point on the earth's surface where I disappear. It is not at all as I had imagined. There are no wolves' (M 151).

There are no wolves, only the wolf-child, a sort of godhead. And like Tournier in *Le Roi des Aulnes*, Malouf plays with the myth of Saint Christopher here, but inverts it: in his version it is the child *qua* Jesus that leads Ovid *qua* St Christopher, saint of all migrants, across the river.

Myth has given us a blueprint of human limit experience and trauma. It offers possibilities of translating trauma, in spite of trauma's resistance to representation. What it means to be human has forever become a questionable category in view of the never-ending crimes against humanity, from the persecution of women as witches to the massacres under Hitler and Stalin, and well beyond to political violence today. This uncertainty about the human condition may explain why some authors choose to approach the representation of these crimes in mythological terms. As a timeless form of representation myth reflects the ultimate inability of representing some of the world's atrocities in realistic terms. It can be argued that if history's most traumatizing moments defer all language and representation – Lycaon attempting speech in vain – myth itself as a form of expression is but a silent field. Nonetheless, at times we see those – Primo Levi, for example – exiled to the field of *lethe* resort to its images: the descent into Hell (Levi's Dante), unspeakable suffering and the futility of human effort (Levi's Tantalus).

What used to be the arbitrariness of the will of the gods in myth has become the arbitrariness of the will of sovereigns in cultures of resentment who compare those seeking better lives and therefore desperately breaking through international borders with verminous animals, condemning them to places where human rights no longer apply, where *homo homini lupus est*. This image too, derived from Plautus's *Asinaria* and Hobbes, Primo Levi was aware of. In *The Truce*, the sequel to *If This Is a Man*, he puts them into the mouth of a Greek concentration camp inmate: 'I had felt it (the concentration camp) as a monstrous upheaval, a loathsome anomaly in my history and the history of the world; he [the Greek] as a sad confirmation of things well known. "There is always war", man is a wolf to man: an old story' (Levi 2007: 224). In such a world it is but a step from the dream to the nightmare.

The power of myth, the power of dehumanizing metaphors, and the damage they cause: my last thoughts are with the wolves, persistently misjudged in our Western, agrarian cultures with their time-worn distrust of vagrancy and fear of intrusion. Overall, unlike migrants, it is difficult to see wolves as they really are, stripped of all metaphors. Barry Lopez once put it this way:

> We do not know very much at all about animals. We cannot understand them except in terms of our own needs and experiences. And to approach them solely in terms of our Western imagination is, really, to deny the animal. It behooves us to visit with a people with whom we share a planet and an interest in wolves but who themselves come from a different time-space and who, so far as we know, are very much closer to the wolf than we will ever be. (Lopez 1978: 86)

It behooves us to visit with the people who misjudge the wolf less than our Western cultures do – the indigenous, hunting and nomadic cultures, which historically have displayed a more intimate knowledge of wolves based on these cultures' closer proximity to nature. Such cultures are, however, as endangered as the wolf is.

They are deeply divisive, these wolves, in the rhetoric and discourses their presence produces. Here too myth matters, myth in the sense of popular superstition shaping a political rhetoric redolent with metaphor and that has stimulated critical artistic reactions over time, especially in view of the politics of human migration. We have seen that both politics and the arts rarely relinquish the wolf myth itself.

The wolf is thus trapped inside the borders of our imagination, its metaphors haunting our psyche. Psychoanalysis may call for its integration as it straddles the boundary between wildness and freedom on the one hand, and domestication and enslavement on the other, but it seems to persist in being locked up as a damaging myth and metaphor. Right-wing xenophobia and fears of immigration are as much manifestations of that locked-up wolf as the new age belief that this undomesticated, border-crossing wolf may have the potential to liberate us.

And yet, we have seen that they may teach us important lessons. Despite their territorialism, wolves cross territorial boundaries and have been known to share territories as do indigenous and nomadic cultures, so that the zoology of wolves and the history of nomadism and indigeneity can teach us about the politics of hospitality, shared land use, cosmopolitanism and an appreciation of diversity, biodiversity and cultural diversity. What remains in the end is my hope, while keeping the dangers of anthropocentrism in mind, that these glimpses into the history of the perception of wolves and migrants may contribute to making us lose our fear of the foreign, think beyond borders, in terms of a politics of hospitality, biodiversity and world citizenship. Oddly enough, Immanuel Kant, who never left Königsberg, thus never experiencing what it means to be *xenos* in the ancient Greek sense of the foreigner who instils feelings of hostility, was among the first modern thinkers to provide us with some of the key ideas of tolerance towards strangers and foreigners. Surely, we would be a step closer to his idea of world peace if one day we could follow writers like Cantù and Ovid crossing the two rivers – the Rio Grande, the Danube – where the cemented borders shielding the United States and the EU become fluid, and if we could then say: there are no wolves here in the way we had imagined them, all our demons are gone, we know now they had only lived inside us.

REFERENCES

Adams, Jad. *Kipling. A Life*. New Delhi: Haus Publishing, 2005.
Agamben, Giorgio. *Homo Sacer: Sovereign Power and Bare Life*. Palo Alto: Stanford UP, 1995.
Agamben, Giorgio. *Remnants of Auschwitz: The Witness and the Archive*. New York: Zone Books, 2002.
Agamben, Giorgio. *State of Exception*. Stanford: Stanford UP, 2005.
Ahne, Petra. *Wölfe*. Berlin: Matthes & Seitz, 2016.
Anahita, Sine and Tamara L. Mix. 'Retrofitting Frontier Masculinity for Alaska's War against Wolves.' *Gender and Society*, 20.3 (June, 2006): 332–53.
Arendt, Hannah. *The Origins of Totalitarianism*. San Diego, New York: Harvest, 1973.
Aristotle. *Metaphysics*. Oxford: Clarendon, 1993.
Arnds, Peter. *Lycanthropy in German Literature*. London/New York: Palgrave Macmillan, 2015.
Arnds, Peter. *Wilhelm Raabe's Der Hungerpastor and Charles Dickens's David Copperfield: Intertextuality of Two Bildungsromane*. New York: Peter Lang, 1997.
Arora, Steffen. 'Die geschürte Angst vorm bösen Wolf.' *Der Standard*. 5 August 2019. https://www.derstandard.at/story/2000107041312/die-geschuerte-angst-vorm-boesen-wolf?ref=article&fbclid=IwAR3Cx0tUJgBBk8CVNpr9ePTZBjgF2GCDkSgjaOB0dzaD3pUzlivPDRTYCHsE
Arpy, Claude. 'The Chinese Are Upset Again.' *Sify News*. 5 May 2008. Web. 14 December 2008.
Augé, Marc. *Non Places: Introduction to an Anthropology of Supermodernity*. London: Verso, 2009.
Baring-Gould, Sabine. *The Book of Werewolves*. (1865) Dublin, Ireland: Nonsuch, 2007.
Barry, Nora Baker. 'Fleur Pillager's Bear Identity in the Novels of Louise Erdrich.' *Studies in American Indian Literatures*. Series 2, 12.2 (Summer 2000): 24–37.
Barthes, Roland. *Mythologies*. New York: The Noonday Press, 1972.
Baschwitz, Kurt. *Hexen und Hexenprozesse. Die Geschichte eines Massenwahns und seiner Bekämpfung*. München: Rütten und Loening Verlag, 1963.
Bayoumi, Moustafa. 'What's a Lone Wolf? It's the Special Name We Give White Terrorists.' *The Guardian*. 4 October 2017. https://www.theguardian.com/commentisfree/2017/oct/04/lone-wolf-white-terrorist-las-vegas
Bender, Hans. 'Die Wölfe kommen zurück.' In: *Erzählte Zeit. 50 deutsche Kurzgeschichten der Gegenwart*. Manfred Durzak (ed.). Stuttgart: Reclam, 1980, 184–9.

Benhabib, Seyla. *The Rights of Others. Aliens, Residents, and Citizens.* Cambridge, Cambridge UP, 2004.
Benjamin, Walter. *Abhandlungen. Gesammelte Schriften.* Vol. I.1. Frankfurt am Main: Suhrkamp, 1991.
Bennhold, Katrin. 'A Fairy-Tale Baddie, the Wolf, Is Back in Germany, and Anti-Migrant Forces Pounce.' *New York Times.* 23 April 2019.
Bennhold, Katrin. 'Wolves Return to Germany, along with Anti-Immigrant Hostilities.' *The Independent.* 14 May 2019.
Bernatzky, Jürgen. 'Der nationalsozialistische Antisemitismus im Spiegel des politischen Plakats.' In: Günther Bernd Ginzel (Ed.). *Antisemitismus. Erscheinungsformen der Judenfeindschaft gestern und heute.* Bielefeld: Verlag Wissenschaft und Politik, 1991.
Bettelheim, Bruno. *The Uses of Enchantment. The Meaning and Importance of Fairy Tales.* New York: Random House, 1977.
Bhabha, Homi K. 'Of Mimicry and Man: The Ambivalence of Colonial Discourse.' In: *The Location of Culture.* London, New York: Routledge, 1994, 85–93.
Biddescombe, Perry. *Werwolf: The History of the National Socialist Guerrilla Movement 1944–1946.* Cardiff: University of Wales Press, 1998.
Biddescombe, Perry. *The Last Nazis: SS Werewolf Guerrilla Resistance in Europe 1944–1947.* Gloucestershire: Tempus, 2000.
Bingener, Reinhard. 'Raubtier Risiko in Deutschland: Der Problem Wolf.' *Frankfurter Allgemeine Zeitung.* 14 February 2018. https://www.faz.net/aktuell/politik/inland/risiko-raubtiere-der-problem-wolf-15445490.html
Bishop, Paul. *The Dionysian Self.* Berlin: de Gruyter, 1995.
Blake, Michael. *Dances with Wolves.* Bath: Lythway, 1991.
Blakeslee, Nate. *The Wolf: A True Story of Survival.* London: Oneworld Publications, 2017.
Blamberger, Günter. *Heinrich von Kleist. Biographie.* Frankfurt am Main: Fischer, 2011.
Bourgault Du Coudray, Chantal. *The Curse of the Werewolf: Fantasy, Horror and the Beast Within.* London: I.B. Tauris, 2006.
Brewton, Vince. 'The Changing Landscape of Violence in Cormac McCarthy's Early Novels and the Border Trilogy.' *The Southern Literary Journal.* 37.1 (Fall, 2004): 121–43.
Bryson, John. *Evil Angels.* New York: Summit Books, 1985.
Buell, Lawrence. *Writing for an Endangered World. Literature, Culture, and Environment in the U.S. and Beyond.* Cambridge/Mass.: Harvard UP, 2001.
Burris, Gregory A. 'The Other from Within: Pan-Turkist Mythmaking and the Expulsion of the Turkish Left.' *Middle Eastern Studies,* 43.4 (Jul, 2007): 611–24.
Burton, Robert. *The Anatomy of Melancholy.* New York: The New York Review of Books Press, 2001.
Buxton, Richard. 'Wolves and Werewolves in Greek Thought.' In: *Interpretations of Greek Mythology.* Jan Bremmer (ed.). London: Routledge, 1987, 60–79.

Canetti, Elias. *Masse und Macht* (1960). Frankfurt am Main: Fischer Verlag, 2011.
Cantú, Francisco. *The Line Becomes a River*. London: Penguin, 2018.
Carter, Angela. *The Bloody Chamber*. London: Vintage, 2006.
Carter, Angela. *The Fairy Tales of Charles Perrault*. London: Penguin, 2008.
Carter, Angela. 'Notes from the frontline.' In: *On Gender and Writing*. Michelene Wandor (ed.). London: Pandora, 1983.
Carter, Angela. *The Sadeian Woman and the Ideology of Pornography*. New York: Pantheon Books, 1978.
Cather, Willa. *My Ántonia*. London: Penguin, 1993.
Cervantes, Miguel de. *La Gitanilla*. The Little Gypsy Girl. http://www.onlineliterature.com/cervantes/exemplary-novels/5/
Chadwick, Douglas. 'Wolf Wars.' *National Geographic*. (March, 2010): 34–55.
Chatwin, Bruce. *The Songlines*. London: Penguin, 1988.
Cheater, Mark. https://www.nwf.org/en/Magazines/National-Wildlife/1998/Wolf-Spirit-Returns-to-Idaho
Cixous, Hélène and Annette Kuhn. 'Castration or Decapitation.' *Signs*, 7.1 (1981): 41–55.
Clark, Colin. 'Severity Has Often Enraged but Never Subdued a Gypsy: The History and Making of European Romani Stereotypes.' In: *The Role of the Romanies: Images and Counter Images of 'Gypsies'/Romanies in European Cultures*. Saul, Nicholas and Susan Tebbutt (ed.). Liverpool: Liverpool UP, 2004, 226–46.
Cohen, Robin. 'Jim, Antonia, and the Wolves Displacement in Cather 's My Antonia.' *Great Plains Quarterly* (2009): 51–60.
Coleman, Jon T. *Vicious: Wolves and Men in America*. New Haven: Yale UP, 2004.
Coonan, Clifford. 'Jiang Rong's *Wolf Totem*. The Year of the Wolf.' *The Independent*. https://www.independent.co.uk/arts-entertainment/books/features/jiang-rongs-wolf-totem-the-year-of-the-wolf-768583.html
Copeland, Julie. 'Interview with David Malouf.' *Australian Literary Studies*, 10.4 (1982): 435.
Cunliffe, Emma. *Weeping on Cue: The Socio-Legal Construction of Motherhood in the Chamberlain Case*. University of British Columbia, dissertation, 2003.
Davis, Charles T. 'Dante's Vision of History.' *Dante Studies*, 118 (2000): 243–59.
Defoe, Daniel. *Robinson Crusoe*. Michael Shinagel (ed.). New York: W. W. Norton, 1994.
Defonseca, Misha. *Surviving with Wolves*. London: Portrait, 2005.
Deleuze, Gilles and Félix Guattari. *A Thousand Plateaus: Capitalism and Schizophrenia*. Trans. Brian Massumi. Minneapolis: University of Minnesota Press, 1987.
Dellamora, Richard. 'Pure Oliver: Or Representation without Agency.' In: *Dickens Refigured: Bodies, Desires, and Other Histories*. John Schad (ed.). Manchester: Manchester UP, 1996, 58–60.
Derrida, Jacques. *The Animal That Therefore I Am*. New York City: Fordham UP, 2008.

Derrida, Jacques. *The Beast and the Sovereign*. Vol. 1 and 2. Trans. Geoffrey Bennington. Chicago and London: University of Chicago Press, 2009.
Dickens, Charles. *Oliver Twist*. London: Wordsworth Classics, 2000.
Douglas, Adam. *The Beast Within. Man, Myths and Werewolves*. London: Orion, 1993.
Draper, John. 'Usury in "The Merchant of Venice".' *Modern Philology*, 331 (August, 1935): 37–47.
Duerr, Hans Peter. *Dreamtime. Concerning the Boundary between Wilderness and Civilization* Trans. Felicitas Goodman. Oxford: Basil. Blackwell, 1985.
Du Maurier, George. *Trilby*. London: J. M. Dent, 1931.
Dundes, Alan. 'Bruno Bettleheim's Uses of Enchantment and Abuses of Scholarship.' *The Journal of American Folklore* 104.411 (1991): 74–83.
Elgot, Jessica. 'How David Cameron's Language on Refugees Has Provoked Anger.' *The Guardian*. 27 January 2016. https://www.theguardian.com/uk-news/2016/jan/27/david-camerons-bunch-of-migrants-quip-is-latest-of-several-such-comments
Eliav-Feldon, "Vagrants or Vermin? Attitudes towards Gypsies in Early Modern Europe," in M. Eliav-Feldon, B. Isaac, and J. Ziegler (eds) *The Origins of Racism in the West*, New York: Cambridge University Press, 2009, 276–291.
Eliav-Feldon, Miriam and Isaac Benjamin, Joseph Ziegler. Ed. *The Origins of Racism in the West*. Cambridge: Cambridge UP, 2009, 276–91.
Erdrich, Louise. *The Painted Drum*. New York: Harper Perennial, 2019.
Erler, A. 'Friedlosigkeit und Werwolfglaube.' *Paideuma*, 1.7 (1940): 303–17.
Fabiunke, Günter. *Martin Luther als Nationalökonom*. Berlin: Akademie Verlag, 1963.
Fisher, Jerilyn and Ellen S. Silber. 'Good and Bad beyond Belief: Teaching Gender Lessons through Fairy Tales and Feminist Theory.' *Women's Studies Quarterly*, 28.3/4 (2000): 121–36.
Fogleman, Valerie M. 'American Attitudes towards Wolves: A History of Misperception.' *Environmental Review*, 13 (1989): 63–94.
Folsom, Raphael Brewster. *The Yaquis and the Empire: Violence, Spanish Imperial Power, and the Native Resilience in Colonial Mexico*. New Haven: Yale UP, 2014.
Forter, Greg. 'Freud, Faulkner, Caruth: Trauma and the Politics of Literary Form.' *Narrative*, 15.3 (2007): 259–85.
Franklin, Ruth. *Lies and Truth in Holocaust Fiction*. Oxford: Oxford UP, 2011.
Fraser, Angus. *The Gypsies*. Oxford: Blackwell, 1992.
Freud, Sigmund. *The Wolf Man and Other Cases*. London: Penguin, 2002.
Fridlund, Emily. *History of Wolves*. London: Weidenfeld & Nicolson, 2017.
Fulbrook, Mary. 'Myth-Making and National Identity: The Case of the G.D.R.' In: *Myths and Nationhood*. G. Hosking and G. Schopflin (eds.). London: Hurst, 1997, 72–87.
Gallagher, Sarah. 'Immigration "Wolves" Take Children across US Border.' *Liberty Voice*. 24 June 2014.

Gardiner, Muriel. *The Wolf Man and Sigmund Freud*. London: Penguin, 1973.
Garloff, Katja. 'The Jewish Crypt: W.G. Sebald and the Melancholy of Modern Jewish Culture.' *The Germanic Review: Literature, Culture, Theory*, 82.2 (2007): 123–40.
Gifford, William. *The Works of Ben Jonson*. In nine volumes. 2nd vol. London: W. Bulmer, 1816.
Gille, Klaus. 'Der Berg und die Seele: Überlegungen zu Tiecks Runenberg.' *Neophilologus: An International Journal of Modern and Medieval Language and Literature*, 77 (1993): 611–23.
Ginzburg, Carlo. *Myths, Emblems, Clues*. Trans. John and Anne C. Tedeschi. London: Hutchinson Radius, 1990.
Glîchezâre, Heinrich der. *Reinhart Fuchs*. Stuttgart: Reclam, 2011.
Gowland, Angus. *The Worlds of Renaissance Melancholy. Robert Burton in Context*. Cambridge: Cambridge UP, 2006.
Grahan, David. *The Atlantic*. 19 June 2018. https://www.theatlantic.com/politics/archive/2018/06/trump-immigrants-infest/563159
Grass, Günter. *Die Blechtrommel*. Darmstadt: Luchterhand, 1986.
Grimm, Jacob. *Deutsche Mythologie*. Göttingen: In der Dieterischen Buchhandlung, 1835; also 1844 edition.
Grimm, Wilhelm. 'Die mythische Bedeutung des Wolfes.' *Zeitschrift für deutsches Altertum*, 12 (1865): 203–28.
Grimm Brothers. *Kinder- und Hausmärchen*. Vol. 1 and 2. Stuttgart: Reclam, 2007.
Grimmelshausen, Hans Jacob Christoph von. *The Adventures of Simplicius Simplicissimus*. Trans. Mike Mitchell. Sawtry: Dedalus, 1999.
Grönbech, Wilhelm. *Geist der Germanen*. Hamburg: Hanseatische Verlagsanstalt, 1940/1942.
Grönbech, Wilhelm. *Kultur und Religion der Germanen*. 2 Bände. Darmstadt, 1976.
Gros, Frédéric. *A Philosophy of Walking*. London: Verso, 2015.
Gupta, Prachi. Trump Calls Undocumented Immigrants 'Animals' Who 'Slice' and 'Dice' Beautiful Teen Girls. *Jezebel: A Supposedly Feminist Website*. 26 July 2017. https://theslot.jezebel.com/trump-calls-undocumented-immigrants-animals-who-slice-a-1797260978
Gurion, Jay. 'The Romantic Necessity in Literary Naturalism: Jack London.' *American Literature*, 38.1 (March, 1966): 112–20.
Halpern, Micah. 'We Must Track and Trap Lone Wolf Terrorists.' *The Observer*. 25 November 2014. https://observer.com/2014/11/we-must-track-and-trap-lone-wolf-terrorists/
Heffernan, Carol Falvo. 'That Dog Again: "Melancholia Canina" and Chaucer's "Book of the Duchess."' In: *Modern Philology*, 84.2 (1986): 185–90.
Helfer, Rebeca. *Spenser's Ruins and the Art of Recollection*. Toronto: Toronto UP, 2012.
Hennen, Peter. 'Bear Bodies, Bear Masculinity: Recuperation, Resistance, or Retreat?' *Gender and Society*, 19.1 (February, 2005): 25–43.

Herf, Jeffrey. *Reactionary Modernism: Technology, Culture and Politics in Weimar and the Third Reich*. Cambridge: Cambridge UP, 1984.
Heyd, David. 'Cultural Diversity and Biodiversity: A Tempting Analogy.' *Critical Review of International Social and Political Philosophy*, 13.1 (2010): 159–79.
Hill, Justin. 'Jiang Rong: The Hour of the Wolf.' Interview with Jiang Rong. *The Independent*. 21 March 2008. Web. 8 December 2008.
Howe, Adrian. 'Chamberlain Revisited: The Case against the Media.' *Refractory Girl*, 2 (1989): 31–2.
Hugo, Victor. *The Hunchback of Notre Dame*. Trans. Keith Wren. London: Wordsworth Classics, 2004.
Hunt, David. 'The Face of the Wolf Is blessed, or Is It? Diverging Perceptions of the Wolf.' *Folklore*. 119.3 (2008): 319–34.
Jane, Lauriat. 'Dickens' Archetypal Jew.' *PMLA*, 73 (1958): 94–100.
Johnson, Diane. 'From Fairy to Witch: Imagery and Myth in the Azaria Case,' *Australian Journal of Cultural Studies*, 2.2 (1982): 90–106.
Jones, Karen. 'From Big Bad Wolf to Ecological Hero: Canis Lupus and the Culture(s) of Nature in the American-Canadian West.' *American Review of Canadian Studies*, 40.3 (2010): 338–50.
Jung, Carl Gustav. *Essays on Contemporary Events: The Psychology of Nazism*. Trans. R. F. C. Hull. Princeton, NJ: Princeton UP, 1989.
Jünger, Ernst. *Der Waldgang*. Stuttgart: Klett-Cotta, 1980.
Kafka, Franz. *Die Verwandlung*. In: *Gesammelte Werke. Erzählungen*. Edited M. Brod. Frankfurt am Main: Fischer, 1989.
Kakridis, I. T. *Greek Mythology*. Athens: Ekdotiki Athinon, 1986.
Kaltenecker, Siegfried. 'Weil aber die vergessenste Fremde unser Körper ist : über Männer-Körper-Repräsentationen und Faschismus.' In: *The Body of Gender: Körper, Geschlechter, Identitäten*. Wien : Passagen Verlag, 1995, 91–109.
Kant, Immanuel (1795). 'Zum ewigen Frieden. Ein philosophischer Entwurf.' *Immanuel Kants Werke*. Edited by A. Buchenau, Ernst Cassirer and B. Kellermann. Berlin: Verlag Bruno Cassirer, 1923, 425–74.
Kershaw, Alex. *Jack London – A Life*. New York: St. Martin's Press, 1997.
King, Scott Alexander. *Animal Dreaming: The Spiritual and Symbolic Language of the Australian Animals*, Glen Waverley: Blue Angel Gallery, 2003.
Korff, Gottfried and Larry Peterson. 'From Brotherly Handshake to Militant Clenched Fist: On Political Metaphors for the Worker's Hand.' *International Labor and Working-Class History*. 42. Tradition and the Working Class (Fall, 1992): 70–81.
Kotrschal, Kurt. *Wolf, Hund, Mensch. Die Geschichte einer jahrtausendealten Beziehung*. Vienna: Brandstätter Verlag, 2012.
Kristeva, Julia. *Strangers to Ourselves*. Trans. Leon Roudiez. New York: Columbia UP, 1991.
LaCapra, Dominick. 'Revisiting the Historians' Debate: Mourning and Genocide.' *History and Memory*, 9.½ 'Passing into History: Nazism and the

Holocaust beyond Memory – In Honor of Saul Friedlander on His Sixty-Fifth Birthday.' (Fall 1997): 80–112.

Landau, Jacob. 'Ultra-Nationalist Literature in the Turkish Republic: A Note on the Novels of Hüseyin Nihâl Atsiz.' *Middle Eastern Studies*, 39.2 (April 2003): 204–10.

Lappalainen, Kaisa. 'Recall of the Fairy-Tale Wolf: "Little Red Riding Hood" in the Dialogic Tension of Contemporary Wolf Politics in the US West.' *ISLE: Interdisciplinary Studies in Literature and Environment*, 26.3 (Summer 2019), 744–67.

Lau, Kimberly. 'Erotic Infidelities: Angela Carter's Wolf Trilogy.' *Marvels & Tales*, 22.1, Erotic Tales (2008): 77–94.

Levi, Primo. *If This Is a Man. The Truce*. London: Abacus, 2007.

Lewin, Nicholas. *Jung on War, Politics and Nazi Germany. Exploring the Theory of Archetypes and the Collective Unconscious*. London: Karnac Books, 2009.

Leys, Ruth. *Trauma. A Genealogy*. Chicago: Chicago UP, 1995.

London, Jack. *Call of the Wild & White Fang*. Oxford: Wordsworth Classics, 1998.

Löns, Hermann. *Der Wehrwolf*. Hameln: Sponholtz Verlag, 2007.

Lopez, Barry Holstun. *Of Wolves and Men*. London, Toronto, Melbourne: Dent & Sons, 1978.

Lusher, Adam. 'Donald Trump Supporters Tell Immigrants 'The Wolves Are Coming, You Are the Hunted – as Race Hate Fears Rise.' *The Independent*. 9 November 2016. https://www.independent.co.uk/news/world/americas/us-elections/donald-trump-wins-racist-racism-race-hate-immigrants-nigel-farage-ukip-brexit-post-referendum-a7407951.html

Mackay, Christopher S. *The Hammer of Witches*. Cambridge: Cambridge UP, 2009.

Mainoldi, Carla. *L'image du loup et du chien dans la Grèce ancienne: d'Homère à Platon*. Paris: Editions Ophrys, 1984.

Mark, Jason. 'Can Wolves Bring Back Wilderness?' *Scientific American*. 9 October 2015.

Maxmen, Amy. 'Migrants and Refugees Are Good for Economies.' *Nature. International Journal of Science*. 20 June 2018. https://www.nature.com/articles/d41586-018-05507-0

Mazzoni, Cristina. *She-Wolf. The Story of a Roman Icon*. Cambridge: Cambridge UP, 2010.

McCarthy, Cormac. *The Border Trilogy*. New York: Knopf, 1999.

McCone, Kim R. 'Hund, Wolf und Krieger bei den Indogermanen.' In: *Studien zum Indogermanischen Wortschatz*. Wolfgang Meid (ed.). Innsbruck: University of Innsbruck Press, 1987, 101–54.

McDonald, Avis G. 'Beyond Language: David Malouf's "An Imaginary Life."' *Ariel: A Review of English Literature*, 19.1 (1988): 45–54.

Mech, David. 'The Challenge and Opportunity of Recovering Wolf Populations.' *Conservation Biology*, 9.2 (1995): 270–8.

Mellinkoff, Ruth. 'Juda's Red Hair and the Jews.' *Journal of Jewish Art*, 9 (1982): 31–46.

Middleton, Arthur. 'Is the Wolf a Real American Hero?' *The New York Times.* 9 March 2014.
Mill, John Stuart. *On Liberty.* Edited by Williams, Geraint. London: Dent, 1968.
Mooallem, Jon. 'How the Teddy Bear Taught Us Compassion.' *Ted Talk.* 2014. https://www.ted.com/talks/jon_mooallem_the_strange_story_of_the_teddy_bear_and_what_it_reveals_about_our_relationship_to_animals?language=en#t-807378
Moore, Olin H. 'How Victor Hugo Created the Characters of *Notre Dame de Paris*.' *PMLA* 57.1 (1942): 255–74.
Morton, Jonathan. 'Wolves in Human Skin: Questions of Animal Appetite in Jean de Meun's "Roman de la Rose."' *The Modern Language Review*, 105.4 (October 2010): 976–97.
Mosse, George L. *The Image of Man: The Creation of Modern Masculinity.* New York: Oxford University, 1996.
Musolff, Andreas. 'Dehumanizing Metaphors in UK Immigrant Debates in Press and Online Media.' *Journal of Language Aggression and Conflict*, 3.1 (2015): 41–56.
Nash, Ralph. 'Shylock's Wolvish Spirit.' *Shakespeare Quarterly*, 10.1 (Winter 1959): 125–8.
Neihardt, John. *Black Elk Speaks.* Lincoln: University of Nebraska Press, 1979.
Nors, Dorthe. 'They Want a Wolf-Free Denmark. Will Migrants Be Next?' *The Guardian.* 16 May 2018. https://www.theguardian.com/commentisfree/2018/may/16/killing-wolf-denmark-migrants-eu-polarisation-of-politics-pack-mentality?fbclid=IwAR1Jzk6dm1EoOHsoCdno0dRi5IGcRm6UkjfIuGOqE04SwWAlGz3fSX1EXzg
O'Donnell, Jim. 'Aimed at Refugees, Fences Are Threatening European Wildlife.' *Yale Environment 360.* 15 December 2016.
Orenstein, Catherine. *Little Red Riding Hood Uncloaked: Sex, Morality and the Evolution of a Fairy Tale.* New York: Basic Books, 2003.
O'Toole, Fintan. 'Trial Runs for Fascism Are in Full Flow.' *The Irish Times.* 12 July 2018. https://www.irishtimes.com/opinion/fintan-o-toole-trial-runs-for-fascism-are-in-full-flow-1.3543375
Ovid. *Metamorphoses.* Translated and with Notes by Charles Martin. New York City: W. W. Norton, 2004.
Panttaja, Elisabeth. 'Going Up in the World: Class in "Cinderella."' *Western Folklore*, 52.1 (1993): 85–104.
Pantucci, Raffaello. 'A Typology of Lone Wolves: Preliminary Analysis of Lone Islamist Terrorists.' *International Centre for the Study of Radicalisation and Political Violence* (ICSR), 2011, 3–39.
Pausanias. *Description of Greece.* Trans. W. H. S. Jones and H. A. Ormerod. Cambridge: Harvard UP, 1918. 8.2.1–6.
Pierotti, Raymond. 'The Role of Myth in Understanding Nature.' *Ethnobiology Letters*, 7.2, Special Issue: Memoirs and Memory (2016): 6–13.
Pierotti, Raymond and Daniel Wildcat. 'Traditional Knowledge, Culturally-Based World Views, and Western Science.' In: *Cultural and Spiritual Values of Biodiversity: A Complimentary Contribution to the Global Biodiversity*

Assessment. Darrell A Posey (ed.). London, Nairobi: United Nations Environment Programme, 1999, 192–9.

Pluskowski, Alexander. *Wolves and the Wilderness in the Middle Ages*. Woodbridge: Boydell Press, 2006.

Poulakou-Rebelakou, E. and C. Tsiamis, G. Pantaleakosi and D. Ploumpidis, 'Lycanthropy in Byzantine times (AD 330–1453).' *History of Psychiatry*, 20.4 (2009): 468–79.

Preece, Rod. *Awe for the Tiger, Love for the Lamb: A Chronicle of Sensibility to Animals*. London: Routledge, 2002.

Provata Carlone, Mika. 'Crying Wolf.' http://bookanista.com/crying-wolf/

Puhak, Shelley. 'Detained: A Genealogy of Whores and Wolves.' *Columbia: A Journal of Literature and Art*, 54 (2016): 70–85.

Quinn, Daniel. *Ishmael: An Adventure of the Mind and Spirit*. New York: Bantam, 1992.

Raabe, Wilhelm. *Der Hungerpastor*. Vol. 6. Göttingen: Vandenhoeck & Ruprecht, 1953a.

Raabe, Wilhelm. *Die Hämelschen Kinder*. Vol. 9.1. Göttingen: Vandenhoeck & Ruprecht, 1953b.

Radin, Paul. *The Trickster: A Study in American Indian Mythology*. New York: Schocken Books, 1972.

Reinhardt, Ilka., Gesa Kluth, Sabina Nowak and Robert Mysłayek. *A Review of Wolf Management in Poland and Germany with Recommendations for Future Transboundary Collaboration*. Bonn: BfN Skripten 356, 2013.

Robisch, S.K. *Wolves and the Wolf Myth in American Literature*. Reno: University of Nevada Press, 2009.

Rong, Jiang. *Wolf Totem*. London: Penguin, 2009.

Rowlands, Mark. *The Philosopher and the Wolf*. London: Granta, 2008.

Salvatori, V. and J. Linnell. Report on the Conservation Status and Threats for Wolf (Canis lupus) in Europe. Councel of Europe. PVS/Inf (2005), 16.

Saul, Nicholas. *Gypsies and Orientalism in German Literature and Anthropology of the Long Nineteenth Century*. London: Legenda, 2007.

Saul, Nicholas and Susan Tebbutt. *The Role of the Romanies: Images and Counter Images of 'Gypsies'/Romanies in European Cultures*. Liverpool: Liverpool UP, 2005.

Schanzer, David. 'We Must Call the El Paso Shooting What It Is: Trump-inspired Terrorism.' *The Guardian*. 5 August 2019. https://www.theguardian.com/commentisfree/2019/aug/05/trump-inspired-terrorism-el-paso

Sebald, W. G. *Luftkrieg und Literatur*. Frankfurt am Main: Fischer, 2002.

Shapiro, Judith. *Mao's War against Nature: Politics and the Environment in Revolutionary China*. Cambridge, UK: Cambridge UP, 2001.

Shariatmadari, David. 'Swarms, Floods, and Marauders: The Toxic Metaphors of the Migration Debate.' *The Guardian*. 10 August 2015. https://www.theguardian.com/commentisfree/2015/aug/10/migration-debate-metaphors-swarms-floods-marauders-migrants

Sharkey, Terence. *Jack the Ripper: One Hundred Years of Investigation*. London: Ward Lock Limited, 1987.
Shipman, Pat. *The Invaders. How Humans and Their Dogs Drove Neanderthals to Extinction*. Cambridge: Harvard UP, 2015.
Smith, Kirby F. 'An Historical Study of the Werewolf in Literature.' *PMLA*, 9.1 (1894): 1–42.
Sorensen, Martin Selsoe. 'Denmark Plans to Isolate Unwanted Migrants on a Small Island. *New York Times*. 3 December 2018. https://www.nytimes.com/2018/12/03/world/europe/denmark-migrants-island.html
Speidel, Michael P. 'Berserks: A History of European 'Mad Warriors.' *Journal of World History*, 13.2 (2002): 253–90.
Spenser, Edmund. *A View of the Present State of Ireland* [1596]. Edited by W. L. Renwick. Oxford: Clarendon Press, 1970.
Stephenson, R. O. 'Nunamiut Eskimos, Wildlife Biologists, and Wolves.' In: *Wolves of the World*. F. H. Harrington and P. C. Pacquet (eds). Park Ridge, NJ: Noyes Publ., 1982. 434–9.
Stoker, Bram. *Dracula*. London: Wordsworth Classics, 2000.
Sugiyama, Michelle S. 'Predation, Narration, Adaptation: Little Red Riding Hood Revisted.' *Interdisciplinary Literary Studies*, 5.2 (2004): 110–29.
Timm, Erika. *Frau Holle, Frau Percht und verwandte Gestalten*. Stuttgart: Hirzel, 2010.
Tournier, Michel. *The Ogre*. Baltimore: Johns Hopkins UP, 1997.
Tretiak, Andrew. 'The Merchant of Venice and the "Alien" Question.' *The Review of English Studies*, 5.20 (1929): 402–9.
Vanderbeets, Richard. 'Nietzsche of the North: Heredity and Race in London's "The Son of the Wolf."' *Western American Literature*, 2.3 (Fall 1967): 229–33.
Varsava, Jerry. 'Jiang Rong's Wolf Totem: Toward a Narrative Ecology of the Grassland of Contemporary Inner Mongolia.' *Interdisciplinary Study in Literature and Environment*, 18.2 (Spring 2011): 283–301.
Verdier, Yvonne. "Little Red Riding Hood in Oral Tradition." *Marvels and Tales*, 11.1/2 (1997): 101–23.
Vine, Steven. *Literature in Psychoanalysis. A Reader*. London: Palgrave, 2005.
Waite, Robert G. L. *Hitler: The Psychopathic God*. New York: Da Capo Press, 1993.
Washington, George. *Letters*, Founders Archives, Washington. https://founders.archives.gov/documents/Washington/99-01-02-11798
Watt, Roderick H. 'Wehrwolf or Werwolf? Literature, Legend or Lexical Error into Nazi Propaganda?' *The Modern Language Review* 87.4 (1992): 879–95.
Wiebe, Robert H. *Who We Are: A History of Popular Nationalism*. Princeton: Princeton UP, 2002.
Wild, Marko. 'Migranten und Wölfe – Zwei Zuwanderungen, ein Prinzip.' *Bürgerstimme – Zeit für Veränderungen*, 31. Mai 2015; no longer available on the web but see also: https://www.antiveganforum.com/forum/viewtopic.php?t=10835&start=1100

Wilson, Patrick Impero. 'Wolves, Politics, and the Nez Perce: Wolf Recovery in Central Idaho and the Role of Native Tribes.' *Natural Resources Journal* (1999): 543–64.

Winder, Robert. *The Last Wolf. The Hidden Springs of Englishness*. London: Abacus, 2017.

Winter, Peter. 'Whipping Boy with Clipped Wings.' Evaluating Anselm Kiefer. Special Issue of *Art International*, 2 (1988): 66–70.

Wiseman, T. P. 'The God of the Lupercal.' *The Journal of Roman Studies*, 85 (1995): 1–22.

Woodhull, Winifred. 'Fascist Bonding and Euphoria in Michel Tournier's The Ogre.' *New German Critique*, 42 (Autumn, 1987): 79–112.

Wyatt, Jean. 'Storytelling, Melancholia, and Narrative Structure in Louise Erdrich's *The Painted Drum*.' *Melus*, 36.1. Ethnic Storytelling (Spring, 2011): 13–36.

Xinjian, Xu, The Chinese Identity in Question: "Descendants of the Dragon" and "The Wolf Totem." *Revue de Littérature Comparée*, 1 (2011): 93–105.

Zanger, Jules. 'A Sympathetic Vibration: Dracula and the Jews.' *English Literature in Translation*, 34.1 (1991): 33–44.

Zipes, Jack. *The Trials & Tribulations of Little Red Riding Hood*. South Hadley: Bergin & Garvey, 1983.

INDEX

abandonment 13, 15, 28, 29, 37, 43, 49, 52, 58, 59, 61, 63, 67, 79, 81, 86, 95, 97, 102, 112, 116, 152, 160, 161, 198
abjection 14, 28, 108, 152, 159, 170, 194
Abraham, Nicholas 193
Adams, Jad 59
Adler, Hermann 46
Adventures of Simplicius Simplicissimus (Grimmelshausen) 16, 25, 39–40, 49–50
Aeneid (Virgil) 31
AfD (Alternative for Germany) 3–4, 23, 50, 132, 133, 143, 174, 179, 180, 185
Africa 140, 148, 169, 198
Agamben, Giorgio 13–14, 27, 41, 55, 123, 194–5
agrarian cultures 8, 53, 70, 79, 96, 150–1, 171, 200
Alaskan Indians 63
alchemy 43
Algonquin 55
alienation 10, 57, 133, 149
Al Qaeda 119
Anatomy of Melancholy (Burton) 107
animal rights 179–80
Animal That Therefore I Am, The (Derrida) 177–8
Annahita, Sine 71
annihilation 80, 164
anthropocentrism 10, 19, 60, 201
anthropomorphization 5
Antígona González (Uribe) 159
anti-hero 33, 120
anti-Huguenot riots 32
anti-Semitism. *See* Jews as wolves
appropriation 3, 20, 70, 74–5, 98, 106, 107, 114–16, 129, 132, 133, 167, 172, 191
Arendt, Hannah 5, 18, 36, 49
Aristotle 27, 55
Arminius 109

Asinaria (Plautus) 14, 200
assimilation 33–4, 67, 68
asylum seekers 174, 198
Ataturk, Kemal 20, 130
Atsız, Huseyin Nihal 129–30, 132
Augé, Marc 14, 145, 161
Augustus 12, 196
Auschwitz 14, 125, 126, 160
Australia 14, 19, 23, 98–103, 168, 196
Austria 3, 129, 131, 174, 178, 187
autochthony, loss of 28

Balibar, Étienne 5
banditry. *See* robbery
Baring-Gould, Sabine 12, 108, 120, 123
Barker, Q. C. 102
Barthes, Roland 189
Baschwitz, Kurt 18, 43, 92
Battle of the Teutoburg Forest, The (Kleist) 109
Battle of Wounded Knee 75
bears 9, 13, 40, 58, 72, 74, 98, 108, 140, 148
bear subculture 73
Beauty and the Beast 40–5
Bender, Hans 163
Benhabib, Seyla 5, 21, 75, 76
Benigni, Roberto 134
Benjamin, Walter 107, 165
Bennhold, Katrin 4, 174
Beowulf 29
berserkers 108–9, 112, 169, 191
Bettelheim, Bruno 84, 89, 90
Bhabha, Homi 151
Bible 53
Biddescombe, Perry 111–12
Bild (tabloid) 178
Bildung 35, 126
Bildungsroman 26, 33, 49, 64, 126, 149–50, 186
billboards 76–7
Bingener, Reinhard 178
biodiversity 6, 7, 22–3, 71, 75, 78, 142, 145, 164, 173–85, 201

Index

biopolitics 1–23, 37, 50, 55, 63, 86, 116, 121, 124, 125, 165, 179, 194, 198
bios 27
Birkenau 160
Birth of Tragedy, The (Nietzsche) 157
Black Elk Speaks (Neihardt) 18, 74–5, 78
Blackfeet 181–3
Blake, Michael 17, 61, 62, 66–70
Blakeslee, Nate 164, 186
Bloch, Albert 133
blonde beast 191–2
bloodlust 2, 29–31, 61
Bloody Chamber, The (Carter) 19, 91
Bluebeard myth 122, 123
Blue Highways (Heat-Moon) 73–4
Boguet, Henri 81
Boitani, Luigi 177, 186
Booker Prize 21, 98
Book of Werewolves (Baring-Gould) 12
border protection 137–61
Breivik, Anders 107, 119
Brexit 21, 22, 140, 164, 166
Brooks, Mel 134
brotherhood 44, 65, 114, 115, 124
Brother Wolf 22, 23, 56, 70–1, 73, 155–61, 176, 190
'Buffalo Hunt under the Wolf-skin Mask' (Catlin) 56
Burton, Robert 107

Call of the Wild (London) 17, 62–4, 66
Cameron, David 2, 39
Canetti, Elias 115, 121, 123–4
cannibalism 11, 28, 31–2, 37, 48, 58, 79, 83, 88, 193, 195
Cantú, Francisco 21–2, 138, 155–61, 176, 198, 201
Capitoline wolf 113–14
Carter, Angela 19, 81, 91–5, 107
Cather, Willa 17, 61–2, 73, 74
Catlin, George 56
Celan, Paul 199
Central Europe 2–3, 7, 11, 94, 139, 163, 165, 174, 175, 176
Chamberlain case 19, 99–103
Chatwin, Bruce 103, 167–8
Cheyenne 8, 54, 70, 73
child abduction/seduction 35, 36–52

Children of Hamelin, The (Raabe) 26, 34, 48, 122, 125, 126
China 22, 71, 166, 167, 168, 172, 173, 179
Christianity 16, 31, 41–2, 64, 71, 83, 108, 128, 191
Chronic Wasting Disease (CWD) 183
Church of Rome 41–3
Cinderella (Grimm Brothers) 84
circumcision 29
city (concept) 27–8, 41, 48, 157–61
clash of civilizations 55, 57
cohabitation 67, 177
Coleman, Jon T. 25, 53, 54–5
colonial wolves 53–78, 150
Company of Wolves, The (Carter) 91, 93–4
concentration camps 14, 15, 51, 96, 125, 160, 161, 198, 200
Copeland, Julie 196
Corbett, Peter 22, 164
cosmopolitanism 17, 29, 33–6, 49, 78, 169, 174, 180, 201
Costner, Kevin 66
creation myths 11, 56, 70, 73
Criminal Prosecution and Capital Punishment of Animals (Evans) 30
Crossing, The (McCarthy) 21, 78, 147–55, 159
Crowds and Power (Canetti) 123–4
cultural diversity 6, 22, 144, 145, 147, 164, 173–80, 181, 185, 201
cultural pluralism 179
cunning 11, 15, 29, 37, 39, 56, 103, 112, 138
Czech Republic 176

Dances with Wolves (Blake) 17, 61, 62, 66–70
Danish People's Party 3–4, 137, 143
Dante 18, 31, 79–80, 159, 194, 199
Dasein 15, 27
David Copperfield (Dickens) 33, 34, 35
Death of the Grey Wolves, The (Atsız) 129
Debit and Credit (Freytag) 33
decapitation 55
deception 56
de Cervantes, Miguel 38–9
deer 54, 68, 78, 118, 126, 140, 148, 175, 198

Index

Defoe, Daniel 17, 58
Defonseca, Misha 19, 81, 91, 95–8, 163
dehumanization 5, 8, 12, 14, 15, 17, 23,
  25–9, 35, 41, 50, 52, 59, 138, 139,
  161, 190, 194, 196, 200
Deleuze, Gilles 74, 157, 159–60, 172
Demian (Hesse) 190
Denmark 3–4, 137, 143
Derrida, Jacques 43, 64, 73, 89, 117, 124,
  142, 147, 152, 171, 177–8, 195
Der Runenberg (Tieck) 83
Der Unhold (Schlöndorff) 124
desire 29, 30, 31, 53, 83, 84, 85, 89–95,
  97, 157, 193, 195
detention camps 2, 14, 160–1
devouring wolf 16–20, 30, 37, 40, 42, 44,
  79–96, 101, 102, 106, 114, 122,
  131, 175
dewolfing 22, 164–73
di Caprio, Leonardo 186
Dickens, Charles 26, 30, 33–5
Die Wölfe kommen zurück (Bender) 163
dingo 19, 98, 99–103
disease 38, 49, 95, 107, 137, 180, 183
Divina Comedia (Dante) 18, 80
dog-become-wolf 64–6
dogs 17, 30, 38, 46, 47, 61, 63–7, 80, 107,
  110, 124, 126–8, 146, 149, 151–2,
  154, 161, 177, 178, 192
Dracula (Stoker) 16, 26, 33, 45–8, 50,
  128, 139, 165, 169, 174
dreams 123, 125–6, 155–7, 189–201
Dryden, John 12
Duane, James 17
du Coudray, Chantal Bourgault 33
Duerr, Hans Peter 89

Eastern Europe 11, 25, 33, 34, 45, 94, 96,
  120, 126
ecocriticism 163
Edict de Nantes 32
Edict of Expulsion 32
Electra complex 195
Eliav-Feldon, Miriam 38–9
Elizabeth I 30, 31, 32
elk 182–4
Else von der Tanne (Raabe) 80
English Fairy Tales 146
Enlightenment 80, 86, 114

environmental studies 176, 183
environment/ecosystem, wolves impact
  on 1, 5–10, 22–3, 53, 55, 57, 62–3,
  71, 76–8, 87, 94–5, 119, 140–1,
  147–8, 163–87
Erdrich, Louise 17, 73–5, 156
Erlking *(Der Erlkönig)* (Goethe) 122,
  124–6
Espulsion de los Gitanos (Moncada) 38
Estés, Clarissa Pinkola 19, 98
Eurocentrism 55
Europa, Europa (Holland) 134
European Union 4, 143, 201
euthanasia 115
Evans, E. P. 30
Every Man out of His Humour (Jonson)
  32
exclusion 5, 13, 15, 17, 27, 37, 41, 42, 74,
  121, 193
exile 2, 13–15, 18, 23, 25, 28, 33–5, 61,
  66, 80, 82, 85, 86, 91, 97, 103, 118,
  138, 151, 153, 163, 179, 189–90,
  192–9
expulsion 12–13, 16, 27, 32, 39, 41, 49,
  51, 80, 86, 106, 124, 158–9, 161,
  163, 166, 179, 194–6

fascism 2, 5, 20–1, 26, 105–35, 169
Fascist Youth Organization 20, 112
fate 13, 15, 19, 36, 52, 83, 103, 131, 196
Faust (Goethe) 128
fear 1–11, 13, 16, 18, 22, 25–52, 56,
  59–60, 65–6, 80, 85, 91–2,
  94–7, 103, 111, 115, 119–20, 137,
  138–9, 144, 145–7, 157, 158, 161,
  165, 173–9, 182–3, 186, 190, 192,
  194, 197, 200–1
Femicide Machine, The (Rodriguez) 159
femininity 18, 71, 72–3, 79, 91, 95, 96,
  101, 150
femme fatale 80
*Feral. Rewilding the Land, Sea and
  Human Life* (Monbiot) 142
Fisher, Jerilyn 84
Fogleman, Valerie M. 17, 54, 57
folktales 10, 18–19, 79–103, 145–6
fox 29, 71, 109, 146, 192
France 7, 43, 44, 45, 58, 81, 111, 121, 128
France, Marie de 29

Index

Frankenstein (Shelley) 51
Franklin, Ruth 14
Frau Holle (Mother Hulda) (Grimm Brothers) 82–3, 88, 101
French Revolution 44–5, 49
Freud, Sigmund 23, 25, 84, 85, 89, 156, 157, 190, 192–7
Freytag, Gustav 33
Fridlund, Emily 98
Friedlos 13–14, 44, 55, 79, 86, 90, 108, 163
frontier myth 4, 17, 54, 55, 60–2, 66, 68, 70–2, 150
Fuhr, Eckhard 57–8

gangs 3, 65, 124
Garloff, Katja 194
Garth, Sir Samuel 12
gas chambers 8
Geist der Germanen (Grönbech) 115
Geneva Convention 76
German–Polish border 50
Germany, wolf reappearance in 7, 8, 22–3, 176
Glîchezâre, Heinrich der 29
Goebbels, Joseph 111, 130
Goering, Hermann 122
gothic genre 33, 41, 48, 111
Grass, Günter 128, 133, 134
Great Dictator, The (Chaplin) 133
Great Werewolf 18, 26
greed 2, 13, 29, 31–4, 37, 40, 54, 76, 79–80, 138–9, 170, 198
Greek mythology 6, 10–11, 14, 15, 23, 28, 68, 82, 97, 108, 160, 192, 193, 198, 200, 201
grey wolf 7–8, 76, 130
Grey Wolves 3, 20–1, 54, 115, 129–35, 167
Grey Wolves Come Back to Life, The (Atsız) 129, 132
Grimaud, Hélène 19, 98
Grimm, Jacob 86, 115
Grimm Brothers 35, 80, 81, 83, 84, 88, 90, 91, 92, 96, 101, 139, 178, 186, 193
Grimmelshausen, Hans Jakob Christoffel von 16, 25, 39–40, 49–50, 97
Grönbech, Wilhelm 13, 28, 115
grotesque 41

Guattari, Félix 157, 159–60, 172
gulags 51–2, 160
Gypsies as wolves 2, 16, 25, 29–30, 36–52, 59, 109, 110, 121, 138, 150, 169

half-breeds 63, 123
Hall, Sarah 21, 140–4, 147, 164–5
Hansel and Gretel (Grimm Brothers) 80, 88, 101, 102, 146
healers 57, 83
Heat-Moon, William Least 73–4
Heidegger, Martin 15, 198–9
Heine, Heinrich 33, 35
Hennen, Peter 73
Hesse, Hermann 23, 25, 49, 190–2, 194
Hilsenrath, Edgar 80
Himmler, Heinrich 111
History of Jews (Johnson) 45
History of Wolves (Fridlund) 98
Hitler, Adolf 3, 20, 21, 110–12, 115–16, 124–5, 129, 139, 191, 195, 199
Hitler salute 21, 131–5
Hitler Youth 112
Hobbes, Thomas 14, 28, 32, 97, 161, 200
Hoffmann, E. T. A. 83
Hölderlin, Friedrich 198
Holland, Agniezska 133, 134
Holocaust 19, 21, 80, 91, 95, 115, 126, 127, 134, 160, 189, 194–6
homelessness 2, 15–16, 28–9, 36–7, 49, 51, 152, 161, 190
hommes naturels 63
homo sacer 11–15, 27–8, 41, 42, 46–51, 54–5, 61–7, 73, 86, 89, 91, 103, 112, 116, 118, 124, 152, 154–5, 159–60, 194–6, 198
Homo Sacer: Sovereign Power and Bare Life (Agamben) 27
hope 1, 6, 144, 145, 157, 161, 192, 201
Hopi 74
hospitality 6, 21, 22, 36, 75–6, 78, 137, 176, 180–7, 201
Hughes, Ted 189
Hugo, Victor 16, 25, 26, 40–1, 43–5, 48–9, 51
Huguenots 32
human rights 9, 76, 120, 137, 180, 200
human sacrifice 43, 46–7, 61

Hunchback of Notre Dame, The (Hugo) 16, 26, 51
Hungary 140, 148
Hunger Pastor, The (Raabe) 16, 26, 33-5, 48-9, 50
Hunt, David 11
hybridity 41, 55, 107, 123, 128, 133, 172, 178

idleness 39, 40, 107
If This Is a Man (Levi) 189, 200
Imaginary Life, An (Malouf) 12, 23, 126, 196-7
immigrants as wolves 137-61, 180
imperialism 17, 20, 27, 75, 79, 106, 129, 131, 134
inclusion 17, 27, 74, 75
Independent newspaper 3, 8, 139, 158
indigenous as wolves 53-78
indigenous connectedness 181
individualism 7, 49, 120
Inferno (Dante) 79-80
infestation 2, 50, 161
initiation rites 82, 86, 89, 96, 103, 124
Inner Mongolia 22, 71, 164-8, 171-3, 187
Inquisition 92
insania lupina 107-9, 119
In the Rukh (Kipling) 60
Inuit 71, 150
irony 17, 41, 47, 74, 92, 112, 120, 121, 128, 146, 170, 172, 192
Ishmael (Quinn) 57, 171
Islamization 23, 143, 174
isolation 18, 87, 140, 141, 177
'Is the Wolf a Real American Hero?' (Middleton) 183-4

jackal 42, 60, 127, 128
Jack the Ripper 46, 119
Jane, L. 35
Jews as wolves 2, 8-9, 16, 25-52, 59, 130-1, 160-1, 165-6, 169, 194-6
Johnson, Diane 99
Johnson, Paul 45
Jones, Karin 181-3
Jonson, Ben 32
Judaism 30, 43
Jung, Carl 23, 108, 156-7, 190-2, 198

Jünger, Ernst 20, 109, 116-21, 124, 128
Jungle Book (Kipling) 17, 57-60, 79, 113

Kafka, Franz 9, 23, 27, 50, 51, 138, 145, 194-6
Kaltenbrunner, Ernst 122
Kaltenecker, Siegfried 131
Kant, Immanuel 6, 21, 36, 75-6, 78, 115, 137, 182, 201
Khan, Genghis 130, 166, 168, 169
Kiefer, Anselm 133, 134, 135
Kim (Kipling) 59
King, Scott Alexander 102
Kipling, Rudyard 17, 57-60, 79, 113
Kipling: A Life (Adams) 59
Kipling, Trix 59
Kleist, Heinrich von 26, 109
Klondike gold rush 62
Kluth, Gesa 176
Krasznahorkai, László 21, 144, 145, 147
Krebitz, Nicolette 19, 81, 91, 94-5
Kristeva, Julia 176

LaCapra, Dominick 160
La Gitanilla (The Little Gypsy Girl) (de Cervantes) 38-9
Lakota 8, 70
'La Lupa' (Verga) 18, 80
lamb metaphor 30-1, 33
Landmarks (Macfarlane) 142
land ownership 7, 22, 70, 76, 142, 173
land use 7, 70, 76-7, 184, 201
Lang, Josef Bernhard 190
Lappalainen, Kaisa 186
Last Nazis: SS Werewolf Guerrilla Resistance in Europe 1944-1947 (Biddescombe) 111-12
Last Wolf, The (Krasznahorkai) 21, 143-5
Last Wolf, The (Winder) 22, 47, 143
Lau, Kimberly 92, 94
lawlessness 95, 109, 152
'Legend of the Friendly Medicine Wolf' 181
Leopold, Aldo 9, 53-4, 182
Le Petit Poucet (Perrault) 122
Le Roi des Aulnes (The Ogre) (Tournier) 20, 116, 120-8, 154, 199
lethe 15, 128, 154, 160, 198-9
Levi, Primo 14, 43, 52, 189, 199-200

life, indigenous philosophy 73–4
Life Is Beautiful (Benigni) 134
Line Becomes a River, The (Cantú) 21, 138, 155–61, 198
Linnell, J. 177
Little Red Riding Hood (Carter) 107
'Little Red Riding Hood' (Grimm's/Perrault) 19, 35, 47, 81, 83–93, 96, 98, 102, 146, 174, 179, 186
livestock and wolves 7, 11, 138, 141, 165, 175, 177, 183
Locke, John 75
locust metaphor 2, 39
logocentrism 198
London, Jack 17, 61, 62–9, 72, 115
loneliness 12, 34, 49, 107, 120, 149–50, 153, 194
'lone wolf' 60, 70, 87, 154
Lone Wolf terrorism 3, 20, 21, 50, 106–7, 116–35, 139
Lone Wolf (Wierusz-Kowalskim) 117
Löns, Hermann 16, 25, 50, 109–11, 131
Lopez, Barry Holstun 15–16, 57, 71, 184, 200
Lopez, Roderigo (Ruy) 30, 32
loss 12–15, 19, 22, 23, 27–8, 34, 44, 48, 50, 60, 74, 82–6, 88, 94, 97, 103, 115, 117, 134, 145, 149–50, 161, 163, 164, 173, 180, 183, 189, 196–8
Lost Words, The (Macfarlane) 142
Luftkrieg und Literatur (Air Raids and Literature) (Sebald) 163
Lupercalia 11, 79
Lupus Institute 176
Lusatia 22–3, 173–4, 185, 187, 198
Lusher, Adam 3, 4, 139, 158
Luther, Martin 31
lycanthropy 5, 10, 12, 20, 25, 29, 33, 34, 43, 49, 50, 88, 89, 97, 107–9, 111, 120, 121, 133, 191, 192, 194, 197
Lycaon myth 11–15, 18, 23, 27–8, 32, 37, 49, 51, 57, 79, 82, 95, 97, 107–8, 119, 120, 153, 154, 159, 179, 189–201
lycophilia 10, 150
lycophobia 2, 10, 150
Lykaios rites 11, 37, 82, 124, 192
lynx 140, 148

Macfarlane, Robert 142
Machiavelli, Niccolo 109
madness 13, 31, 70, 107–9, 135, 186
Malleus Maleficarum (Hammer of Witches) 18, 26, 42–3, 81, 83
Malouf, David 12, 23, 126, 196, 198–9
'Man of the Crowd' (Poe) 34
Mark, Jason 8, 70
Martin, Charles 12
masculinity/male fantasies 18, 62–3, 71–3, 96
May, Karl 111–12
Mazzoni, Cristina 79, 112–14
McCarthy, Cormac 21, 23, 78, 147–55, 157, 159, 161
McDonald, Avis 196
McIntyre, Rich 76, 186
Mech, David 175
media coverage 3, 19, 21, 99, 103, 120, 139, 178, 183–4
Mediterranean 2, 28, 138
Mein Kampf (Hitler) 111
melancholia canina 107
Mellinkoff, Ruth 35
Melville, A. D. 12
Mengele, Josef 125
mental illness 39, 119, 190
Merchant of Venice, The (Shakespeare) 16, 30–3
Metamorphoses (Malouf) 12
Metamorphoses (Ovid) 12, 13, 23, 28, 79, 153, 189, 196–7, 199, 201
Metamorphosis (Kafka) 9, 23, 27, 50, 51, 138, 145, 194, 195, 196
Mexican Cartels 148
Middle Ages 6, 13, 16, 18, 25, 28, 29, 31, 37, 40, 46, 48, 49, 55, 64, 99, 109, 143, 179
Middleton, Arthur 183–4
Mill, John Stuart 179
Mix, Tamara 71–3
Monbiot, George 142, 166
Moncada, Sancho de 38
Mooallem, Jon 6, 7
More, Brookes 12
Mormon wolf hunts 53
Mosse, George 130–1
multiculturalism 6, 21, 143, 145, 147, 161, 174, 179, 184

Musolff, Andreas 139
Mussolini, Benito 20, 79, 110, 112–14, 116, 131
My Ántonia (Cather) 17, 61–2, 73
myth, concept of 129, 189–90, 199
mythical realism 124–5
Mythologies (Barthes) 189

naivety 33, 39, 102, 125, 126, 127, 128, 182
Napoleon 45, 109, 125
Nash, Ralph 30
nationalism 3, 20, 26, 27, 55, 75, 109, 115, 129–35, 167
National Socialism 6, 20, 27, 40, 109, 110, 111, 120, 128, 129, 130, 133, 134, 161, 178, 191
nation building 26, 33, 49, 60, 115
nation-state 1–2, 21, 27, 28, 46, 48, 49, 51, 55, 137, 139, 150, 157, 160, 161, 176, 182–3
Navajo 56, 73, 82
Nazi and the Barber, The (Hilsenrath) 80
Nazism 3, 105–35, 191, 194–5
Nazi Werewolves 110–12, 123, 126–7, 133
Neihardt, John G. 18, 74–5
neo-fascism 5, 115, 129, 135
neurosis 114, 190, 194, 195
New York Times 183
Nez Perce tribe 7, 23, 54, 76, 184–5
Nietzsche, Friedrich 63, 157, 191
Night Wolves 3
nomadism 20, 121, 167, 201
non-places 14, 145, 161
Nordic supremacy 35, 46, 63, 120, 122, 125, 129, 169
Northern Europe 7, 16, 46, 64, 124
Northern Plains tribes 8, 70
Notre Dame de Paris (Hugo) 40–5, 48–9
nurturing 11, 18, 19, 21, 59–60, 72, 73, 79, 81–2, 84, 85, 88, 89, 90, 96–7, 112, 114, 130, 149, 153, 154, 157

Obama, Barack 9
Ocasio-Cortez, Alexandria 160
Occupations (Kiefer) 134
Odin myth 82, 114, 125
O'Donnell, Jim 140, 148
oedipal relationship 84, 85, 89–92, 194, 195

Ojibwe 56, 73–4, 156, 181
Old Ways: A Journey on Foot, The (Macfarlane) 142
Oliver Twist (Dickens) 26, 34, 35
One Clear, Ice-Cold January Morning at the Beginning of the Twenty-First Century (Schimmelpfennig) 21, 143, 145–6, 174
On the Genealogy of Morals (Nietzsche) 191
Opera Nazionale Balilla 20, 112
Operation Werwolf 20, 111, 121
Opolka, Rainer 3, 4, 20, 21, 116, 132–5
Origins of the Bourgeois Tragedy (Benjamin) 107
Origins of Totalitarianism (Arendt) 49
O'Toole, Fintan 2, 115
Our Mutual Friend (Dickens) 35
outlaws 4, 5, 10, 11, 13, 16, 25, 28, 29, 41, 46, 59, 64, 86, 95, 108, 123–4, 139, 143, 151–3, 160, 181, 190, 194, 198
Ovid 12–13, 23, 28, 79, 153, 189, 196–9, 201

pack, idea of the 25–52, 110, 115–20, 123–4, 128
Painted Drum, The (Erdrich) 17, 73, 156
Pankeiev, Sergei 192–3, 195
Panttaja, Elisabeth 84
Pantucci, Raffaello 119–20
Papal Bull Summis Desiderantes Affectibus 18
parasite 4, 9, 11, 38, 49–50, 70, 138, 139, 180
Parmenides (Heidegger) 15, 198
parody 80, 120–1, 126, 128, 131, 133, 134
Pausanias 192
Pawnee 56, 156, 181
peace 27–8, 163
Pegida (Patriotic Europeans against the Islamization of the Occident) 23, 132, 174
Perrault, Charles 83, 84, 91, 92, 122, 123, 125
persecution 1, 6, 8, 9, 16, 18, 26, 27, 41, 42, 44–5, 78, 80, 83, 88, 98, 108, 121, 124, 131, 138, 150, 151, 157, 165, 184, 185, 199

Index

Philosopher and the Wolf, The (Rowlands) 118–19
Pied Piper legend 122, 125, 126
Pierotti, Raymond 70–1, 181, 186
plague 36, 37, 38–9, 49–50
Plautus 14, 200
pleasure 89, 108, 193, 195, 196
Pliny 192
pluralism 75, 161, 179
Pluskowski, Alexander 29
Poe, Edgar Allen 34
Poland 145, 176
polis 15, 25–8, 32, 34, 45, 50, 51, 55, 63, 65, 157–8, 160–1
political violence 2, 5, 199
polos 15
Pope Innocent VIII 18, 26
populism 1–5, 8, 20, 27, 40, 69, 76, 133, 137, 150, 174–5
Powell, Robert Baden 112
pride 80, 110, 167
Prince, The (Machiavelli) 109
Producers, The (Brooks) 134
provincialism 35, 49
psychoanalysis 23, 82, 84, 107, 156, 189–201
Puhak, Shelley 110
Putin, Vladimir 3

Quinn, Daniel 57, 171

Raabe, Wilhelm 16, 26, 33–5, 48–50, 80
racism 3, 5, 16, 20, 21, 26, 40, 45, 48, 49, 60, 63, 66, 130, 131–2
Radinger, Elli 9–10, 19, 98
rage 13, 82, 96, 107–8, 119, 120, 191
Rais, Gilles de 20, 39, 120, 122–3
rape 14, 31, 43, 89, 90–1, 93, 96, 109, 159, 160
Readman, Paul 142
realism 21
recolonization, prevention of 176, 186
Red Army Faction 119
Reinhardt, Ilka 176–7
Reinhart Fuchs (Glîchezâre) 29
resistance wolves 105–35
res nullius 75
rewilding 21–3, 141–3, 163–87
Reynolds, George W. M. 33

Rights of Others, The (Benhabib) 75
right-wing politics 2, 3, 19–20, 50, 132, 133, 143, 173–80, 201
rituals 41, 55, 73, 89, 131, 192
robbery 39–40, 143
Robin Hood 124
Robinson Crusoe (Defoe) 17, 58
Rodriguez, Sergio Gonzalez 159
Roman de Renard (Saint-Cloud) 29
Roman mythology 11, 79, 196
Romantic period 48, 68, 111
Romany as wolves 16, 26, 36
Romulus and Remus 11, 18, 60, 79, 114
Rong, Jiang 22, 129–30, 166–75, 179
Rousseau, Jean-Jacques 63, 95
Rowlands, Mark 118–19, 126
Russia 3, 61, 73, 145, 193–4

sacrifice 9, 37, 43, 46–9, 55, 61–2, 73, 101, 103, 112, 129, 194–5
Sadeian Woman, The (Carter) 93
Saint-Cloud, Pierre de 29
Salvatori, V. 177
sanctuary, idea of 6, 14, 23, 28, 48, 50, 94, 95, 159
Sandys, George 12
Schimmelpfennig, Roland 21, 143, 145, 146, 147, 174, 176
Schlöndorff, Volker 124, 134
Sebald, W. G. 163
seduction 35, 36–52, 82–3, 93
self-defence 110
Séminaire: La bête et le souverain (*The Beast & the Sovereign*) (Derrida) 152
semiology 189
Seton, Ernest Thompson 60
sexuality 33, 80, 82–3, 88–90, 93–5, 99, 113, 129, 134, 194, 195
shadow, Jungian 190–2
Shakespeare, William 16, 30
Shapiro, Janet 168
Shelley, Mary 51
she-wolf 18–19, 31, 60, 78, 79–103, 113–14, 147–55
Shipman, Pat 54
Sieg Heil (Opolka) 21
Silber, Ellen S. 84
Sinti and Roma as wolves 9, 29, 36–52

Index   221

Slavs as wolves 26
solitude 60
Sombart, Werner 35–6
'Son of the Wolf, The' (London) 63
Sonoma Desert 28
sorceresses 81
sovereignty 64, 73
Spenser, Edmund 53
sports hunting 72
'Springtime for Hitler' (Brooks) 134
Steiger, Vincent 118
stepmothers 84
Steppenwolf (Hesse) 25, 49, 190
Støberg, Inger 137
Stoker, Bram 16, 25, 26, 128
Storied Ground: Landscape and the Shaping of English Identity (Readman) 142
superstition 2, 16, 40, 78
Surviving with Wolves (Defonseca) 19, 91, 95–7
symbiosis 67, 77
symbolism 60, 74
syphilis 38

Ted Talks 6
teleology 131
territorialism 2
terrorism 3
'Thinking Like a Mountain' (Leopold) 53–4
Third Reich 108
Thirty Years' War 39, 50, 80
Three Little Pigs (Disney) 110
Three Pigs (Jacobs) 146
Tieck, Ludwig 83
Times 46
Tin Drum, The (Grass) 128, 134
To Genet (Kiefer) 134
Torok, Maria 193
Tournier, Michel 20–1, 120–8
trauma 52, 80, 189–90, 199
    and memory 59
Traumzeit (dreamtime) 89
Tretiak, Andrew 32
trickster 56
Truce, The (Levi) 200
Trump, Donald 1–2, 50
Turkey 3, 20, 21

Ukraine 3
ultranationalism 107, 109–10, 129–35
undocumented migration
    populist perception of migrants 1–2
Ungeziefer (vermin) 9, 38–40, 49–50
United Kingdom 2, 39
    Act of Union 141–2
United States 7, 23
    Congress 54
    Division of Predator and Rodent Control 54
    Federal Bureau of Biological Survey 54
    Fish and Wildlife Service 140
Universal Declaration of Human Rights 76
Unternehmen Karneval (Operation Carnival) 111
Uribe, Sara 159
US Army, 1865 campaign 8
US–Mexico border 2, 21–2, 147–55
utopia 6, 157

vampire 45
Vanderbeets, Richard 63
vargr/vargr i veum 15, 28–9, 46, 48, 55
Varus 109
Venice 32
Venus 83
Venus figure 83
Verdier, Yvonne 85
Verga, Giovanni 18, 80
vermin 56
Vermont wolves 58
Victorian Age 33, 45–6
View of the Present State of Ireland, A (Spenser) 53
'View of the Present State of Ireland' (Spenser) 17
Virgil 30–1
Volk 130
voraciousness. *See* greed

Wagner the Werewolf (Reynolds) 33
Waldgänger 20
Waldgang (Jünger) 116–28
Washington, George 17
Watt, Roderick 111
Weltbild (world view) 75

Weltbürgertum (citizenship of the world) 75
Weltfrieden 6
Werewolf, The (Carter) 92
Werewolf, The (Löns) 16, 25, 50, 109–10
werewolves 81, 110
Werwolf: The History of the National Socialist Guerrilla Movement 1944–1946 (Biddescombe) 111
Western Europe 7
White Fang (London) 17, 62, 64–6, 115
'Who Is Afraid of the Big Bad Wolf' (song) 110
Wierusz-Kowalskim, Alfred von 117
Wild (Krebitz) 19, 91, 94–5
Wild, Marko 4, 143
Wild Animals I Have Known (Seton) 60–1
Wildcat 181
wilderness 70
Wild Places, The (Macfarlane) 142
Wilson, Patrick Impero 184
Winder, Robert 22, 47
Wisdom of Wolves (Radinger) 9–10, 19, 98
Wiseman, T. P. 11
Wissen ist Macht (knowledge is power) 34
witch-burning 81
witches 80–1
Witch Hunt 18, 26, 82
Wolf: A True Story of Survival, The (Blakeslee) 186
Wolf and Seven Kids, The (Grimm Brothers) 83, 90, 102
Wolf Border, The (Hall) 21, 140–3
wolf conservation/protection 176, 179–80
wolf greeting 130, 131
wolf heads (wulfesheud) 55

wolf killing/hunting 174–5, 180–1
wolf man 156
Wolf Man's Magic Word: A Cryptonomy, The (Abraham and Torok) 193
wolf metaphor, discourse of 1–23
wolf migration 176–7, 181–2
wolf reintroduction 76–7
Wolfsonate (Grimaud) 19
Wolf Statue 'NSA Man' (Opolka) 3, 4
wolf totem cults 57
Wolf Totem (Rong) 22
Wolf Trail 181
'wolf wars' 76
wolf zoning 175
'Wolves Are Back, The' (Opolka) 3
women's liberation 57
Women Who Run with Wolves (Estés) 19, 98
working class 33
World Migration Report 1
world peace 6–7, 21, 36, 75
'Wotan' (Jung) 191
Wotan myth 25, 82

xenophobia 2, 7, 26, 77
xenos 176

Yaqui Indians 78
Yeehats 64
'yellow peril' 63
Yellowstone National Park wolves 7, 23, 176, 180–7
Yukon 62

Zavisca, Jane 138
Zeitgeist 174
Zimen, Erik 58
Zipes, Jack 27
zoe 27

www.ingramcontent.com/pod-product-compliance
Lightning Source LLC
Chambersburg PA
CBHW060950230426
43665CB00015B/2144